The OUTSIDER'S EDGE

THE MAKING OF SELF-MADE BILLIONAIRES

BRENT D TAYLOR

BICENTENNIAL
1807
WILEY
2007
BICENTENNIAL

John Wiley & Sons Australia, Ltd

First published 2007 by John Wiley & Sons Australia, Ltd
42 McDougall Street, Milton Qld 4064

Office also in Melbourne

Typeset in Berkely LT 11/13.2 pt

© Brent D Taylor 2007

The moral rights of the author have been asserted

National Library of Australia Cataloguing-in-Publication data:

Taylor, Brent D

The Outsider's Edge: the Making of Self-Made Billionaires.

Includes index.
ISBN 9780731407316 (pbk.).

1. Billionaires - Case studies. 2. Wealth. 3. Success in
business. 4. Finance, Personal. I. Title.

332.02401

Front cover (clockwise from left to right): Oprah Winfrey, Frank Lowy, Bill
Gates, Warren Buffett and Richard Branson

Front cover: Newspix/Newspix/AFP Photo/Timothy A Clary

Back cover: Newspix/Newspix/Ross Schultz

Wiley bicentennial logo: Richard J Pacifico

Author images © Merran Kelsall

Printed in Australia by McPherson's Printing Group

10 9 8 7 6 5 4 3 2 1

Disclaimer

The material in this publication is of the nature of general comment only, and
does not represent professional advice. It is not intended to provide specific
guidance for particular circumstances and it should not be relied on as the basis
for any decision to take action or not take action on any matter which it covers.
Readers should obtain professional advice where appropriate, before making
any such decision. To the maximum extent permitted by law, the author and
publisher disclaim all responsibility and liability to any person, arising directly
or indirectly from any person taking or not taking action based upon the
information in this publication.

Contents

About the author

Brent D Taylor was born and raised in several small towns in New Zealand. He gained a bachelor of engineering from Auckland University and then worked as a professional engineer in New Zealand and Papua New Guinea. On leaving the profession he became a professional photographer and settled permanently in Australia. Brent returned to study at the University of Melbourne where he gained an honours degree in psychology. For the past twenty years he has worked as a successful market researcher for government and large corporations.

Brent has long been fascinated by extreme achievers and as a researcher he was constantly frustrated by the lack of explanation as to why extreme achievers are as they are. This was the catalyst for the long, exploratory journey that has resulted in *The Outsider's Edge*.

As a researcher, Brent is used to looking beyond conventional wisdom to find answers where others have tried and failed. In this case the explanation was in plain sight for all to see. Having discovered the secret, he was driven to write this book because no-one else was going to.

Brent is currently exploring the issues raised in this book and is running a survey on his website <www.brentdtaylor.com>. The findings from this survey will be used to form the basis of his forthcoming book; he would greatly appreciate your responses.

This book is dedicated to all the outsiders in the world who have so enriched us with their edge, particularly to the outsiders in my life, some of whom have used their edge to achieve great things and to the others who have not yet got there. No matter how small or large their achievements, all of them continue searching. For their ongoing support of this project, particular thanks go to all those friends who have helped me with encouragement, sage advice and infinite patience. Also, thanks to the first important outsiders in my life—my father and mother and those other important outsiders, my children Grace, Luke and Sam.

Preface

The Outsider's Edge is the result of my long-held fascination with psychology and human behaviour, and, in particular, extreme achievement in business, politics, science and the arts. Wealth is an easily quantifiable form of outstanding success.

Initially, my interest in human behaviour led me to study psychology, in which I achieved an honours degree from the University of Melbourne in the 1980s. Since that time I have worked continuously in business as a market and social researcher helping clients understand individuals in social and business systems. Research methods I employ include focus groups and surveys, and I have conducted over 200 000 interviews. My clients are spread across a range of industries and include major retailers, developers, manufacturers, tollways, accident insurers, utility providers, education institutions, hospitals and government organisations.

Despite the different problems my clients present me, they all want to know the same thing—what makes the biggest impact for their organisation? They also want to be told the answer in a simple and, if possible, positive and entertaining way. They don't want all the details—they just want to know that the findings are underpinned by data and scientific methods.

After five years' intensive research I wrote *The Outsider's Edge* because I wanted to share my discoveries. It has been investigated and written using the principles I apply as a professional researcher every day. In the book I discuss what makes a difference and then clearly and concisely explain my findings.

You will not find this book weighed down by excessive use of technical terms. Nor does it get lost among the many disciplines that it traverses.

I have briefly covered some topics that many learned books are dedicated to, and in which scientific and academic debate is heated. These topics include brain development, intelligence testing, learning theories, educational practice and the impact of genetics versus environment. There is plenty of reading to be done in all of these areas, so I have included a starter set of references for anyone who is interested in researching these topics further.

I apologise in advance to those with detailed scientific knowledge for any omissions in detail or if the arguments for their discipline aren't fully presented. Only those parts relevant to the understanding of what makes self-made billionaires have been included in this book.

I would like to thank the large number of family, friends, colleagues and clients who have given me support, encouragement and critical advice over the five years I have been researching and writing this book.

Also, I would like to thank Michael Hanrahan for his early editing and encouragement, as well as the team at John Wiley & Sons for its support and help.

Part I

INTRODUCTION

Chapter 1

Why haven't I got what Bill Gates has?

'Why is Bill Gates rich and not me?' Many people wonder why they haven't got a fortune as they struggle to pay the mortgage, send the kids to the dentist or buy economy airfares for the family to somewhere not very exotic. After all, Gates is just a human. Like everyone else, he was born of woman, had a father, was a baby once and, like us all, wore nappies and was spoonfed by his parents. He learned to walk and talk, and even now he still has to do most of the normal everyday things we do. It's a fair bet that he, like us, showers naked. So, *why him?* That's what I'm going to investigate in this book.

Gates, with apparently normal beginnings, miraculously became the world's richest man with over $50 billion. He has a bigger cash flow than some small nations and can buy just about anything he wants. Gates certainly doesn't have any problem paying for his children's dental care, he can buy a plane any time he wants to travel, and he could buy the exotic resort and the island it is on as well.

Oprah Winfrey has a mere 3 per cent of Gates's wealth, weighing in at only $1.5 billion. Yet $1.5 billion is a phenomenal amount of money for any person to have, let alone to earn from a standing start. This is especially impressive considering Winfrey's background—a dirt-poor, abandoned and abused African-American woman from rural US. Most of us would be excited to have even 3 per cent of her wealth. Like Gates and everyone else, she was a baby once too, and to all intents and purposes functions like a normal woman. Like Gates, it is a fair bet that Winfrey showers naked too. So, *why her?*

Some people theorise that maybe it was just luck, but such wealth is so statistically improbable that luck can't explain it. Maybe it was God's will or it was just meant to be. Possible, but this explanation is ultimately unsatisfactory as we all like to think we have some kind of control over our own destinies. Most people want their destinies to include more money, so God's will or luck are ultimately unhelpful in their day-to-day struggle.

So what could possibly have led these two—and the 1000 or so other billionaires on the *Forbes* world's billionaires list—to have so much money?

Chapter 2

Seeking the causes
of extreme wealth

Surprisingly there was no consistent explanation for the self-made billionaires' wealth up until this book was written. Certainly there are money-making 'recipe books' that have attempted to fill the void, but there aren't any universal rules that the billionaires have all applied. Author Dale Carnegie famously proposed that the way to wealth was to 'make friends and influence people', but just looking at Gates and some of the other billionaires throws the friendship model into doubt. Donald Trump trumpets his own particular brand of money making while Richard Branson has a different take on making money, which seems to include having fun. But who is right? Who knows, as there is no way to test this.

The billionaires can't tell us why they became wealthy

Unlike Trump and Carnegie, most billionaires are silent when it comes to explaining why it was them that became wealthy. Most do not even hazard a guess! Certainly they all have their own particular style—and in the case of Trump, peculiar style—but is it style that counts?

Gates said that 'business is a good game. Lots of competition and a minimum of rules. You keep score with money' (Lowe 1998). All very well for him to say but that isn't how Winfrey plays it. Buffett annually pontificates on money matters but doesn't ever reveal why he got rich instead of his buddy at school.

Even John Sperling, with a doctorate and a lifetime's work in education, and who shares over $3 billion with his son (together both are major shareholders in the world's largest for-profit education institution), is silent on why he is so rich. This is despite writing an autobiography that is remarkable for its candidness regarding his personal journey.

So, why is it that billionaires don't impart the secrets of their success to the rest of us? It is because they actually *don't know* why it is them and not someone else, and they probably don't care. Certainly they know what they did but they don't really know *why* they did it. How can they? They are human like the rest of us, and very few of us can untangle the influences that led us to where we have ended up. If we want to know about ourselves, inevitably we seek professional help to untangle the skeins of our lives.

This book sets out to do just that—untangle the skeins of seventeen self-made billionaires' lives so that you might understand what caused their extreme wealth.

Developing a 'theory of everything' for becoming extremely wealthy in a lifetime

Albert Einstein was of the firm view that there was a 'theory of everything' that could be used to explain the physical universe. He failed to solve this problem, but he has inspired physicists to keep looking. Despite not finding the theory of everything, Einstein did propose key theories that have become the cornerstones of how we understand the physical universe and this may eventually lead to someone else solving what many consider to be the ultimate problem.

Einstein developed his famous theories by taking what was known about the universe at the time and looking for consistencies *and* inconsistencies. He examined the evidence and then proposed his theories. Others later confirmed them through experimentation. His task was Herculean. Not only was the problem he was trying to solve colossally complex and the difficulties compounded by it being unobservable, the problem was also steeped in centuries of conventional wisdom, which went way back to before Greek civilisation.

Prior to beginning my search, there has been no theory of everything when it comes to understanding how individuals become extremely wealthy. So I started with a proposal that it is possible to find a theory of everything about why some people become extremely rich. It may actually be that it is not possible to find such a theory but it will be fun and informative to try, and that is what this book sets out to do.

The problem I am setting out to solve is unlikely to be as complex as Einstein's, and it certainly isn't hidden by conventional wisdom. What little conventional wisdom that does exist can be dismissed fairly easily. The method used in this book is similar to that used by Einstein. While my research capabilities fall well below those of Einstein's and the subject matter is undoubtedly simpler and different, the method he used is still valid in these circumstances. It is to examine all the available evidence for consistencies and inconsistencies, propose hypotheses to explain the patterns, and then test them.

Looking for secrets in the right places

Like Einstein, or any other scientist for that matter, I have had to identify what data is available and the best method to illuminate the problem.

First, it is obvious how second or latter generation billionaires have come by their wealth. They may have grown or lost the family pile, but beginning with a fortune changes the starting conditions. Their wealth is dependent on others more than themselves.

I only want to deal with people who made their own wealth—in other words, they are self-made. But what is self-made? Again, there are shades. Ted Turner started in his father's billboard advertising company with a turnover greater than $20 million. Rupert Murdoch was given a newspaper by his father. Both have turned what appears to be a relatively meagre start into global media empires that are now in competition with each other. Despite growing their businesses thousands-fold, they did begin with a considerable stake compared with what most people can expect to start with. They are only semi–self-made!

This study excludes all billionaires that are not absolutely self-made, where self-made will be defined very strictly to include only those who did not start in the family business or had a substantial family stake. Therefore, Ted Turner and Rupert Murdoch do not qualify.

Second, self-made billionaires have to be found. Money, as Gates says, is a great way to keep score and the people that keep score brilliantly are *Forbes*. *Forbes* publishes an annual world's billionaires list, which is available going back a number of years. The *Forbes* list has the great advantage of being an industry standard. If a billionaire is reported as having a certain level of wealth and is on the *Forbes* table then that is probably as good an estimate as can be achieved. *Forbes* do not make the distinction of self-made as adopted for this project, but their list is an excellent starting point.

Third, like have to be compared with like. This doesn't mean those chosen have to be the same gender or in the same industry or country or anything like that. But they need to have been brought up and live in more or less the same political and economic system. The only way to make a fair comparison is to ensure they were brought up in approximately equivalent times. For this reason, the criterion will be that they must be on the *Forbes* 2007 world's billionaires list (meaning they are alive in 2007). While all will have been born at different times, they will all have a large number of overlapping years. What is more, their money is measured by the same unit — 2007 US dollars. It would be great to include, for example, Henry Ford but he was born before his model T-Ford became a ubiquitous form of transport, did business through World War II and died before the personal computer revolution. Too many influences were different in his life compared with living self-made billionaires. It may not make any difference to the final conclusions but it does eliminate a possible source of error.

The recently deceased Sam Walton, founder of Wal-Mart, also has to be excluded because he is dead. If he was alive, he would be wealthier than Bill Gates. Certainly his life overlapped considerably with Warren Buffett's and Bernie Ecclestone's but scientific rules are rules. Einstein would have approved.

Fourth, there must be information available. Given the generally secretive nature and general unavailability of self-made billionaires for interview it will be impossible to carry out 'experiments' on a sufficient number to test hypotheses. Besides, there isn't really any hypotheses to test yet, so it would be a waste of time to start with interviews of billionaires and randomly dredge for information. Anyway, they probably don't know.

Luckily there is information available. There are biographies and autobiographies on a smattering of self-made billionaires. This will suffice. But books on billionaires vary considerably. They usually concentrate most of the detail on the minutiae of business after the billionaire was on his or her way, often just starting at that point as if all that went before is not important. But what came before has to be important — we become who we are through a complex interplay of genetics and environment. From birth this ongoing interaction develops personality, hence childhood development cannot be ignored as a factor that separates self-made billionaires from the rest of the population. This may turn out to be the only place to look, since the minutiae of adult business dealings are picked over daily and are yet to answer the question, *why them?*

Like books on any subject, books on billionaires vary in quality and tone. Some are hostile, some are sycophantic, some skip important early detail, others drill down. For this project, books about billionaires have been chosen only if they report sufficient major early events as the billionaire was growing up. Certainly some are sketchy but there needs to be sufficient evidence in the book to at least infer what happened. In addition, it will be important to ignore any inference that other writers make about the source of a particular billionaire's wealth since inference from a sample of one is always a risky business and is usually wrong. This book makes inferences after reviewing the lives of seventeen billionaires.

Fifth, the final step once the input data has been found is to do as Einstein did—look for patterns that explain the outcome. To do this we need to see what happened to the billionaires, what they did as they grew up, how they behave in adulthood, and then compare and contrast—concentrate on what they have in common.

I have identified seventeen self-made billionaires with books about them that fit my criteria. This is sufficient to find a pattern and develop a theory of everything about becoming extremely wealthy.

The next part of the book will examine each billionaire's life. It will not go into the minutiae but concentrate only on the big events. Each summary or mini-biography is split up into three sections. The first concentrates on the billionaire's achievements. The second discusses the circumstances of his or her development, particularly family background, mother, father, other family, schooling and friends. This section will take you up to the founding of each billionaire's wealth-creating business. The third part of each mini-biography is an interpretation of the first two sections and identifies key elements in each of the developing billionaires' lives.

The chapters following the mini-biographies will reveal the common pattern running through each of their lives, and will discuss this pattern in a broader context.

Now that the data has been assembled and the method decided, all that is required is to find the pattern. It is now time to set sail into uncharted waters to find out why Gates, Winfrey, Sperling, Lucas and all the rest became billionaires? *Why them?*

Part II

BIOGRAPHIES

Chapter 3

Bill Gates

Forbes information 2007
Rank: 1
Citizenship: United States
Wealth: US$56 billion
Industry: software/service

Bill Gates plays games with the world. In fact, Gates plays the world. He plays very serious, very successful games with extreme vigour. He plays games that affect the lives of millions, games that have enriched thousands of employees and stockholders and millions of users, but they are games nevertheless. Gates has been quoted as saying, 'business is a good game. Lots of competition and minimum of rules. You keep score with money' (Lowe 1998). But Gates doesn't look like he is game playing; he looks like he is building the most successful software house in the world and making a fortune at the same time.

Achievement

After gaining valuable programming experience (and earning money from it) with friends at school, Gates was excited by the future of computing and its potential. He dropped out of Harvard to rejoin his school friend Paul Allen and together they set themselves on the visionary path of putting a computer on every desk and in every home. This was a visionary goal because at the time computers weighed tons, filled rooms with hot flashing tubes and huge whirring tape spools and used as much power as a small town. On top of this, those behemoths had less computing power than a standard mobile phone.

Personal computing was the fantasy of sci-fi nuts, along with Dick Tracy's watch phone. Gates and Allen were among the thousands of electronics and computer nuts that spotted the now famous *Popular Electronics* cover of 1975, which showed the latest thing in personal computing—barely more than a box with flashing lights and toggle switches. The box had no easy means of interaction as we have come to expect from present-day computers. There was no internal electronic memory, disc drives, keyboard, screen or printer and the now ubiquitous internet and email were twenty years in the future. Yet Gates and Allen, and a few others (including Steve Jobs and Stephen Wozniak of Apple), saw this unpromising box of flashing bits as the future. It's possible that they didn't see this box as the foundation of an industry, but boxes of bits like this worked in sci-fi imagination so why not in the real world? Gates, like any isolated computer nerd, read this genre avidly and watched *Star Trek* along with everything sci-fi available on TV and at the movies. Sci-fi is a genre replete with mysterious boxes with flashing lights and amazing functions. Computing was a short step in their imagination and a large step to application, but for a couple of antisocial lads with time and little else on their hands it looked like the future. There was no holding them back!

With Paul Allen, Gates started Microsoft. Their first software development was an adaptation of an existing program, BASIC, to run on a new hobbyist's computer developed by another company. Making a mistake that he was never to make again, Gates allowed some of the licensing to be held by the client company. An early indication of Gates's business orientation was that he and Allen formed Microsoft and moved to Albuquerque, New Mexico, to be close to their client—something normal computer 'nerds' didn't do. When the company didn't perform in relation to sales of BASIC, Gates mounted a law suit and won back the rights to the program. This program became the basis for Microsoft's early cash flows.

Microsoft moved to Bellevue, Washington, and continued to work with BASIC. In 1980, IBM came looking for an operating system for its first PC. Gates referred IBM to an aligned company that had an operating system. Talks between that company and IBM failed, due in large part to the lack of vision and professionalism of that company's managing director—he was off flying his new plane that day and just couldn't be bothered meeting with IBM. IBM came back to Microsoft and Gates, seeing the opportunity, immediately bought the rights to the DOS operating system from the other software developer. Gates and Allen further developed the software into MS-DOS and licensed it to IBM.

Gates, having learned from his previous licensing mistake, brilliantly negotiated the licensing deal for the operating system to IBM. This deal is both a testimony to Gates's negotiation skills and IBM's desperation to get into personal computing because it was unheard of for IBM to give up rights. With its computers running Microsoft's operating system, IBM used its existing brand presence to become an early leader in personal computing; at one time IBM and personal computing were synonymous in the same way that Xerox was synonymous with photocopying. Since Microsoft owned the rights, Gates was able to license other PC makers to use the operating system, which he set about doing. This decision to license rights for MS-DOS became the cornerstone of the Microsoft empire as MS-DOS—and later, Windows (based on MS-DOS)—became the industry standard due to the proliferation of computers using Microsoft's operating system.

This decision was pivotal in Microsoft stealing the march on other operating systems, particularly that of Apple. Apple had tried to do what IBM had done in the past and would have loved to have done with PCs but couldn't—inextricably link its operating system to its hardware. But since Microsoft made money out of software irrespective of whose hardware it was operating on, it was in Microsoft's interests to get its system onto as many computers as it could. Microsoft, operating as a pure software house, did this, eventually swamping Apple in the market. IBM could not keep up with other personal computer makers and eventually became an also-ran company in the personal computing market while Microsoft became a leader.

Microsoft grew and grew and grew. There were many changes of allies and competitors, and there were constant battles. Through a vigilant focus on business and deals, Gates became the youngest billionaire ever at the age of thirty-one.

Gates, reported to be a hard and uncompromising boss, set up an industrial process for developing software. He bought in management and very cleverly took its advice. Gates's role became one of technical guru and the marketing face of Microsoft—a very deliberate strategy by Microsoft management. Most importantly he was the deal doer, the economic force behind Microsoft's expansion.

Today Microsoft is the biggest and most successful software company in the world. It is significant that it has achieved this mainly by being derivative. While the marketing hype portrays Gates as a programming genius, most—if not all—of Microsoft's products began their life in the hands of others. This is particularly so for the cornerstones of its early business, BASIC and then MS-DOS, then later spreadsheet and word processing packages. While there is no doubt that Gates is a very good programmer, his genius is not in programming. Gates's genius has been in spotting how to keep control of and exploit his intellectual property, and in negotiating ever more lucrative deals. His negotiations are tough, and Gates is tenacious and focused. Microsoft products have not usually been the best, just the most successful. So successful, in fact, that many have gone on to become the industry standard.

Microsoft products have not usually been the best, just the most successful.

Unlike many founders, Gates knows he isn't good at everything. To his credit, Gates allows others to run his company; he did so before getting kicked upstairs like many other founders.

Development

Born in 1955, Gates is the middle child of three and the only son. He is a descendant of early settlers of Washington State—a family of influence.

Gates's father, Bill Senior, had served time in the army during World War II, ending as a first lieutenant. On discharge, he enrolled at university and obtained a law degree, served as an assistant city attorney and then as a partner in a prominent Seattle law firm. Gates's grandfather ran a small furniture store.

His mother, Mary Gates, was from money, the men in her family having been prominent bankers for generations. She was very much the socialite, nicknamed 'Giggles' when she was growing up. This name belied her status in Seattle. Originally a teacher, she took to organising the school's mothers' club, she had a very hectic social calendar and she sat on the governing boards of many prominent west coast companies.

Gates's parents have the appearance of being loving and supportive in a fierce kind of way. Gates had poorly developed social skills and was often in conflict with his parents. He would have been extremely difficult to live with, especially for his mother, a tidiness freak, since he was extremely untidy in his personal habits. The eventual compromise after an extended battle between Bill and his mother was to leave his door closed.

Mary gave up teaching after Bill was born. She became a community volunteer, as her own mother had done. From all accounts she was an extremely active and energetic volunteer—probably dedicating as much time to that as she would to a full-time job. She also had board seats on several of the northwest's largest corporations. Mary was the driving force in the family. She was the socialite and extrovert, Bill senior was the introvert. At Mary's behest the Gates's threw many parties for Seattle's wealthiest and most powerful citizens.

While there was no question that Mary was a loving and devoted mother, she sounds like she gave fierce, demanding, obsessive love:

> Always exceedingly well-organized, she had a weekly
> wardrobe battle plan for Trey [Bill Gates] throughout the
> year that included color-coordinating his clothes for each
> day, matching shirts, pants, and socks ... Mary would post
> dinner menus for the entire weekend on the refrigerator.
> Each meal was carefully planned out, along with dinner
> times. Everything fit into a schedule. It is a trait she has
> passed on to her son, who brooks no wasted time either at
> work or play (Wallace 1993).

Mary is reported to have continued this habit with her son until well after he left home—she was always in his life, organising clothes, food and domestic staff. It is no wonder Gates is reported to be obsessive. Gates's father, meanwhile, was a rock-solid citizen who also set strict and firm standards for his children. He was known to be difficult and demanding, traits also often attributed to his son.

Gates's parents fostered a competitive environment, and in this he thrived. In family sports and games Gates loved to win and hated losing. Much is made of playing games in the Gates family. He played with everyone, especially his grandmother. There is a very strong sense that love and approval was contingent on winning games. The family frequently played bridge when Gates was young.

Young Gates underperformed at his first school and had behavioural problems. A psychologist said that it was useless to force Gates to learn or be more obedient since he learned prolific amounts of information and had a virtually photographic memory if he was interested in the subject. If not, he refused. This is the hallmark behaviour of a bright and headstrong, but bored, child.

Aside from changing schools to go to the exclusive Lakeside when he was twelve, Gates's whole life up until he went to Harvard was in Seattle, Washington. When he was twelve, he was enrolled in a small school known for its exceptional students. While Gates is now a moderately tall man at five foot eleven inches, when he was growing up he was usually among the shortest in his class because he was accelerated two grades. While he might have been an average-sized child for his age, he was not in his age group at school. Gates was an awkward child with big feet. He was also left-handed, small and skinny.

As he was in his junior school, Gates continued to be bored and often displayed behavioural problems, routinely scoring low grades in subjects that didn't interest him and getting into scrapes with teachers. He also learned that if he wanted to be accepted he would have to dumb down a little. Gates deliberately got lower marks in all subjects other than reading and maths.

Dumbing down didn't help much. Gates was definitely not a hit with the girls when he was growing up and there are no reports of girlfriends. He and Allen had the job of organising class seating and Gates would often find himself surrounded by girls in class, but he did not gain any relationship advantages from it. He may have been in contact and available but there were no takers, and to make matters worse he often avoided social events that his peers attended.

Gates couldn't be like everybody else. He had no conception of what it took to socialise, to fit in, and he had few friends: 'Gates could be cold and aloof like his father' (Wallace 1993).

> Gates did not suffer fools gladly ... 'That's the
> stupidest thing I've ever heard of!' became a Gates
> catchphrase ... 'but as it turns out, he's almost always
> right' ... To those who didn't mesh with the scrawny,
> arrogant kid, he could be 'an extremely annoying person.
> He was very easy to sort of dislike. And I think that
> probably me and a lot of people took a little extra pleasure
> in sort of bumping him while passing him in the hall and
> basically giving him a little bit of a hard time'
> (Manes 1994).

Given Gates's obvious differences from most of his classmates right through school, it was inevitable that he was an outsider there. He is reported to have had an obsessive personality and was compulsive about being the best. Compounding this he was arrogant and had sufficient intellectual horsepower to humiliate his classmates, two years his elder. Not a great mix for social acceptance, and coupled with being low on the boys' sports-determined pecking order, Gates was almost guaranteed unpopularity. Gates is good at some solo sports such as waterskiing and tennis but was never very interested in team sports—despite encouragement from his parents. Team sports were not for him.

With his shift to Lakeside school at the age of twelve, Gates's work improved and he achieved some excellent results. One of his teachers estimated that he had an IQ in the 160s or 170s, which was one of the highest she had ever experienced. At Lakeside, Gates was precocious, even for a student at an accelerated school.

It was at Lakeside students' club that he met Paul Allen. The club programmed a 'computer' given to it by the mothers' club run by Gates's mother. Allen was two years Gates's senior, as were all his classmates. Allen is reported to be exceptionally shy—another social misfit. Gates was such a handful that he was ejected from the informal students' club with Allen because they considered him to be too immature. But the club couldn't do without him so they invited him back. Gates became the boss and he set the terms. The club couldn't do without him because he was the one who did the deals with local companies to get computer time and made money from it. Very much a sign of what was to come.

Computers and programming dominated a large proportion of Gates's time during high school, he says: 'It was hard to tear myself away from a machine at which I could so unambiguously demonstrate success. I was hooked' (Gates 1995). Gates is describing an obsession that, along with deal making, became the cornerstones of his empire. Critically he could demonstrate that success to a small group of other, older boys. He had found something that he could be admired for and this formed the core of his social standing. He had found a place to belong and a way to stay there.

Gates's parents paid for his schooling, but he had to find the money to pay for his computer time. This is what got him thinking about the commercial side of computing. Gates got himself and some of the others in his computer club summer programmer jobs, making an extraordinary $5000 each per summer. Gates and his group worked in a computer company after hours and developed a 300-page manual called the Problem Report Book. Because they loved working on software so much they often worked right through the night. Before leaving school, the group also wrote programs for traffic counting (reported to have earned $20 000) and for solving problems in a power grid.

At Harvard, Gates missed classes and spent days in the computer lab working on his own projects. It has been reported that he sometimes went up to thirty-six hours without sleep. He also spent time isolated in his room in a deep philosophical funk trying to work out what to do with his life. Obviously it didn't occur to him to go out and have some fun until Steve Ballmer—later Microsoft's CEO—took him to parties. More likely, Gates was terrified of socialising—he had little in the way of social or sporting skills to help him fit in.

His academic record at Harvard was patchy and his social participation poor, but he kept up his extracurricular programming activities with Allen. At times they would monopolise the university computer to develop their software.

Despite being supremely bright and perfectly capable of graduating from Harvard, Gates dropped out. Undoubtedly it was due to his inability to belong socially as much as his frequently reported view that business school was irrelevant. Besides which, Gates now had something exciting to do—build the personal computing revolution.

About leaving Harvard, Gates said: 'Let me put it this way. Say you added two years to my life and let me go to business school. I don't think I would have done a better job at Microsoft. Let's look around these shelves and see if there are any business books. Oops. We didn't need any' (Lowe 1998). He made it up as he went, although he was quite willing to hire people who had the formal training to manage his company once it was large enough.

Bill Gates is reported to be aggressive, competitive, obsessive and a workaholic. Between 1978 and 1984 Gates took only fifteen days off. He is reported to be difficult to work for, shouting and being abusive to staff. And he expects his staff to be likewise. 'Like any successful cult, sacrifice and penance and the idea that the deity is perfect and his priests are better than you works at Microsoft. Each level, from Gates on down, screams at the next, goading and humiliating them' (Cringely 1992). Humiliation is par for the course.

Much of the criticism that Gates attracts is in relation to his antisocial behaviour, and he has made plenty of enemies. He is reported to be confrontational, rude and condescending. This is how a typical staff meeting was described:

> ... Gates exploded. For an hour, he screamed, waved his arms, shouted, interrupted, delivered himself of cruel and sarcastic insults, and generally berated his charges, who kept trying bravely to make their points without sending him over the homicidal edge ... Finally, the meeting ended with Gates sitting silently in his chair, rocking rhythmically back and forth, lost in thought. Then he said, quietly, 'OK ... sounds good ... go ahead' (Lowe 1998).

Despite his image, Gates is not principally a computer nerd. His success comes from his skills as a businessman and his toughness as a negotiator. Warren Buffett said that if Gates had sold hot dogs instead of software, he would have become the hot dog king of the world. Microsoft is also known for the way it targets rivals, and it has thwarted many a competitor that had a better product but could not withstand an attack from Microsoft.

Microsoft's products are not revolutionary, and they are often not even the best available, but through his obsessiveness and drive Gates has pushed Microsoft to massive success. His negotiating skills have always been the key to his extreme wealth. Right at the start of Microsoft he negotiated himself a 60/40 split with Allen. He negotiated for the rights to BASIC and then retained the rights to MS-DOS in his deal with IBM. He stared down Ross Perot and the US Supreme Court.

Gates certainly has no fear of litigation. Microsoft has received and initiated many law suits, and this is part of the culture at Microsoft. Gates runs his business the way a hard-nosed lawyer probably would. It's legal until proven otherwise, but he pushes the letter of the law to the limit. Gates, like any successful lawyer, is a consummate game player. He plays brinkmanship games and interpretation of the law games. There is little in his business practices that looks benign. It is interesting that in 2007 Harvard gave Gates an honorary Law degree, probably as recognition that he behaves much like a lawyer in business.

> Gates, like any successful lawyer, is a consummate game player.

Without a doubt, Gates was an outsider. In his book *Accidental Empires*, Robert Cringely rightly compares Gates to Henry Ford—both technically gifted, self-centred and eccentric. He says that both were ahead of their time, and capitalised on this by creating an industry out of something that was just a hobby to most others.

Says Gates, 'You can't count on conventional wisdom. That only makes sense in conventional markets. For the last three decades the market for computer hardware and software has definitely been unconventional' (Gates 1995). One gets the sense, however, that no market would have been seen as conventional by Gates.

Despite being the world's richest man, Gates obsessively searches for the next big thing. He is still as driven today as he ever was, and he is always looking for new ways to generate profits.

Gates had few long-term female relationships but finally married at thirty-eight to a mid-level Microsoft executive with an MBA. The couple had dated for six years. Gates, mystified by personal relationships, was surprised at being attached to a woman and feeling like getting married. He reports that it was against all his rational thinking. Continuing with his rush of irrationality he fathered three children, but he says he likes being a parent.

He has few other friends. His original partner, Paul Allen, retired sick prior to Microsoft's public listing in the 1980s. Steve Ballmer, his

Harvard pal, was brought in as CEO but there is little evidence of any others. He has 'friendships' with other billionaires, notably Buffett with whom he plays bridge and is engaged in a friendly competition with—to see who can become the richest man in the world.

Interpretation

It seems very likely that Bill Gates had a highly stressed upbringing.

> From the start the newest Bill was a high-energy kid.
> Whenever his mother visited his cradle, a family heirloom
> on rockers, the baby would be swaying to and fro. In his
> early years he would spend hours riding a coil-springed
> hobbyhorse. 'I think that got to be a very comforting,
> comfortable kind of motion for him,' his mother recalled.
> No doubt: He carried his rocking habit into adulthood
> and Microsoft, where it would become his most widely
> imitated personal trademark (Manes 1994).

Continual rocking in infants is often taken as a sign of stress. Rocking that goes on for years is a sure sign that something is permanently wrong, and it must have gone on for years since it became a behavioural trait. It is most likely that his mother was the major cause of this stress. She was reportedly both obsessive and intrusive on the older Bill, right through his adolescence and into adulthood, rigidly laying out colour-coordinated clothing regimes and drawing up family schedules to last the whole week. If she was obsessive and intrusive when he was older, it is even more likely that she was the same when he was a helpless infant.

Obsessive and intrusive people interrupt and interact with others according to their own highly unbalanced and unpredictable emotional needs. Such unpredictable and intrusive interactions are exactly what a developing infant doesn't need. What infants need is warm, responsive predictability; they have no defences against intrusion. Infants have to cope the best they can, and one of those defences, or rather comforts, is rocking. What is worse is that infants treated this way don't learn how to interact with people appropriately. Baby Bill probably had to scream and throw tantrums to get his mother's attention or to leave him alone, behaviour that has persisted throughout his life.

The child Gates was primed to be a misfit at school. Clearly he didn't know how to interact properly with other children or teachers and this caused problems for himself and others. His social problems were compounded by his high intelligence. Nobody likes a smarty, especially one who can humiliate his elders and those who should be his intellectual betters.

Gates's social problems were further compounded when he was accelerated two grades. From that time on he had no hope socially. Despite being a relatively normal-sized boy for his age, acceleration meant that he was physically two years younger than his classmates. He had no chance of competing physically with them and consequently did not willingly play team sports. He did become good at some solo sports like waterskiing, so coordination was not his problem. Gates couldn't get a girlfriend, and on top of this his classmates would have been angry at this obnoxious young boy who showed them up intellectually.

Undoubtedly Gates was lonely, but he didn't know how to moderate his behaviour. He wouldn't play games that he would lose, and he would have had plenty of experience of losing against his much older and bigger peers. Actually it is most likely that his older peers, angry at the humiliations they received in class from Gates, returned the compliment on the sports grounds and in the schoolyard. To say he wasn't interested in team sport is probably a wild understatement — he was undoubtedly humiliated and hurt when he played them.

During his family time, Gates's successes came from playing bridge and other games. This is where he gained his approval, and for a little boy hungry for approval, winning at such games would have been emotional gold — so much so that it became an obsession. He would always have a deep emotional link with winning games. Everyone loved him for winning games — his grandmother, his father and even his mother. Gates didn't just play for fun, he played for love and approval. After he left home this behaviour continued; Gates's play was just as intense as his work.

Those who have tried computer programming will not need to have it pointed out that it is an intellectual game that can be played solo or in teams. The teenage Gates was in his element when computing was introduced to his school. He had found a game he could excel at with a group of nerdy friends. For the first time in his life he was playing a team sport and loving it! But he couldn't keep his unruly personality in check, and they ejected him from the club. Gates was devastated.

His despondency was not to last. Gates conceived and executed his first significant deal. Making money and having unlimited night-time programming on a corporate computer was a fledgling computer nerd's dream, and Gates negotiated it. He became the boss of the group and he could do just about whatever he wanted so long as he could keep negotiating deals to keep the group intact.

Naturally it didn't last. Gates and his cohorts graduated from school and went their various ways. Harvard did not deliver the intellectual or emotional stimulation Bill wanted. Bill was an outsider with an unfortunate personality and wasn't able to put together a group on his terms. In particular, Harvard did not deliver the emotional charge of being the boss of his own computer development team. Well out of his social comfort zone, Gates suffered a meltdown and went looking to re-experience the thrill of running his own boys' club again.

Undoubtedly Gates was excited by the prospect of putting a computer on every desk, but he was even more excited by reuniting his boys' club. This being the only group Gates had ever really belonged to. The *Popular Electronics* magazine fired the starter's pistol on the personal computing revolution. It gave him a reason and he had motivation. Gates reconnected with Allen and built up another little band of software developers, his own personal boys' club, and the rest is history.

Gates knew he needed to be boss because no-one would put up with his difficult behaviour unless there was a good reason. He also knew that in order to be the boss and to stay the boss, he had to keep feeding better and bigger deals into the system, and that is what he did. Microsoft grew and grew, principally on the deals that Gates made.

Gates's brilliance is not in computing, it is in spotting the deal and closing it. He did deals in computing before it was even imagined as an industry. His trading comes from both sides of the family. His ancestors on his mother's side started and operated banks, and while his father was a solicitor, his forebears were small businesspeople.

Litigation is a way of life for Gates. In addition to his competitive nature, he has little fear of litigation because he has learned from his father. He knows it is just another business game to compete in.

Microsoft became an outgrowth of the school boys' club and Gates is reported to continue to behave as if it still is. Business became an extension of adolescent games and Gates behaved that way. Any behaviour short of illegality is okay. To win the game is the thing!

References:

Cringely, RX 1993, *Accidental Empires*, Penguin Books, London.

Gates, B 1995, *The Road Ahead*, Viking, United Kingdom.

Lowe, J 1998, *Bill Gates Speaks*, John Wiley & Sons, New York.

Manes, S and Andrews P 1994, *Gates*, Touchstone, New York.

Wallace, J and Erickson, J 1993, *Hard Drive: Bill Gates and the Making of the Microsoft Empire*, HarperBusiness, New York.

Chapter 4

Warren Buffett

Forbes information 2007
Rank: 2
Citizenship: United States
Wealth: US$52 billion
Industry: investing

Buffett is essentially a small businessman from a country town whose work happens to generate colossal wealth for both himself and his investors.

The secret of his phenomenal wealth comes from a relentless testing of the logic of investment. The market sometimes misvalues a business because investor group think has not identified an opportunity. Buffett, the rugged individualist, actively eschews group think. Through an obsessive immersion in financial balance sheets and subsequent analysis, Buffett is adept at seeing the opportunity to make money by investing in companies before others do and then backing his own judgement with mountains of money. He listens to what the data says, not what insiders say. Right from the outset he did unorthodox deals conservatively.

Early on he confounded the markets when a company he owned, a New Bedford fabric mill, acquired an Omaha insurance company. Buffett's logic was that insurance companies collect premiums up-front but claims are paid out later, so insurance companies have large cash buffers known as a float. These floats were usually large and conservatively managed, but Buffett saw the huge potential of this money. This approach was unusual at the time, but it soon became commonplace.

Achievement

Buffett started with a small financial stake in the mid 1950s and began investing in companies. While his family origins are in stockbroking, Buffett is an investor not a stockbroker. Unlike stockbrokers, he does not trade in and out of stocks for clients. Instead he takes an investment from a client and does with it what he will. He never tells his investors what he is doing with their money. This was quite a leap of faith for clients in the early days when he was just starting out and had no track record. It is a credit to Buffett's natural persuasiveness and enthusiasm for what he was doing. With absolute confidence in his own abilities, and fuelled by some arrogance, he started an investment program using some of his own money and a considerable pile of money from others.

Unlike stockbrokers, Buffett is only open for business one day a year. He is not at the beck and call of clients or investment advisers. His major point of contact with his investors and now fairly much the whole investment world is his much heralded public address for Berkshire Hathaway. Buffett made his fortune almost entirely alone. He specifically instructed brokers not to contact him. He didn't want to know about their 'hot' tips.

> Buffett made his fortune almost entirely alone.

Naturally Buffett's success caused a great deal of resentment in the broking and financial industry. Buffett was doing what any small investor could, theoretically, do, but unlike small investors all over the world, he made billions. His method involves total immersion in business performance statistics. He reads thousands of business documents every year, identifying the best prospects and then investing in them. Prior to the 1990s he had neither computers nor teams of analysts mining the balance sheets for nuggets to invest in. His key then and now is single-minded focus on the data along with rugged individualism when it comes to making decisions. He consults no-one for anything other than data. Buffett is a trendsetter not a follower.

The industry has long believed Buffett has a huge network of tipsters helping him, for how else could he do it? The truth is much simpler—he buries himself in the information, remembers large amounts of it, looks for his own patterns, carries out independent fact or trend checking and makes up his own mind. His investments are often counterintuitive to those made by insiders. Naturally Buffett is resented and many people in the industry are jealous of him—but to others, particularly his investors and many in the media, he is a god!

Many believe his success is just an unnaturally long run of good luck, but there is no luck in it. Beating the stock market every year for forty years is not luck. Buffett has made losses and mistakes, as any investor does, but in aggregate he is always way ahead of the market.

The truth is more unbelievable. He does it himself. He is so single-minded about investing that the process of searching and investing appears to be his only true love. He is prodigiously intelligent (in this area), can calculate very large sums in his head, is reputed to have a photographic memory (certainly he can remember balance sheet details for years), and is deeply fascinated and obsessively immersed—all critical for his particular kind of success.

Development

Born in 1930 in Omaha, Nebraska, Buffett was the second of three children and the only son.

Buffett's grandfather and great grandfather (on his father's side) were crusty small-time grocers in Omaha, good at business but very frugal. His father was a small-time stockbroker, a very conservative and highly ethical man who later went on to become a senator for Nebraska in Washington. This move was to have mixed results for young Buffett.

His mother's parents were small newspaper publishers and she was said to have a great head for numbers. Unfortunately she was also emotionally unstable, which made her unpredictable to live with.

> Without warning, that good-humored woman would
> become furious beyond words, and rage at her children
> with an unrelenting meanness, sometimes not letting up
> for hours. She scolded and degraded her children. Nothing
> they had done measured up (Lowenstein 1996).

Buffett coped by avoiding conflict wherever possible. This also had the effect of pushing him away from his mother and seeking and luckily gaining approval from other relatives, notably his father, grandfather and grandmother. Buffet's father, Howard, was said to be serious and kind—a conservative, liberal pillar of society, both exceptionally honest and frugal.

When Buffett was ten, he visited Wall Street with his father. He became fascinated with the way the prices were chalked up. Back home

27

he was allowed to do this in his father's stockbroking business. His father obviously thought this was cute and as a result directed Buffett's prodigious interest in numbers towards investing.

Despite the variability in his mother's emotions, Buffett had a liberal upbringing for the times. He had considerable regard for his father and identified strongly with him. He was allowed to be with his friends and carry out his activities relatively unimpeded. These activities always involved counting and, as time went on, money. This included tipping horse races, salvaging golf balls for money, and paper rounds. Luckily there were no great sporting or social expectations placed on him, as he had no interest in either.

He had loving grandparents with whom he had a great deal of contact. His grandfather Ernest seems to have had one of the most formative influences on Buffett. His philosophy, developed during the Great Depression, was to save his credit, because credit is better than money. Buffett almost never spends money—he wants credit.

His father gave him regular lectures on the importance of sticking to his guns. This sounds very much like the annual lecture given by Buffett at the Berkshire Hathaway meetings. Howard was an extremely ethical person, a trait he inherited from his father and passed to his son. Howard would refuse work junkets and other benefits, which many politicians accepted as their right.

Howard Buffett established a stockbroking business during the Great Depression. Times were tough but they had turned around by the time Buffett was six. This early experience of tough times apparently had a lasting impact on Buffett. It is reported that before he was five years old, he had already resolved to become extremely rich. Maybe this time of financial hardship did fuel some of his drive to become rich, but millions of people suffered through the depression without emerging from it as Buffett did—the depression years probably affirmed the direction he was already heading in. Buffett received approval for making money; he can make money and it gave—and still gives him—his place in the world.

Buffett's father was elected as a senator to Washington when Buffett was eleven. It was at this time that Buffett's father started moving the family around, which totally dislocated Buffett. He was taken away from his friends, and his father was away from the family during the week. Buffett became very homesick and sad. He developed a mystery allergy and sleep disorder. He wrote to his grandfather that he was unhappy, and arrangements were made for him to finish eighth grade back in Omaha. He worked in Grandpa's store where he received approval from Aunt Alice, a free-spirited economics teacher, and Grandpa Ernest, an instinctive teacher. Miraculously his problems went away.

28

Buffett's reprieve did not last. At twelve he was forced out of Omaha to Washington where he was well out of the social stream. His grades weren't very good, and having skipped a grade he was young for his class. Buffett's only joy was his paper round. At the end of the year he ran away, which shocked his parents. When he was recovered he was given an ultimatum—shape up or lose his paper round. He shaped up and threw himself into the paper round.

At school Buffett was the leader of a small group of semi-outsiders. He had a particularly close friend in Omaha when he was young, but his friendship groups became dislocated when he was forced to move on several occasions with his father. But he wasn't without friends. He almost always had one or two friends who subordinated to him in business ventures. Clearly he learnt that he could escape emotional pain by being busy and successful in business, an orientation that never left him.

Now a tall, relatively awkward man, at school he was a tall, awkward boy and did not have a girlfriend growing up. Socially inept and unfashionable, he was very much the outsider and he didn't try to be otherwise. Buffett wore sneakers to school, and was different in appearance and behaviour. It seems that he enjoyed being different, or maybe he just didn't know how to fit in. While not unpopular he was rather disconnected socially. He would drift in and out of contact, even when he was playing a team sport.

At fourteen and still at school, Buffett took on a new paper round. He systematised it and soon had five paper rounds. He then expanded his line into magazines and learnt how to spot the most likely targets for subscriptions. He was earning $175 a month, the same salary as a young man in a full-time job. He took his $1200 in profits and bought a farm. In his senior year he developed a pinball business with a friend, which he later sold. By the time he left school he was earning more than his teachers.

Buffett went to two humble colleges in the US mid-west. Not quite fitting in socially, he rushed to finish in three years, worked nearly a full-time job supervising newspaper boys, played bridge and finished with straight A's. He failed to gain entry to Harvard Business School, probably because he didn't distinguish himself in any way except academically. He had no sport and unlike Gates, didn't come from a high-status family. However, he was accepted to go to Columbia to study under the great Benjamin Graham, a guru of the stock market at the time.

At college, Buffett kept to himself. But he did gain approval by pontificating to groups in the same manner his father did at home. Warren could entertain a party with his talks on, for example, the gold standard. It became a routine that by the end of a night Buffett would be surrounded by an attentive audience.

It was under Graham that he learned many (but not all) of his basic trading philosophies. Buffett's primary philosophy is to invest when prices are far below their intrinsic value based on the fundamentals of the stock. The fundamentals are what the business is doing and what its future appears to be. He also believes that the value of poor trading 'good' stocks will eventually be recognised and the stock price will rise to match the fundamentals. This correction may take some time, which is why he is an investor rather than a trader.

While with Graham, he started his own investing. At the time Wall Street was very conservative and there were many bargains around. Graham, having come through the stock market crash of the 1920s, was even more conservative than Buffett, so Buffett began investing in many stocks that his teacher rejected. By the time he left college and under the tutelage of Graham, he was familiar with most stocks and bonds in existence. He would read more than a thousand annual reports a year and remember them.

Buffett is always his own man. He always makes up his own mind without consultation and absolutely eschews advice givers and public opinion. A particularly indicative story concerns an American Express subsidiary that had inadvertently become embroiled in some shady dealing, which had become public. The conventional financial wisdom around the stockbroking scene was that the company was in trouble and consequently the shares took a tumble. Buffett went to several restaurants and watched consumers use their cards and concluded that the scandal had made no difference to the real market—consumers. Irrespective of what value the stockbrokers placed on the shares, the fundamentals of the business had not changed. He bought a big stake and profited. Berkshire Hathaway remains one of American Express's largest shareholders.

He is typically gloomy when the Dow Jones is doing well and buoyant when others are gloomy. Buffett is a counter-cyclic man! This is, of course, because there are no bargains in a bull market and lots in a bear market. Hence, by being independent of market think, he profited where others did not. Unlike many people, investors included, Buffett wants to be right, not in step with the market, and he and many others have profited from his being out of step.

Buffett is almost totally focused on investment to the point of excluding anything else. He is famous for being frugal and not engaging in excessive spending, despite his tremendous wealth. He still likes hamburgers and lives in a modest family home in a typical street. Buffett doesn't have much use for other people if they aren't investors (source of capital), collaborators or an audience for his now famous lectures.

Buffett's catchcry is: 'It's not that I want money. It's the fun of making money and watching it grow' (Lowenstein 1996). Money is for investing and growing, and that is the sole point for Buffett. It is a huge testimony to his concentration that he grew a modest pile of cash into such a huge pile of cash and made the lives of many investors richer along the way. But Buffett's life has been very single focused. It excludes actually running companies; in fact, it excludes just about everything else, including family and community. People are just bit players in Buffett's life.

> Money is for investing and growing, and that is the sole point for Buffett.

By the 1990s, Buffett was a billionaire and had become the guru that he is now. People were starting to recognise him in public. His only real concession to wealth was to buy a private jet so that he didn't have to mix with the public. He found the constant interruptions, gratuitous advice and deal offers made by total strangers in airports annoying.

Buffett is honest and hard working. He takes his responsibilities for other people's money very seriously, and he delivers year after year. Buffett is an investor and a very good one.

In the mid 1990s, he employed fewer than fifty people and bought into companies that were already established. His essential business model is to buy stocks that are trading at less than their intrinsic value and hold them for a long time. He limits his risk by doing his homework and not investing in start-up businesses, particularly hi-tech. Buffett's happy to let everybody else take the risk on that!

Despite having the will to be a philanthropist, he struggled. He was constantly asking if people knew any good charities, but few met his criteria—he was concerned that people or organisations that were given his charity might actually use the money instead of investing it.

Buffett's ongoing lack of civic generosity has been a constant source of irritation to the Omaha community. They had one of the world's richest people living among them and yet there was no evidence of it nor much benefit from it. There were no hospital buildings, libraries, not even an injection of capital with the building of a new office building. Buffett worked out of down-market commercial premises and never employed many people. And he never sold a share of Berkshire, his only investment vehicle.

Until recently the words Buffett and philanthropy were rarely heard together. When asked for donations he gave homilies not cash. In recent times he has given up trying to be a philanthropist in his own right and joined much of his fortune with that of Bill Gates to be administered through the Gates Foundation. He does, however, have time for Bill Gates. Gates and Buffett have a rivalry over who is top of the *Forbes* world's billionaires list and they play bridge.

Buffett's early relationships were focused mainly around transactions. He was committed to his obsession—numbers and business. He courted only one woman, Susie, a woman he won more by persistence than dash. Once she was won, family became entirely the responsibility of his wife. Despite working from home much of the time, he was largely absent from all things related to family. For all family and social matters, Buffett was totally dependent on his wife; he worked to the exclusion of all else. He was not much of a companion or husband. When his wife 'left' him when she was forty-five to pursue a music career, he was mystified about why she had left.

He was hardly separated from his first wife when another woman, Astrid Menks from Omaha, moved in with him. Clearly this is a testimony to the attractiveness of billionaires rather than the intrinsic attractiveness of the man. Big piles of money are often compensations for other inadequacies. The ex-wife and the new woman got on and Buffett was often seen in public with both. He never divorced his first wife and she occupied a place on the *Forbes* list until she died. Buffett recently married his long-term companion, Menks.

Buffett had a peculiar relationship with his close and wider family. He was always aloof when it came to his children. When they were growing up, he was around but not available. Warm, but distant. The family benefited little from Buffett's investment skills. For example, his sister Doris went broke trading shares and he let her.

He has given his children very little in terms of money (or attention for that matter). When he helped his son into a farm, he insisted on setting the terms of a market rent. Buffett absolutely refused to go to the farm even just to share the experience with his son—he just wanted to see the balance sheet. He gave his children small parcels of Berkshire shares, which they sold early to finance the normal sorts of things young people want to buy, and that was that—there was no more coming from Warren.

Buffett is a talker rather than a conversationalist. He doesn't care much for parties and generally eschews anything that is not directly related to investing; it would be praising him to say that he is socially inept. There is a story about him sitting next to a woman at a dinner party held shortly after the collapse of his marriage. Buffett was single and had just become well known. The woman sitting next to him asked him to cut her steak. Suspecting that she was motivated to start a relationship,

Buffett literally turned his back on her. The reality was that she had her arm in a sling and couldn't cut her own meat. All she was asking for was a simple act of kindness, and Buffett was so wrapped up in his own world that he didn't notice her difficulty.

Interpretation

Buffett comes from a loving family with an unstable mother. He could never be certain whether he was going to receive love or abuse from her. Buffett would have been ashamed of his mother and avoided bringing other children home because he could never be sure what humiliation she would heap on him or his friends. He may also have been teased about his mother. She would not have been integrated into the mothers' networks, therefore increasing the isolation the already awkward young Buffett would have experienced. Because any interaction with his mother was bound to be unpredictable, he would have been unable to learn about loving and dealing with day-to-day conflicts and normal interactions. Such instability is formative on an infant and would have driven the infant Buffett to concentrate on doing the small number of things he could do and gain approval for.

He could be certain of approval from his austere father by demonstrating an interest in numbers, finance, stocks and shares. Buffett had close times with his father on their trip to Wall Street and when he played at his father's work chalking up stock figures. His father's office would have been an oasis of calm and approval in contrast to home, which was unpredictable and frequently emotionally dangerous. While trading was in the family, Buffett would have had any such tendencies reinforced by 'working' in his father's business. He would have learnt as a small boy that the office and work is safe and rewarding, while home is a problem. This later became his pattern even though his wife was nothing like his mother.

His grandfather and aunt also provided Buffett with formative approval, which locked in interest in small business, frugality and economics. Despite the size of Berkshire Hathaway's investments, it is a small business run on small business principles modelled on his grandfather's store and his father's small stockbroking business.

As an infant, Buffett was obsessed with counting. Counting evolved into a strong interest in money. Early games with his friend involved counting bottle caps to determine the strongest brand in the market. He would spend hours reading his father's stock tickertape. By nine he had a thriving business salvaging golf balls and reselling them—this business he returned to time and again until he went to college. From the time he was six, Buffett was constantly doing business, as business has its own rewards.

An early trip to Wall Street with his father increased Buffett's fascination with stocks. At eleven he was charting his own stocks and had bought three. He developed a tipping system for horse racing and sold the tips—he was shut down for operating without a licence. He was obsessed with numbers.

Always an outsider, Buffett was a tall, awkward, bright boy, and one who could never make friends easily. He would have been always a little off centre in the way he thought and because he was constantly uprooted he was never able to maintain a place in his peer group. His obvious high intelligence, awkwardness and poor social skills would have further isolated him at school, and since he didn't concentrate on sports he had no easy means of connecting with other children. His shying away from interactions with other people would have led him into what is essentially a technical job. He is not good with people, and he buys and sells companies at arm's length without actually 'getting dirty'; in other words, avoiding dealing with people issues. He is a technician.

He probably started with limited social or emotional intelligence, but his interactions with his mother and constant upheavals during growing up put paid to any continuity in whatever limited way those intelligences were going to develop. He compensated for lack of genuine social skills by becoming a technician—he had to manage very little and build nothing except investment. His focus is extremely narrow and extremely deep.

In public he comes over as warm and folksy. This is Buffett the guru. In fact, it is Buffett emulating his hero, Buffett Senior, the man who lectured the family at the dinner table and became the senator for Nebraska. In reality Buffett is neither warm nor folksy.

Buffett was an outsider right from the beginning. His natural brightness and talent for numbers ensured that he would always be slightly different from the herd. But given his mother's emotional instability and all the moving around as a young man, he was always going to be knocked well and truly off centre. He gained some stability and admiration through developing businesses and always seemed to manage to get a small group of friends together to help. These groups gave him the acceptance he craved. Always socially awkward, being in business with some fellow school children gave him some control of the situation; it gave him a reason to belong. So long as he had work for his followers to do, they were bound together. Buffett's model of belonging was transactional—he obviously felt that as soon as the transactions stopped he was likely to lose friends. Earning more than his teachers was an added incentive to do business.

His business achievements would have given him many emotional rewards from his father and other close relatives. Later, at college, he also gained approval for being able to hold forth on economic matters. Students would get him started and let him lecture.

With business tendencies inherited from both parents and a fascination with numbers inherited from his mother, Buffett was born for and steered by his environment to his ultimate destiny. He was doing business from a very young age—it was what gave him comfort and approval in his unstable upbringing.

He picked up a smorgasbord of starter ideas and encouragement from father, grandfather and aunt, and his investment guru, Benjamin Graham, and through trial and error worked out that he could rationally think his way through any (rational) situation. In particular, he trusted his own advice because experience taught him that the advice of others was virtually worthless. If you could earn more than your teachers while at school, what use was anything they had to say?

This pretty much explains the origins of Buffett's business—a small enterprise, run by an outsider, with the assistance of his now best friend. The business is based on Buffett's deep affection for numbers and his equally deep understanding of stocks. Buffett's business is protected by his extreme frugality and distrust of conventional wisdom, and driven by his intense, single-minded focus on his work.

He could have chosen to remain largely invisible or less enigmatic, but Buffett loves pontificating in public to gain the approval he craves. This may be the main reason that Buffett started and continues to lecture on behalf of Berkshire Hathaway (aside from the fact that guru status will undoubtedly be good for his stock price).

By the time Buffett was twenty-five he was more or less set on his course. There was a great deal of learning to do and a huge amount of trading, but essentially it was along the trajectory already established. The rocket was fuelled and had taken off.

References:

Kilpatrick, A 2001, *Of Permanent Value: the Story of Warren Buffett,* McGraw-Hill, New York.

Lowenstein, R 1996, *Buffett: the Making of an American Capitalist,* Weidenfeld & Nicolson, London.

Chapter 5

Ingvar Kamprad

Forbes information 2007
Rank: 4
Citizenship: Sweden
Wealth: US$33 billion
Industry: retail

Ingvar Kamprad has never worked for anyone but himself. The quintessential outsider from the rural back blocks, he started retailing and a mail-order business when he was five and has been growing it ever since.

The IKEA name was adopted by the young Kamprad at seventeen and while still at school as an outgrowth of the mail-order business he operated out of a tiny shed. It was a family affair, started first on the remote Swedish family farm and then later moved to the local village. Once he left school, driven to succeed, Kamprad evolved the business progressively and eventually had to abandon mail order only business because the fierce competition drove down prices to such an extent that quality had to be compromised.

Achievement

IKEA advertised furniture for the first time in 1948 when Kamprad was twenty-two. Kamprad sourced his furniture locally—people ordered from him and the factories delivered direct to customers. Cutting out the middlemen made the product cheaper, and this was sufficient until complaints about quality began. He bought a local empty factory and converted it to retail premises and on 18 March 1953 opened for business, after first distributing a mail-order catalogue. The idea was to use the catalogue to tempt people into the store. Customers could bring their catalogues into the store and browse, and test out the furniture they had seen. They could then place an order and would receive their goods via mail. Serendipitously Kamprad had combined the cost benefits of mail-order buying while reducing customers' uncertainty about what they were buying. Success was immediate. In the first years after opening, tens of thousands of people travelled from all over Sweden to visit the store in Almhult.

Devaluation of Sweden's currency in 1949 accelerated the nation's export industry. Any businesses that had survived the devastation of industry during World War II were poised to make money, and Sweden's gross domestic product grew rapidly right through the 1950s and 1960s. Sweden prospered, and its products were in demand. People were moving around, building was at record levels and people needed furniture. Kamprad had started the right business at the right time.

Naturally such popularity and cheap prices threatened the existing furniture retailers, who applied cartel-like pressures on manufacturers to prevent supply to IKEA. Kamprad was also banned from trade fairs—important events at the time. This caused him to seek all sorts of expedient measures to secure suppliers. One of his innovations was in being one of the first, and then later one of the largest, buyers from and investors in suppliers in Poland.

Since the boycott prevented IKEA from buying pre-existing designs from local suppliers, it had to design its own furniture. It was during one catalogue photoshoot that one of IKEA's most profitable design ideas was stumbled upon. While packing up, the designer commented that table legs take up a lot of space and that they should be taken off and packed under the table. From this simple suggestion IKEA developed flat packs, with the furniture assembled by the purchaser. The self-assemble table was included in the 1953 catalogue, and by 1956 IKEA had a whole range of self-assemble furniture. There were many advantages to be gained from this method. The number of products that were damaged during delivery was reduced, and since the bulk of items was reduced, so were all the handling and transport costs, particularly the cost of delivery to customers.

IKEA moved towards 'democratic design'—that is, a design that is not just good, but is also suited to machine production and therefore cheap to produce. This, in combination with self assembly, helped to dramatically reduce the production and shipment costs for IKEA, which helped keep prices down for customers. From an early age Kamprad had wondered about the large disparity between prices at the factory and prices in the stores. He concluded that distribution was a major contributor to this difference and his design innovations and his practice of shipping direct from manufacturer to IKEA store and self assembly were major factors in controlling costs. As IKEA grew it also achieved cost-saving economies of scale and much more negotiation clout with suppliers, further driving down costs.

After a time the cartel became unimportant because IKEA had grown so large—with a presence in major towns—that exclusion from events and advertising was no longer of market consequence. Instead of forcing IKEA out of business, the boycott had the opposite effect. Kamprad innovated his way out of trouble and developed an almost invincible retail formula. While Almhult has remained the central IKEA 'shrine', it was outgrown in 1965 and a new flagship store was built in Kungens. Having developed his retail formula, Kamprad continued IKEA's relentless expansion. Growth was easier in Europe than in the US because existing European furniture suppliers were traditional, which left a large gap in the market for a new consumer-based furniture retailer, whereas the US already had an established consumer market so competition was much tougher. The incursion into the US, while ultimately successful, took much longer to become established than in Europe.

Unusually for many modern retailers, IKEA both owns and operates most of its sites. This means that as well as operating incomes, it also receives capital gains from real estate investment.

Development

Ingvar Kamprad was born in 1926, and his sister four years later, on a remote farm (Elmtaryd) in southern Sweden, close to the small but remote village of Almhult. This is the origin of the name IKEA—I(ngvar) K(amprad) E(lmtaryd) A(lmhult).

His grandmother was the illegitimate child of an innkeeper, while his grandfather was a man from a good family and a long line of foresters. After their marriage, the stigma of her illegitimacy prompted the couple to emigrate to the forests of southern Sweden, only for them to suffer the double stigma of illegitimacy and foreignness.

They purchased the forested property sight unseen from a mail-order company. Times were hard and the grandfather took to drinking. They were undercapitalised, and on failing to get a bank loan Kamprad's grandfather committed suicide.

His grandmother was a stern, strong and stubborn woman. Despite being left alone in an unknown country to care for her children, she managed to became a respected employer. Given her poor start in life it is unsurprising to find that she became controlling. She controlled everyone and everything in her orbit. Grandmother dominated all, and eventually her son, Ingvar's uncle, also committed suicide.

Ingvar's father (Franz Feodor), refused permission by his mother to follow another career, took over the farm. He married the local village shopkeeper's daughter. Kamprad's mother, Berta Nilsson, was from a leading trading family in Almhult; her father ran Almhult's largest country store. Franz brought his bride to live in the family home with his mother, who Kamprad described as being a clever woman who influenced the entire family. But of course there was tension between his domineering grandmother and his mother.

Luckily Kamprad's grandmother liked him, so he did not suffer her wrath. He says she 'protected' him from the outside world. When Kamprad began his business career buying and selling things at the age of five, his grandmother became his best customer. She would buy things she didn't need to support his endeavours. This gave young Kamprad the confidence to expand and start selling to his neighbours. Kamprad's paternal grandmother doted on him.

Kamprad says that trading is in his blood—he spent a lot of time at the store with his maternal grandfather and would run errands for him. It was a typical country store of the time, selling just about anything a family in such an isolated community could need. Kamprad and his grandfather were very close—he encouraged the young boy's imagination and made him believe that anything was possible. The very first real IKEA store stands on the site of the old store, and remains a shrine to IKEA.

Everything that couldn't be purchased in the local general store had to be purchased by going to the nearest towns and cities—a challenge in those pre-automobile days—or, most commonly, bought from mail-order catalogues. You can imagine the excitement the young and isolated

Kamprad must have felt when a new catalogue came out or goods arrived by mail. It is no wonder the boy was drawn to mail-order selling.

Life on the farm would have been like being brought up on a boat that occasionally puts to shore. Kamprad's family appears to have been loving in a tough, dysfunctional kind of way and the extended family was considered important. Kamprad's strongest relationships were with his family.

School went badly for Kamprad. He was uninterested in sport and dyslexic. He says that the books he has finished reading could be 'counted on the fingers of one hand' (Torekull 1998). His family was stigmatised by the local community for being both new and German with a grandfather and uncle who committed suicide and an illegitimate grandmother. At best Kamprad was probably treated as dumb and ostracised, possibly even bullied. School would not have been fun.

In Kamprad's latter years of schooling he went to two boarding schools. He was bullied at both. These schools operated a system not unlike that of English boarding schools where the younger students are systematically bullied to perform servant duties for older students.

At that time, he joined a secret political party and drew swastikas, but all that seems like a simple boy flirting with the power politics of the day. When Kamprad was moved to senior school in another city he attended Neo-Swede (Nazi) meetings. The local leader was the biology teacher, who Kamprad says was very nice.

Lonely young Kamprad was under the influence of his family—the people he loved. Both his grandmother and his loved father had strong pro-Nazi leanings. His father was considered pure Nazi locally—not necessarily a point for ostracism as pre-war Sweden was Nazi tolerant. When the local teacher came around to play cards, there was much talk of Germany and the positive influence of Hitler. Kamprad's grandmother also admired Hitler and his plans for a greater Germany.

The family received a lot of propaganda material from Germany. With the naiveté of youth, Kamprad thought Hitler was doing a lot to help Germany, including his grandmother's relatives. He was also moved by the Nazi ceremonies. He says that at the time he admired both Hitler and Lindholm (a local Nazi leader), which he was later ashamed of. He put up Lindholm posters and attended a Lindholm camp for Nordic Youth in 1941. The camaraderie was enticing to a young boy with few friends his own age. But while attracted to the pomp and camaraderie of Nazism, Kamprad obviously didn't follow the party line very closely. One of his closest friends at the time was a German-Jewish refugee.

Kamprad later converted to the Engdahl movement. At sixteen he went to a meeting and was seated next to Engdahl, who greeted him warmly. The lonely Kamprad was noticed, and naturally he was flattered by this attention. Eventually his flirtation with the Nazis lapsed and he reverted to his first love, the mail-order business.

His flirtation with the Nazi and Neo-Swede movements has haunted Kamprad on two occasions. He weathered the storm by open disclosure and a lot of scrutiny. A rabbi working in the Simon Wiesenthal Center in Los Angeles was convinced that Kamprad's company had never discriminated against Israel, and that for a long time it had actually purchased from Israeli suppliers and sold to Israeli customers. The Center also accepted Kamprad's regrets over his Nazi involvement when he was young.

Kamprad's first marriage dissolved acrimoniously. He says that he and his wife had a few happy years while they lived on the farm but she didn't like his obsessive concentration on work. Kamprad was away often, and the marriage slowly disintegrated. His second marriage has endured.

Interpretation

Mothers are usually the most important people in an infant's life, yet Kamprad barely mentions his, choosing to concentrate on his domineering grandmother. Without a doubt, there were unusual and tense interplays between mother, grandmother and the infant Kamprad. The adult Kamprad now admits to breaking down in tears quite often when under stress, and to being an alcoholic. Grandmother would have been both obsessive and intrusive. Equally undoubtedly, Kamprad would have had split loyalties—he would have been present when his grandmother chastised his mother and bullied her about how she should run the family. Kamprad probably could not easily reconcile his relationship with his mother with family life.

Kamprad began buying and selling from the age of five, with strong family encouragement

Kamprad began buying and selling from the age of five, with strong family encouragement. Such a money-making activity guaranteed the admiration of his domineering grandmother and turned her into a supporter, a very privileged relationship in the fraught family. In such a fractious family, making money was admired and it was safe—everyone agreed that this was a good activity. Kamprad and his mail-order business ventures were protected, promoted and admired.

Grandmother was the most important person in the young Kamprad's life. Whatever love she gave would have been tough love. After all, she had lost a husband and son to suicide and was almost certainly a contributing factor in both.

Kamprad would have been drawn to mail-order business because of the excitement surrounding the arrival of catalogues and orders. His involvement at such a young age would have brought sweet approval when his life outside home was socially bleak.

Kamprad tells of one of his first ever business transactions, at around the age of five. His aunt helped him purchase one hundred boxes of matches, which he sold for a large profit. He still remembers the good feeling that gave him. Young Kamprad had just pulled off what he felt was a major retail success and the family gave him accolades. And so it continued — lingonberries, garden seeds, bicycles, typewriters, fountain pens. Kamprad experienced a continual heady mix of turnover, profit and family approval. He remembers his father talking about things they could do if only they had some more money, and this only added more fuel as Kamprad could see himself as the family's saviour. Selling became an obsession.

His business methods are all self-learned and he freely admits to many mistakes. He knows that he is odd and an outsider. He is also deeply insecure. He hates to be late, and says he arrives at the airport an hour and a half early so that he feels safe. He is known to break down and cry when addressing staff and is a self-declared alcoholic.

Today Kamprad is still troubled by self-doubt, despite his prodigious success. He still sees himself as an underdog, and strives to prove that he is good enough. Being a multinational businessman does not seem to come easily to him. He eschews the trappings that normally come with such a life, such as nice clothes and accessories and expensive cars — he drives an old Volvo wagon. And he runs his company the same way. IKEA staff travel economy class, as does Kamprad, a culture that is deeply ingrained at IKEA.

He suffers from twin insecurities. First there is the hunger of a peasant living always in the shadow of tough times, right on the edge of survival. The constant fear that crop failure will bring disaster and the only help is the family. No-one other than the family can be relied on in tough times.

Kamprad insists on calling IKEA employees his family even after IKEA grew to over 200 stores globally. Non-family cannot be relied on. This is especially so for banks. After all, Grandpa killed himself when turned down for a bank loan. Consequently, not since the early days has IKEA had a loan. It is built up entirely from re-investment from cash flows.

Second is the fear that if he doesn't keep getting better in his business, he will not be loved. His sense of love as a young boy was based on being successful in his mail-order business. His entire family was undoubtedly stingy when it came to expressing uncontingent love, but they did express love and approval for young Ingvar's business. This was especially important for achieving the love of his grandmother. Young Kamprad alone was the recipient of her love while everyone else received a tongue lashing. But his grandmother's love could not be relied on to continue indefinitely; it was contingent on continuing to produce an increasing number of little joys by mail.

These feelings of joy Kamprad experienced through being a retailer would have been reinforced by his maternal grandfather. He provided love and approval in the safe haven of the local general store. No wonder Kamprad was compulsively drawn to both being a shopkeeper and running a catalogue-based business. IKEA is the embodiment of both.

Undoubtedly, Kamprad was left with the feeling that he was only lovable if he was doing well at business—aside from that he had no worth at all. He still seeks acknowledgement and approval. Such feelings would have induced an obsessive need to be successful in business to get love, and a sense of worthlessness because he was only lovable if he was doing business. This would explain why he often cried and this may also contribute to his being an alcoholic. He felt unworthy and unlovable in his own right. He certainly doesn't seek the thrill of being rich for its own sake. But there was a cost. Kamprad spent a huge amount of time as a boy and adolescent working, when other children were having fun.

IKEA started as a family concern in Kamprad's home village. Everyone was involved. As a young businessman his first customers were family members, and as the business grew his family could always be called upon. His father became chairman and kept the books, and his mother was always around to help. After a while the business dominated the family home. Kamprad has tried to keep the family feel at IKEA, even as the business grew into a multinational; he needs to think of it as an extended family. And in keeping with it being a family concern he has resisted floating the company on the stock exchange. In the early days Kamprad interviewed every recruit as though he was taking on a son- or daughter-in-law.

The sixth statement in the IKEA Furniture Dealer's Testament is 'Doing it a different way'. Kamprad worked against the odds from the start. Starting a company in a small place like Almhult would not usually be considered a road to international success. Kamprad prides himself on the fact that IKEA is different, and believes this is part of the company's success.

Since he 'invented' his business, it has always been different. He had no formal retail training nor has he ever worked for another retailer. Even the great Sam Walton of Wal-Mart, another farm boy, started off in other retail businesses. Kamprad grew his company entirely from outside the established industry. It is an outsider company run by an outsider.

It is no coincidence that Sam Walton was also a country boy who began his business in small rural towns, honing his model and then finally moving out of the countryside to take on the big competitors in large centres across the US. Sam Walton, if alive, would be the world's richest man but Kamprad would be catching up.

Kamprad couldn't help being an outsider—a dyslexic, isolated farm boy with a disposition to trade. His trading was fuelled by positive feedback from his family with overtones of impending doom due to harsh living conditions, undercapitalisation and incessant crop uncertainty. The need for business success would be far more than just providing physical requirements, it would have a strong emotional overlay due to the suicide of his grandfather and uncle, as well as loving and being loved by his controlling paternal grandmother. Wealth staves off the death of loved ones—this gave Kamprad his essential hunger. There can never be enough love or material surplus for Kamprad—IKEA will never be big enough!

References:

Kamprad, I & Torekull, B 1998, *Leading by Design: the IKEA Story*, HarperBusiness, New York.

Lewis, E 2005, *Great IKEA! A Brand For All the People*, Cyan books, London.

Chapter 6

Larry Ellison

Forbes information 2007
Rank: 11
Citizenship: United States
Wealth: US$21.5 billion
Industry: software

Larry Ellison is the co-founder, visionary and leading light of Oracle Software, the database company. Currently he is Oracle's CEO.

Ellison's compulsive need to appear the hero created in him a highly developed ability to embroider the truth, to spin and to overpromise. Once Ellison had his own company and was the leader of a team that actually had to deliver on his promises, some of this overpromising became reality. Ellison's compulsive invention became 'vision' and was the engine that drove Oracle's innovation and success. This meant that Oracle not only appeared to stay ahead of the competition, but actually did so. In the early days of Oracle there was a tendency to over promise and under deliver. But Oracle rapidly improved on its own products. It also leapt ahead of the more technologically precise but slower-to-market competition and eventually drove them out of the market. This proves that fast to market with spin beats technological precision every time!

Achievement

After moving from Chicago to California after having been expelled from the University of Illinois for lack of performance and dropping out of the University of Chicago after one semester, Ellison drifted from job to job. Ostensibly he was a programmer, but by all accounts he didn't do very much programming. Ellison is characterised by talking. He reportedly never closed his mouth. But he is charismatic, and is the kind of person that other people will follow.

As he moved from job to job, he met people, notably Bob Miner and Edward Oates, who would later become his partners. This is one of the most notable computing partnerships; others include Gates and Allen (Microsoft), and Jobs and Wozniak (Apple). Each partnership worked as a team, with one dominating as an entrepreneur and the other a programmer with strong technical skills.

Ellison landed a job as vice-president of systems engineering for a company attempting, unsuccessfully, to make mass data storage units. The company made hardware and needed software to drive it, so they called for suppliers to provide this under contract. Ellison brought Miner and Oates over as contractors and they started a contracting company to write the driver software for the hardware. Ellison had 60 per cent of the shares. While the software 'worked', the project was a technical failure in the sense that the hardware was too unreliable to perform properly.

Ellison did not have a vision for the future of software and his place in it. He was solely motivated to be his own boss and by the selling process. The owners of the fledgling company did not like being contractors. As contractors they needed to continually write different pieces of software on demand with no ownership of the final product. For this they got only the contracted sum.

The partners had the key idea to write a single program and sell it over and over again, in essence changing their business model from being boutique commissioned software developers to being something much more like a traditional manufacturer. This was a novel idea at the time as the software industry wasn't yet an industry but a collection of academics, boffins, hobbyists and big hardware companies such as IBM. The large hardware companies were only interested in software because it was needed to run their few incredibly expensive machines. In the days before software houses, Oracle, like Microsoft, became a software manufacturer, whereas Apple was developed in the IBM model of software tied to and in the service of specific hardware.

As with many start-ups it was an idea looking for a product, so there remained the problem of what software to write. At that time there was talk of relational databases being developed at IBM so, in the tradition of software companies, the fledgling Oracle 'borrowed' the idea. This relational database software would eventually become the cornerstone of Oracle's business.

The key to Oracle picking up market share in the relational database market was that it was fast to market and it overpromised its performance capabilities. It got into the market with a semi-viable product before IBM had even moved its equivalent product out of its research division. IBM was slow because its business ethos, as a market leader, was to never release untested or unreliable product, as it would be damaging to their reputation. Oracle, as the impertinent upstart, felt no such restraints.

While Ellison's company was fast and shoddy, they found a small number of early adopter tech buyers that were happy to pioneer a new product. These pioneers never expected the product to be perfect, nor able to deliver on all its promises, but they wanted products like that developed anyway and were happy to take on a far less-than-perfect product for the sake of kick-starting the industry. These customers, typically in strategic government positions, also believed that it was their duty to support new product to ensure that it actually became viable over time. Undoubtedly these clients were boy enthusiasts of sci-fi and believed in the future of computers.

Typically, people try to diminish Ellison's achievement by saying he was in the right place at the right time—luck in other words. But nobody handed either the initial idea or his ultimate success to him on a plate. The information about relational databases was available to all through published papers. He saw the opportunity and built a huge company and personal fortune on the back of that idea.

Ellison considers that there are always opportunities available. He built his fortune through tireless work and determination, and by being himself.

Early contracts for Oracle came in from the CIA and Navy Intelligence. While they were generally accommodating clients, they demanded that the database run on three different types of machines. There was no dominant computer operating system at the time so, with what turned out to be a stroke of brilliance on Ellison's part, the decision was made to make the software portable—in other words, able to work on any computer and any operating system. This became a very powerful selling point.

The software didn't deliver its basic database requirements—let alone the portability claim—for several versions, but sales kept growing. This was a testimony to Ellison's spin abilities and the tolerance of early clients to support product development. At times the company was considered to be selling 'vapourware'. But Oracle weren't the only ones—Microsoft has been accused of doing the same many times over the years.

Like just about all companies started by entrepreneurs, the early Oracle company was chaotic. Recruitment and budgeting were ad-hoc and often Oracle struggled to meet salary. Ellison saw life and business as a contest, and he was always striving to prove himself. He wanted to win at everything. 'Ellison seemed willing to do or say almost anything to get business' (Wilson 1998). There was no doubt that he was charismatic, and people would follow him—at times without knowing why.

It is generally recognised that average technology and good marketing will beat good technology and average marketing. In a number of cases, his opposition had superior technology but lost on marketing. Ellison the relentless marketer simply ran over the top of technically superior but marketing-inferior competition.

Ellison's continual overpromising had benefits—he stretched his product developers and the product. During interviews or sales pitches he invented new capabilities for his software and then demanded his partners and staff deliver. They didn't often deliver as much as promised but they were always stretched—consequently the product was always being improved much faster than any competitive software was. Ellison, like Gates, also used overpromising to checkmate the opposition. Clients would hold off buying other company's products to wait for the new Oracle product.

Ellison's management style left a lot to be desired. He hated doing anything that would make him unpopular, so he hated doing that very worst of management jobs—firing people. It is reported that Ellison often avoided this task by hiring someone else and letting them do the firing of the incumbent.

Oracle continued to grow. It was handed a coup when IBM's software language was adopted as an industry standard for mainframe computers, because that was the language Oracle used. Oracle's main competitor, who had been using a competing language, effectively fell by the wayside even though its product was technically superior—its demise was helped along by Ellison's relentless marketing and that company's own slow to market 'academic', technically perfect orientation.

The working culture at Oracle was unrelentingly tough. In addition to stretching the software development teams, Ellison insisted that sales targets were met. He pursued growth relentlessly, doubling sales revenue every year. The sales force was aggressive and so were the deals. Sales kept doubling. By the mid 1980s Bob Miner, the technical guru, was worn out and left, unfortunately, to die of cancer soon after.

Oracle and Microsoft both listed as public companies in 1986. Ellison ended the opening day with $93 million and Gates with $300 million. The competition between Gates and Ellison was just beginning—over the years it has extended to houses, cars and media coverage.

By 1990, Oracle had become a large company but its small start-up company mentality nearly made it hit the wall. Bad accounting and management meant it wasn't staying on top of money owed to it. It had a huge amount of cash owed in outstanding and defaulting bills. In addition, the software market was maturing. The early clients were allies in software development but now the clients, like the software, were becoming more mainstream. Software was becoming an essential business tool that had to be reliable, so clients became more demanding. Pesky clients began to insist on software working before they paid for it, resulting in re-working of product and delays in bill payment.

To top off Oracle's woes, the economy was weak. Growth rates that had fuelled and made possible bad cash management caught up with Oracle. The sales force was re-motivated with a campaign called 'Go for Gold', which actually paid in gold. Staff numbers were drastically cut to help control overheads. Even so, in late 1990 the stock price was anaemic and sales remained poor. While other people sold their shares in Oracle, Ellison held on to his. He refused to admit (at least publicly) that there was anything wrong with the company. The stock price caused him problems because he had financed his lavish lifestyle by borrowing against its value. Ellison came close to losing his job and was humbled publicly. A new chief financial officer (CFO) commented that he had heard that Ellison was very arrogant, but that he definitely seemed to have been taken down a few pegs by events at the company.

The new CFO implemented much-needed financial management discipline. Growth rates plummeted to 12 per cent, down from 102 per cent in 1989. They had to slow down because the practices needed to sustain the high growth rates were ultimately damaging the company.

The pain and humiliation associated with changing business practices at Oracle lasted several years. Eventually Oracle and Ellison emerged from the hard times and business took off again, this time with more discipline.

Over the lifetime of Oracle, Ellison has been frequently in the news and seems to love it. He had very public feuds with Bill Gates, who is equally competitive and attention seeking. To the outsider, it would appear that Gates and Ellison were mortal enemies, but the truth seems to be that they put on a public show, which helped both of them get media attention while admiring each other in private. There is nothing like a fight to generate headlines and these two are nothing if not adversarial and attention seeking.

Ellison wanted more wealth and fame, particularly fame—there could never be enough. He was needy for it. In 1993 *Fortune* ran a piece that changed everything for Ellison—'Gates and Microsoft are perhaps the only CEO and company in the industry that match Ellison and Oracle for aggressiveness, drive, tenacity, chutzpah, and unbridled self-confidence' (Wilson 1998). This increased Ellison's national profile dramatically, and it was a great compliment to be seen as a rival to Bill Gates. A media fight between Gates and Ellison guarantees national—if not global—attention, and given that both run market-oriented companies this can only be good for sales and credibility. It is a game they both play.

Development

Ellison was illegitimate, born in 1944 to an unmarried woman in New York. His birth mother tried to raise the boy but suffered pneumonia and almost died. Nothing is known about his father.

He was adopted by his mother's aunt and her husband and raised in a middle-class Jewish home, firstly in the affluent north side of Chicago and then later on the south side of Chicago (when it was still affluent). Little is recorded about his relationship with his birth mother from that point on. Ellison obviously knew about her and that he was adopted; he is reported as saying that it is a sensitive subject. Just when he found out about the adoption and under what circumstances is not recorded. Given that his birth mother was a relative of his adoptive mother it is most likely that he had some contact with his birth mother over the years, and this probably fuelled a sense of abandonment and, if not that, at least a sense of otherness in contrast to the rest of the children growing up in his conservative neighbourhood.

His adoptive father was a quiet Jewish accountant who could find nothing in the young Ellison to praise. He was a repressed Russian Jewish refugee and adored the US so intensely that he believed everything that was decreed by US authorities was right. This brought him into constant conflict with young Ellison because Ellison was very much a law unto himself, perhaps as a reaction to the extremely rule-bound attitude of his adoptive father or maybe simply because that was the way Ellison was. In any event, the adoptive father was totally convinced that Ellison was going to be a failure and told him so, constantly. Ellison says:

> Oh, it was a powerful motivation ... If fire doesn't destroy
> you, you're tempered by it ... I'm not sure I would
> recommend that everyone raise their children like this.
> There's got to be a better way. But it certainly worked
> (Wilson 1998).

Friends report that Ellison hated his adoptive father who had two children from his first marriage. These two were older, had grown up and left home before Ellison arrived. Ellison's adoptive mother was the husband's second wife. She never had children of her own and is reported by Ellison as being wonderful. She was a bookkeeper and, unlike the other mothers in the neighbourhood, she worked. Due to this she could not be around to provide lunch for Ellison as many of the other mothers did, but she did arrange for other families to feed him. The Ellison's financial situation was modest, and this embarrassed Larry.

Ellison started school on the north side of Chicago and moved in his sophomore year. Nothing is recorded about his schooling on the north side but his leaving must have been a dislocation. He made hardly any impression at South Shore High School. He kept to himself. He did not socialise much or participate in sports or clubs, and he was an average student. He describes himself as quiet, withdrawn and out of the mainstream—in other words an outsider.

He describes himself as quiet, withdrawn and out of the mainstream— in other words an outsider.

While he may have been quiet, Ellison was anything but rule bound; if he didn't want to do something, he wouldn't—in particular, he wouldn't read prescribed texts if they bored him. He spent a lot of time reading but would only read books that interested him. Ellison was wilful and difficult. He is quoted as saying:

> I never accepted conventional wisdom. This got me in a lot
> of trouble. It served me well later in life, but it got me in
> terrible trouble in a school system that tries to get you to
> conform (Wilson 1998).

Ellison, while never the school favourite, always had a few good friends of the semi-delinquent type. He and his friends played up in unconventional ways, such as 'launderating' by climbing into big clothes dryers and spinning around or by simply hanging about telling jokes and tall stories—Ellison's particular skill.

He claims that he was passionate about basketball, but while he practised for hours shooting hoops, he seldom played on the school team, supposedly because he didn't want to be told what to do by a coach. There is a story about him playing once for a team and scoring a goal for the opposition. This incident was reported in the newspaper and

Ellison's father used the article to humiliate Ellison. This event indicates that Ellison was poor at sport and given his problems with authority, was unsuitable for team sports. In any event, sport was closed as a way for Ellison to gain approval from his peers.

He now owns the very successful Oracle America's Cup yachting team. He may not be a sportsman but he, like a number of others such as Bernie Ecclestone, Richard Branson and Frank Lowy, shares in the reflected glory of sport. In addition, it is a great status show!

As Ellison progressed through school, he became better and better at embroidering the stories of his life. He had no problem enhancing his life with events of his own creation, and often to his own glory. This seems to be the enduring 'skill' that Ellison developed, from which he has gained a lot of benefit and plenty of criticism. He is accused of embellishing just about everything about Oracle and his life. Friends recall Ellison spinning some really elaborate stories with positive effects, such as a time when he talked his way out of a speeding ticket.

He envied the cars and possessions of friends, and one friend recalled that Ellison had an endless need for attention and to impress people, resulting from feelings of inadequacy. He began telling tall stories. His small group of acolytes had a good time with Ellison so his storytelling became a great source of approval.

Ellison went to university, but again couldn't keep to the syllabus. He read widely but off subject, just as he did at school. Unlike school, however, a fail is a fail and he was dismissed after not achieving a C average for two semesters in a row. Ellison seems to care intensely about not having a degree and frequently changes his history by claiming that he does have one.

Even before becoming wealthy, Ellison was successful at starting relationships but not at maintaining them. He charmed and won his first wife and they lived together for seven years. During that time he bounced from job to job with champagne tastes on a beer budget. They owned and renovated a house, and Ellison bought a boat but made the financial stresses his wife's. Worrying about Ellison's ways with money caused her to develop an ulcer, and after some unsuccessful counselling, the couple parted. She left him everything. They have remained friends and Ellison seeks advice from her from time to time. He has since helped her in a number of ways. His first ex-wife says:

> I was worn out. He's beyond anything I've ever
> experienced. And I'm sure that's what accounts for his
> enormous success now. He has incredible intelligence, and
> he applies it with incredible intensity (Wilson 1998).

Ellison was introduced to his second wife while buying a car. They married soon after. She was very smart and outgoing, but it only lasted eighteen months. She sold her interest in Ellison's company back to him for $500.

Failing to adhere to the prohibition about 'fishing from the company pier', Ellison's third marriage was to an Oracle employee. The knot was finally tied after a long 'courtship' period in which Ellison dragged his feet. Obviously he had some serious misgivings. A few hours before the wedding, he produced a prenuptial agreement and refused to proceed until it was signed. Even though the bride signed, she naturally felt cornered and this cast a pall over the marriage. It failed in slightly less than three years. In this time the couple produced two children. After separating, his wife went to court and had the prenuptial agreement overturned. Ellison had to pay a greater settlement than he had hoped.

Being the boss's lover obviously tips the power balance between the lover and other managers within the organisation. This can lead to complications, and Ellison continued with the very dangerous practice of finding lovers within Oracle. He claims they recruited him. One fateful day he met Adelyn Lee in the elevator. She pursued him vigorously and, after some resistance on Ellison's part, bedded him frequently. She began making email requests for expensive gifts and 'loans', which Ellison deflected. Quite predictably, her sleeping with the boss caused difficulties for some Oracle managers and other staff because Lee threw her weight around and was very demanding.

It became a particular problem when her manager wanted to fire her for poor performance. Ellison was asked and agreed that his relationship with her had nothing to do with her continued employment. This may have been a fair call but it was dangerous, especially as he dated her three days before she was fired. Lee was furious and apparently sent an email to Ellison attributed to her manager saying 'I have terminated adelyn [sic] per your request' (Wilson 1998). Oracle and Ellison were sued for wrongful termination, failure to prevent discrimination and negligent mental stress. The trial turned into such a media circus that Ellison settled out of court. But he did not leave it there. He convinced the district attorney that there was a case for criminal charges, proved that the email had originated from a source outside Oracle, and won his money back. Lee was sentenced to a year in prison for perjury.

Ellison is not fascinated with software or technology at all. It could be anything, so long as it is his something that can make money and fame. He seems most fascinated with being rich and getting attention. His core behaviour is related to spin and overpromising. He can spin anything and is almost compulsive about it but along the way he inspires staff and markets. Being optimistic, competitive and needy add fuel to his progress.

Interpretation

Ellison's upbringing was shadowed by three problems—being illegitimate, adopted and continually criticised by his adoptive father. Being illegitimate and adopted almost certainly caused feelings of neglect, abandonment and shame. While his adoptive mother was probably loving and attentive, early neglect from his real mother would have interfered with his development.

Despite Ellison finding his adoptive mother loving, she was probably no antidote for the negativity and dogmatism of her husband. His adoptive father was continually critical and Ellison felt that criticism acutely. No matter what he did, he would be criticised for it. Quite possibly Ellison's 'poor' origins were a source of contempt and held up as a source of derision. His adoptive father may also have been angry at having another child after his own biological children had grown up.

Ellison claims that his father's constant criticism had something to do with Ellison's need to win, but it probably didn't because people need to win sometimes and be rewarded for it for it to actually have a positive effect. More likely, Ellison needed to win to prove his worth to his small number of friends. His ability to win was confined to a very narrow range. It excluded sport and school work, but included storytelling and public exploits.

His experiences at home and at school would have led to his later attitude that people were either for him or against him—there were no neutrals. Ellison is deeply distressed by resignations, which obviously cause strong feelings of abandonment. Ellison's behaviour is not symmetrical, however; while he demands absolute loyalty from others he is not particularly loyal to those around him. After he left school, Ellison didn't contact his 'close' school friends—his buddies in mischief and early audience.

It is not recorded by his friends what happened if Ellison lost a friend at school, but his subsequent rage when an employee 'disloyally' resigned indicates that he felt such abandonment acutely. It is probably a hangover from feelings of abandonment by his birth mother as well as any loss of friends as he was growing up.

Ellison was ashamed of his parents and probably ashamed of being both illegitimate and adopted. Ellison almost never invited friends to his place and almost never invited his parents to see him do anything.

Ellison obviously has high intelligence, but he was unengaged at school. This is most probably because it bored him or maybe he just couldn't concentrate — he couldn't see the point and, like many bright children, if he can't see the point, he simply will not cooperate. While he would have liked praise from his father, being good at school was never going to earn him compensatory praise.

He was an outsider at school, disengaged with schooling and unwilling or, more likely, unable to play sport. Since he moved from one school to another, any early friendship groups were dislocated. He couldn't conform nor get approval by succeeding in conventional ways, so he achieved it through unconventional means.

He needed attention and admiration from his peers, so he learned to embellish his life story. He also found expensive trappings gained him admiration. These strategies worked well and he received attention from a small number of friends (but never from his father), and as he got better at it he attracted more attention from it. What started as a strategy to meet an early need for attention developed into a fully grown compulsion to win admiration and devotion.

> He couldn't conform nor get approval by succeeding in conventional ways, so he achieved it through unconventional means.

Not only could Ellison spin a great story, he had to spin stories to make himself feel good. He was extremely quick at thinking on his feet. He became so good at manipulating feelings that to many in close contact he became almost godlike. Ellison was a storyteller and performer whose skills were honed in the schoolyard. He needed admiration and his embroidered stories about his life gave him some of that. Money gave him more. His eloquence eventually landed him in a position in the software industry and his hunger and intelligence made him see opportunities where others didn't — Oracle was born.

Ellison's need for approval led directly to his overpromising of software benefits and delivery times to clients. In turn, his overpromising led to stretching his development team so that at least part of the promise was delivered. This is why Oracle not only appeared to stay ahead of the competition but actually did stay ahead of the competition.

Over a period of time, Ellison became firm friends with Steve Jobs, the co-founder of Apple — an interesting choice since Jobs was also an adoptee. President Bill Clinton, another person raised by surrogates and who never knew his father, became firm friends with Ellison. Clearly cloudy parentage and being raised by surrogates was very important to Ellison.

References:

Stone, FM 2002, *The Oracle of Oracle*, Amacom (American Management Association), New York.

Symonds, M 2003, *Softwar: an Intimate Portrait of Larry Ellison and Oracle*, Simon & Schuster, New York.

Wilson, M 2002, *The Difference Between God and Larry Ellison*, HarperBusiness, New York.

Chapter 7

Carl Icahn

Forbes information 2007
Rank: 42
Citizenship: United States
Wealth: US$13.0 billion
Industry: investment/takeovers

Carl Icahn, the warrior trader, wreaked retribution on corporations by using against them the very same prejudices he experienced while growing up—prejudices about him being an outsider and Jewish. His revenge was strongly motivated by his loathing of 'robber barons', inherited from his parents; for the indignities served up to him at school, Princeton University and Wall Street; and finally for the indignities he suffered as a neophyte takeover king. He was on the attack against corporate privilege.

Icahn was not interested in money as a young man. He was a philosopher of considerable intellectual power, and it is that intellectual power combined with oblique outsider strategies that he now uses on unwitting businesspeople to completely derail them during negotiations. Negotiations he conducts with a relentless determination to win.

Achievement

At the beginning of Icahn's investing career he was refused a board position at an undervalued company he held a large stake in. Actively repelled by the very idea of having Icahn on its board or anywhere near its privileged positions, the company offered him a considerable cash margin on his investment to go away. This was a defining experience for Icahn. He realised that managers generally do not have a large stake in the companies they run and naturally enough want to protect their benefits. They often pay themselves large salaries with executive perks, such as corporate jets, and run fiefdoms at their shareholders' expense. Managers do not want an outsider coming in and upsetting their privileges, particularly an outsider like Icahn, who does not fit any of the criteria of belonging to their 'club'.

Once Icahn had his epiphany he started engaging with his takeover targets using five strategies, any of which could make him money. He would buy a sufficiently large stake in an undervalued stock and then attempt to control the destiny of the company by:

- trying to convince management to liquidate or sell the company

- waging a proxy contest

- making a tender offer

- selling back his position to the company at a generous margin to himself

- becoming an owner and having a position on the board.

While accepting 'go away money' was the easiest, Icahn was always in a position to win since he had no investment in the company besides money. He certainly had no emotional connection or privilege to lose, and undoubtedly it gave him satisfaction to see managements and boards squirm. He was always in a position to win, whereas the companies were always in a position to lose, especially if Icahn became an owner and took a position on the board. The latter being a fate too horrible for most companies to contemplate!

CEOs, boards of directors and other company heavyweights knew that to have an awkward man like Icahn on their board would disrupt their corporate lifestyles. This is why many managements caved in to his demands. One of the management groups' prime goals was to protect their own lifestyles—power and high incomes—or what is euphemistically called corporate culture. Icahn had the guts and the nous to challenge them, particularly as he made sure he could never lose. When he became a threat, they would often buy him off just to get rid of him, resulting in a large and quick profit.

At times Icahn made noises about what was beneficial to shareholders, but there was only ever one shareholder he was interested in—himself. If others benefited as well that was fine, but this was never an objective in itself.

Icahn's negotiating style is off-centre and persistent—he wears his opponents down. He negotiates for hours on end—often into the night—and chatters on aimlessly as a deliberate tactic to distract the other side. He'll unexpectedly change a detail just when an agreement appears close, to throw his opponents off balance, or bring in such irrelevant topics as artificial insemination of sheep in the middle of negotiations. Icahn just keeps going until he gets his way, no matter how long it takes or how much acrimony there is. He has a mental agility and toughness that allows him to completely flummox, frustrate and infuriate his adversaries, and he certainly is not distracted by the need to be liked. Icahn grinds his opponents down and blindsides them into submission. He also negotiates every last detail, picking up the odd $10 million or so here and there where other negotiators close the big deal leaving others to work out the details.

Icahn went on to apply his technique to a list of undervalued companies. He had a relatively short association with junk bonds and Drexel in the 1980s but for the most part he finances each deal separately. Icahn was investigated for shady practices over the use of junk bonds but was cleared. Starting relatively small he worked his way up to Howard Hughes's old national airline, TWA.

In taking over TWA, Icahn succumbed to the ultimate vanity that many wealthy people fall for—to own an airline. In addition, he made the near fatal mistake of believing that he was smarter than management and decided to run the company himself. But running a company is very different to and more difficult than buying or selling one—it requires different skills.

It turned out that Icahn had few management skills. Believing he could run a company and interact with staff the same way he interracted with management as a trader was nearly his undoing. Never strong on interpersonal communication, he first wooed and then burned off unions and other allies, becoming mired in long-run complications. Like Charles Schwab, he was not fascinated with the process of running an effective back-office operation, and ran afoul of the Securities and Exchange Commission (SEC) for a number of minor administrative infractions.

After many beleaguered years, he managed to deal himself out of both TWA and onerous pension fund liabilities.

Like many billionaires, he was a lousy manager. Icahn related to numbers and deals, not to people. In his trading he had one faithful employee who was with him for years, but never cut him into the business. It has been suggested that this employee benefited by shadowing Icahn's deals.

Once out of TWA, Icahn continued his trading and has shown no evidence of slowing down. Still using his old tactics he has dealt himself into a communications company, three casinos and sundry other companies. He has also donated $10 million to build a track-and-field stadium in New York.

Development

Icahn was born on 16 February 1936, in lower middle-class Bayswater, New York. His mother, Bella, was a strict, strong-minded, frustrated public school teacher who had wanted to pursue a music career. Her husband, Michael, trained as a lawyer but never practised. He was a dedicated, if not poor and shakily employed, musician. Bella provided the major part of a modest, but stable, income.

Both were strongly 'small c capitalist'. They had an aversion to privilege and like many people in the wrong job, they were angry. Both constantly railed against the huge difference in incomes and lifestyles that the rich enjoyed and both had the view that big capitalism was institutionalised theft for the benefit of robber barons. It was personal for them—not only was big business theft in general, but it was their money that was being stolen. Icahn could not help but be influenced.

Undoubtedly there was a great deal of friction between his parents, with one a frustrated and impecunious musician and the other a frustrated, domineering breadwinner in the wrong occupation.

Icahn's parents could be called tough but fair. His mother was forceful, intrusive and dominating. Nothing was good enough. She wanted Icahn to be a doctor because of its professional status and the fact that doctors are never out of work. His father was cold and aloof with a prodigious intellect, which he used to challenge others. He would sit for hours and talk, and anyone who interjected would be given a tongue lashing. Icahn's father discussed philosophy with the young Icahn. He never played games with him.

As a child, Icahn received little unconditional love and approval. Approval from his father meant succeeding at combative intellectual word games, games that Icahn would one day incorporate into his trading practices.

Despite this there was money around. Icahn's uncle married into money and was rich, and Icahn visited often enough to get a taste for the high life.

Icahn was bright and had a fascination with books, and excelled at maths. He won a scholarship to a private college, Woodmere. In a bizarre act of inverted snobbery, his parents turned this down because they didn't like the school's values—in their eyes, the school and its students were too privileged. However, staying at his old school probably helped turn him into the fighter he became—a bright boy with great disdain for learning. Importantly he learned to take opportunities before others did, and not to trust anybody.

He did not stand out at school despite having demonstrated considerable intellectual ability by winning the scholarship. Like many bright people in boring and difficult circumstances, he probably only devoted part of his mind to his school studies; it may also have been a deliberate ploy to keep out of conflict.

Icahn is a moderately tall man. Like Buffett, he is a man for whom height seems to be more an issue than an asset. He is six feet three inches, ungainly and pigeon-toed. He developed a set of eccentric and diminishing characteristics that led people to underestimate him. As a trader he appeared to be erratic and awkward, and didn't dress like a wealthy businessman. He did not give the impression of being a formidable corporate raider. In his rumpled suit and cheap shoes, he looked like what he was—an outsider—and he used this as a weapon to unsettle people. But, of course, being underestimated and misunderstood at the negotiating table has always been a considerable advantage for Icahn. He never let anything as trivial as looking and acting the part upset a good corporate 'kill'.

It is probable that his stature brought him unwanted attention at school, probably with smaller kids wanting to test their strength by challenging him to a fight. Icahn is not known to have played any sport and stories of his school days are few. One story to surface sums up Icahn quite well. Some tough boys were bullying him and trying to intimidate him, but one day Icahn stood up for himself and sent the message that they were never to mess with him again. Unpopular and alone he may be, but take him on at your own peril.

Icahn had a stable upbringing in the sense that he remained in one neighbourhood until he left for university. Despite finishing second in his high school year, teachers tried to dissuade Icahn from applying to Princeton or Harvard—poor kids from poor schools just didn't go to Ivy

League colleges. Icahn applied anyway and achieved a full scholarship to Princeton University.

Naturally enough, Icahn was an outsider at the Ivy League college. Princeton had elite clubs that selected members, and Icahn was one of the small number not selected. This experience compounded the anger and distrust he had of privileged groups, a trait he inherited from his mother and father. He did, however, manage to find a home in a non-elite club.

Icahn studied and excelled at philosophy, winning a prestigious prize. Unsurprising, given his intellect and that the limited quality time he had with his father was spent discussing philosophy. Icahn achieved an undergraduate degree with first prize in philosophy from Princeton University. Like George Soros, philosophy is believed to have contributed to Icahn's success by instilling in him the desire to see events in a bigger context than simple profit and loss. He needed to understand the meaning of things, and this set him apart from the usual Wall Street number-crunchers. More than anything, philosophy would have given him the intellectual and verbal flexibility to confound most people in business. Outsiders don't argue the same as other people.

Icahn tried medical school, the stridently favoured preference of his mother. He hated it so much that he dropped out, simply walking out during a tour of a tuberculosis ward, never to return. His father talked him out of going into law.

> He hated it so much that he dropped out, simply walking out during a tour of a tuberculosis ward, never to return.

To bide his time and avoid his mother's pressure to become a doctor he joined the army. There he became a formidable poker player, a natural! Cards allowed him to take advantage of his affinity with numbers and his natural ability to leverage a good hand and bluff a bad one. Poker provided him with his initial investment stake and, more importantly, gave him skills to 'play poker' with company executives for the control of their companies. Undoubtedly he learnt all about having a poker face and bluffing while in the army, playing poker.

Once out of the army, he began a career in investing and worked on Wall Street. Like Soros, he identified the emerging options-trading field as a good area to work in, especially as it was unregulated. He began building up clients and then borrowed money from his uncle to buy a seat on Wall Street.

When the money started rolling in, Icahn began to make the rounds of hot spots and parties, and dated attractive women. Always the egghead loner, he was never socially comfortable and his stint as a carefree bachelor was short-lived. He married a Russian émigré, a former ballerina who had served as his secretary for a short time. The marriage lasted and the couple have children.

He was also totally out of his depth with reporters. Interviews tended to go horribly wrong. Icahn either didn't pay attention or he would cut them short for no reason. Once an outsider always an outsider.

Interpretation

Icahn was obviously an outsider by birth, upbringing and inclination. He was an odd boy from an odd family. He wasn't entirely antisocial—he did play chess. He said of himself, 'I was never a well-adjusted kid—never really happy' (Stevens 1993).

His mother was intrusive and domineering; and his father was intrusive and cold. The little affection Icahn received from his parents was contingent on achievement through playing intellectual or philosophical games, and signing on to the belief that people in big business are thieves and should be punished severely. In adulthood, winning intellectual games was important to Icahn since it was the only consistent approval he received, and who better to win against than the stated enemies of his parents—big business.

In adulthood Icahn has joined the enemy, but he seems to be able to reconcile that by claiming to make his billions for the good of everyone. He probably also plays the 'but I'm different' card used by many people to justify their actions. The philosopher in him should be able to spot the sophistry in both arguments!

School was obviously a torment. He got through mainly by making himself invisible—no sport and no supreme achievements. Icahn simply carried on because he had no other options. He was a very bright, gawky boy growing up in a tough school with unconventional parents. He was bullied, and developed inner strength, mistrust and skills to counter it. Winning over bullying is its own reward. While at Princeton he suffered social humiliation at the hands of the establishment and its sires but gained approval for intellectual achievement.

Poker was a source of success in the army. It was almost like it was part of his calling, waiting to be discovered. His means of bluffing his way to a fortune. By the time he left the army, he had the motivation and the skills to take on the establishment. Every win was a source of satisfaction. It was Icahn against the establishment. He obviously sees every engagement as a battle, and has a strong dislike for the 'elite' who run the companies.

Despite trying to justify his actions as being a champion of shareholders' interests, he mounts his raids with scant concern for the consequences of the company or its shareholders. While personal benefit was always his main goal, in maximising his gain Icahn was maximising the damage done to the company and the damage he could do to other companies in the future. It was never money for money's sake alone! Every win ensures more attacks in the future.

Unlike many self-made billionaires, Icahn was not a teenage entrepreneur. This indicates that he probably was never very interested in money for its own sake. There is no doubt that he was angry at injustices wreaked on him and he was interested in the damage he could do to people with money — revenge in other words. His relationships with the other soldiers in his poker games are not recorded, but one can be sure that Icahn gained considerable pleasure in taking them down: an exercise of power and revenge that he had never experienced before.

Icahn's investing started off fairly slowly, but always the outsider, he developed his own operating philosophy about how the market worked. He believes that there is a pattern behind everything, he just has to figure out what it is. Since he 'invented' his own way of looking at the investment world, it was understandably idiosyncratic — a huge advantage for him.

Icahn has the outsider's edge of owing no loyalty to any establishment and having the intellectual power and drive to seek his profit from, and revenge on, insiders. While he plays by the legal rules, and uses them often, he does not obey any formal negotiating rules. He negotiates like he is playing a combination of chess and poker, winning a mind game by any means possible. He is doing what his father did to him, using his intellectual power to bully opponents.

His business ethos is to make money at the expense of the establishment. He is only interested in his own shareholding stake, but if other shareholders benefit from the value he finds in companies, then fine. Despite claiming general shareholder value as a rationale, Icahn is only interested in the outcome for Icahn.

Icahn is fighting a battle started by his parents and reinforced by the humiliations of school, Princeton and his early days on Wall Street. He wanted revenge and revenge he got. He wanted revenge on the establishment because his parents hated it, he wanted revenge on the Ivy Leaguers who had humiliated him at college, and he wanted revenge on all those comfortable board and management 'clubs' that would never have him. Icahn turned being reviled into a lucrative business advantage and got rich out of 'go away money'. If he didn't get 'go away money', he got the company and then his revenge was exacted in other ways.

Icahn is angry and after revenge, and he is bright enough and determined enough to go and get it. He takes on the biggest companies and exacts his revenge in hundreds of millions of dollars.

References:

Bruck, C 1988, *The Predators' Ball: the inside story of Drexel Burnham and the Rise of the Junk Bond Raiders*, Penguin, Melbourne.

Stevens, M 1993, *King Icahn: the Biography of a Renegade Capitalist*, Dutton, New York.

Chapter 8

George Soros

Forbes information 2007
Rank: 80
Citizenship: United States
Wealth: US$8.5 billion
Industry: hedge funds

George Soros may have become the world's richest man if he hadn't had an almost compulsive need to be philanthropic. Due to childhood trauma sustained during World War II, Soros developed a paradoxical need to both earn large amounts of money and to give it away. Soros's need to have money to ensure survival in tough times conflicts with the deeply held belief, gained from his father, not to have money for money's own sake. His covert trading during the war helped save many Jewish people from the Nazis and deeply ingrained in him the value of making money and the value of giving it away.

Achievement

Soros left Hungary after World War II. On completing his degree in the UK, Soros went to the US and through contacts landed a job in a broking company. He proved to be very capable.

After he set up a couple of investment funds that invested in anything and everything, Soros identified hedge funds, an emerging financial vehicle at the time, as being for him. In their infancy, hedge funds made up their own rules free of the wishes of investors or the interference of regulators and governments. This was blissfully unrestrained game playing and it obviously suited Soros's guerrilla style of investment learnt during the war.

He proved to be very good at it, and his hedge funds grew rapidly. Like Icahn, he had a strong interest in philosophy and developed a model of how the global financial system worked. He had a rapacious appetite for information and he effectively mapped the international finance system in his mind. He traded in anything. As a migrant he brought knowledge of the European financial system to the then inward-looking US investment scene and built up large investments overseas. He is most famous for being the man who 'broke the Bank of England' in 1992 through speculating in British pounds.

> He is most famous for being the man who 'broke the Bank of England' in 1992 through speculating in British pounds.

The Bank of England had for some time been vehemently assuring the world that it would not devalue the pound. Soros's chief analyst did not believe this and went to Soros with the case as to why the pound would be devalued. Soros rounded on the analyst, not for getting the analysis wrong but for suggesting that they only bet two to three billion dollars on the Bank of England doing so. Soros laid his huge bet against the Bank of England, the Bank of England devalued, and he raked in an outrageously high profit of over a billion dollars.

Soros has been in turns vilified for acting in an ungentlemanly manner and admired for his gall. He has, however, offered to help fix the international money trading rules, but has also said that he will play any existing rules to his advantage, which he did in the case of the Bank of England and continues to do around the globe.

Soros's success has been attributed to his natural courage and conviction to pull the trigger when necessary. While he is calm under pressure, highly intelligent and a good analyst, he has two key advantages. He is adept at spotting the opportunity and he is willing to make exceptionally big moves. He is equally willing to take a loss and move on if he believes that's the right move. He has a competitive nature and the courage of his convictions. Soros is very unsentimental about his investments—they are purely business. He has no favourite companies or investment vehicles and, as in the war, he goes where the opportunity arises.

Critically for Soros, business is a game. It is something not to be taken too seriously. He plays his game hard and competitively, but it is a game nevertheless. Because Soros treats investing as if it were a game, he is capable of taking higher risks, which sets him apart from most investors.

Being rich and famous did not make him content or happy. While Soros was becoming rich, he was also becoming increasingly anxious. He was good at making money, but it was meaningless to him. Asked when he first realised that he liked making money, he said, 'I don't like it ... I'm just good at it' (Kaufman 2002).

His hunger, a wartime legacy, remained with him. He worked himself into the ground to try to overcome this, but the more money he made the unhappier he became. Despite being compelled to make money, money was not what he wanted. He had inherited three drives from his father—philosophy, making money and giving money away. Soros had failed at being a philosopher but he was outrageously successful at making money. However, he could only relieve his anxiety by turning to his father's third legacy—philanthropy.

Initially he tried to influence governments to provide meaningful assistance to countries behind the Iron Curtain. As he had experienced with his philosophy, the political gatekeepers rebuffed him, but this time he wasn't powerless—he was rich and becoming richer. He began to funnel more and more of his own money into causes to open up society behind the Iron Curtain. This flow of money ended up being hundreds of millions of dollars per year.

Soros became one of the single biggest sources of overseas aid in the world, a one man foreign affairs bureau. His aid was pumped into turnkey and often unconventional operations that affected the openness of society. These projects were inherently subversive because they allowed people to communicate with each other without government approval or control. He experienced the forces of repression under the Nazis and then communists in Budapest. He has a deeply held view that repression can only be sustained if the repressor controls information. Consequently, many of his projects have been about breaking state control of information.

One of his original subversive projects in Hungary was to fund photocopiers at universities at a time when any photocopying required permission from authority. He has also funded the installation of internet facilities at Russian universities.

Not all projects were subversive in that way. He also funded projects that retained or built capability behind the Iron Curtain. At the time of the collapse of communism, the Russian government could not pay salaries. Soros paid the salaries of top Russian scientists for a year so their skill and expertise was not lost to Russia.

Soros is a dedicated philanthropist. He has been seriously considered as a candidate for the Nobel Peace Prize, and he is one of the most philanthropic private citizens in the world. He has had a significant influence in many countries. Breaking the Bank of England has also had some unexpected spin-offs. This has raised his profile from a mere speculator to the status of a man who can make or break economies. Governments deal with him now and he has increasing access to government leaders.

Soros is a guerrilla in his philanthropic activities as he is in his trading, again a legacy of the war when any long-term activities were bound to be uncovered and brutally punished. He only invests in short-term activities with high impact. He never funds philanthropy projects for long or indefinite periods. He also prefers anonymity, something that he can no longer manage. Soros felt that publicity could be harmful to what he was trying to do.

Unlike many businesspeople, Soros has in the past had a strict policy of keeping his business and philanthropy separate. When asked to do a philanthropy project in India, Soros declined because at that time he had huge investments there. He has a rule of not being a philanthropist and an investor in the same country, so that there are no conflicts of interest.

During the 1980s and 1990s he worked frantically on building both his hedge fund and his aid programs. Had he been more interested in money for its own sake, he could have become the richest man in the world. He had the capacity, but in the end his main objective for having the money, beyond the fact that he could make it, was to help people emerge from oppression. He didn't want anybody to suffer as he and his family had, firstly under Nazi occupation, and then Soviet occupation of Budapest.

Soros was not playing the *Forbes* world's billionaires list game with Buffett and Gates; if he was he wouldn't have given money away. Gates has only relatively recently started his philanthropy program and Buffett has only just joined the philanthropy team. Soros began his philanthropy program in the 1980s with extensive targeted gifting and he still has achieved $7.4 billion and eightieth place on the *Forbes* list.

Development

George Soros was born in Budapest, Hungary, in 1930, and was the second of two sons. The family was well off and both his parents were from well-to-do families — traders and successful shop owners. His father was an unenthusiastic lawyer who practised only two hours a day. Mostly he looked after investments made by the mother's side of the family.

Soros's mother admits to being not very maternal. In fact she claims that it was her husband who provided much of the affection to George. She seems to have been present, possibly benign but not very engaged emotionally, and intrusive if she interacted at all. Soros is quoted as saying 'she had violated my space. She was very intrusive' (Kaufman 2002).

His father was a liberal amateur intellectual and philosopher who was not particularly interested in making money. It is claimed that this is because he lost vigour due to internment in Russian prison camps during World War I. Whatever the reason, the Soros family had sufficient money to have a townhouse and to spend summers at an exclusive island holiday house. The difference in temperament and aspiration between mother and father caused considerable conflict, conflict that was exacerbated by the father's philandering. There was tension and fighting in the relationship, and Soros disapproved of how his father treated his mother.

Soros's father did not play physical games with George, he played mind games. He was very intellectually challenging and demanded that George think philosophically about issues. The father was particularly keen on instilling values about money, emphasising that money was not simply for accumulation but for use. George's father was also a committed philanthropist, encouraging George to get his first public acclaim by way of a newspaper article for philanthropy before the war. There are parallels with Icahn's father, except Icahn's father radiated class conflict rather than philanthropy — note how both boys learnt their respective lessons well.

At school in Budapest before the war, Soros was an indifferent student. He was not very good at maths as he had fallen behind when he missed several weeks of school due to illness. Somewhat short, he played individual sports, such as boxing and tennis, but not team sports. He is also a very slow reader, and his wife wonders whether he is dyslexic but has not had her suspicions confirmed. Soros participated in sport and games in junior school.

His childhood was disrupted when the Nazis invaded Hungary in 1944. Drawing on his experiences with hostile authority during World War I, Soros's father immediately went into crisis management, saving the family where other families perished. In order to survive, his father gave the family members non-Jewish identities, split the family up, and distributed them around various willing non-Jewish families. His father, a lawyer before the war, became active in the underground movement by, among other things, arranging for fake identities, exits from Hungary and cashing in gold for money. Young George was actively involved in these activities, including trading gold for money. Of the war, Soros is quoted as saying:

> This was the most exciting time of my life … For an adolescent to be in real danger, having a feeling he is inviolate, having a father whom he adored acting as a hero and having an evil confronting you and getting the better of it, I mean, being in command of the situation, even though you're in danger, but basically maneuvering successfully, what more can you ask for? (Kaufman 2002).

He has said that the bets he now makes in business are nothing compared with the chances he took with his father when he was young. One false move then could have killed him; now he just stands to lose money.

Soros stresses the excitement of his work experiences and overlooks the trauma. His insatiable drive, however, must come from the trauma. He was very much his father's boy, with the added compulsion that comes from honing skills while your life depends on it.

At the end of the war, Hungary was taken over by the Soviets. Hard times continued, so at seventeen, Soros moved alone and with great difficultly from communist Hungary to London via Europe. Isolated from his family, he was very lonely, frustrated and unhappy. For the nine years he was in London, he was very much the outsider and emotionally unfulfilled. He was also a virgin, and the lack of physical contact added to his loneliness and isolation. He tried to meet women but without success. He describes himself as an outsider during this time.

Originally he worked and then he began studying at the London School of Economics. Soros did not receive any funding for education so he had to work at menial jobs and accept what charity he could find. This may explain why he is such a generous supporter of education.

Soros graduated from the London School of Economics with a bachelor's degree. He went on to work for several years as a management trainee for a firm that sold custom jewellery. Soros was not a success in his next job either, working as a bookkeeper in a London stockbroking firm run by two ex-Hungarians. Soros decided to move to the US and begin his trading career.

There is no doubt that Soros was interested in girls as he grew up. But the vexed relationship between his parents caused him some problems. He had a long-standing first marriage that produced two children, but ultimately ended. His second marriage has endured. Soros says that he had always been ambivalent towards women, and that he was afraid of the intimacy women demand, finding it too penetrating and persistent. This gives a clue as to how his mother probably was. He is reported to be a demanding and critical father—not particularly loving. Like father, like son!

At work, his bonding was anything but permanent. To be sure, Soros has a small number of people that worked closely with him for a long time, but in general he sees work relationships purely from a business perspective and for the benefits they offer. As with everything, his project focus is short term, and he doesn't get too close to business associates; indeed he has been known to fire people simply because they have been around too long or because they tried to get too close. Wartime mistrust of associates obviously runs deep.

In contrast, Soros was extremely loyal to his parents and his brother, most likely as a result of the times when they depended on each other just to stay alive.

Soros trades in much the same way as he did when he was cutting his trading teeth during the war. Then it was necessary to trade hard and fast, taking any financial loss or gain without sentiment so long as it was not the loss of his or his family's life. He bet the lot—the lives of himself and his family—on a minute-by-minute basis for over a year, and won.

In addition to courage, there was a need during the occupation years to learn quickly, instantly appraise the situation and to rapidly adjust to what was being done to suit the conditions. To decide now and accept the consequences immediately. Life and death conditions could change in a moment, rules needed to be formed quickly and abandoned if they did not work. A sharp mind was often all that stood between Soros and death.

> A sharp mind was often all that stood between Soros and death.

Soros was a semi-outsider even before the Nazis occupied Budapest. From that time on, his formative training alongside his hero father ensured that he developed patterns of behaviour that enhanced his chances of survival. He suffered being an outsider in London for nine years and the failure of his aspiration to be a renowned philosopher. For Soros, broking was a poor option compared to being a philosopher, but it was one in which he could make a living. He could thrive rather than merely survive!

Being a foreigner in the US trading market gave him a further edge. At the time he began trading he had an international view of the world and was particularly focused on European opportunities. This set him apart from his contemporaries. It was relatively rare for Wall Street to be concerned with markets outside the US in the 1950s and 1960s. Soros was very much aware that having a conventional view of investment was a handicap rather than a help. For this reason, when he hired staff he deliberately avoided anybody from Wall Street. Soros says of himself:

> I took pride in being in the minority, an outsider who was capable of seeing the other point of view. Only the ability to think critically, and to rise above a particular point of view, could make up for the dangers and indignities that being a Hungarian Jew had inflicted on me (Kaufman 2002).

It is hardly surprising that Soros's philanthropic venture is called Open Society, having experienced closed societies under both Hungarian communism and British democracy.

Interpretation

Soros was an underachieving, bright, possibly dyslexic Jewish boy growing up in an upper middle-class family with relationship problems between the parents. His mother was intrusive but otherwise emotionally detached, and as such would have disturbed some his early development patterns.

His father, whom Soros hero worshipped, was a lawyer of Socratic style who, like Icahn's father, 'played' with Soros by challenging him philosophically rather than actually playing with him. Soros achieved approval from his father by being philosophic; in others such approval might have led to the child becoming a philosopher (as it did for Icahn). But later this emphasis on philosophy would turn out to be a source of frustration. Soros had difficulty writing due to possible dyslexia; on top of this English was not his native language, which meant he was unable to deliver sufficiently good work. It is also possible that Soros, as a refugee outsider, was discriminated against in his attempts to break into British academia from the bottom.

For all the difficulties he faced at home, Soros appeared to be fairly well adjusted. He went to school and achieved middling results and he played some individual sports in junior school. Unfortunately for Soros his fairly normal family life came to an abrupt end when the Nazis occupied Budapest. Soros's father used the survival skills he learned in World War I concentration camps and his skills as a lawyer to survive. He saved the family where many less-fortunate and less-experienced Jewish families were exterminated. Soros also learned extremely valuable lessons at that time from his father, including which rules should be obeyed and which rules should be broken.

When the Nazis occupied the city, Soros developed many of the traits that led him to become both rich and a philanthropist specialising in occupied societies. He helped his family to survive and he assisted his father to help fellow Hungarian Jews escape persecution by, among other things, trading gold on the local black market. He learnt the game of the financial markets and to have scant regard for authorities, who were obviously dangerous and self-serving.

In this context, George's first financial experience came towards the end of the war, trading on the black market. There can be no doubt that these events were core formative experiences encompassing adversity and approval both from father and the people he helped. He saved lives by trading; what better benefit could there be?

While George struggled at school before the war, he was not noticeably an outsider. He may well have experienced problems in the classroom due to poor reading skills, but the social impact of this was offset by his early proficiency at sport. Once the Nazis invaded Budapest, he, along with the whole Jewish population, became outsiders. Social networks were disrupted and everyone, even family, friends and neighbours, became potential sources of betrayal.

Soros has obviously internalised the very harsh lessons he learned during the war. To survive he could not afford friends. Everyone except his family was a potential threat. To this day he does not maintain friends and only gets into very short-term projects. While Soros may have a long view as to what his ultimate purpose is, his war experiences mean that he is both a guerrilla trader and a guerrilla philanthropist. When he grew up and survival was no longer a daily issue, he still carried with him the lessons, attitudes and techniques he had learned during this time in his life.

There was trading and business on both sides of the Soros family. His and others' lives depended on his skill at getting the best deal. Soros's principal training was during the war, where he learnt the day-to-day need to take life-threatening risks to survive, including trading and helping people.

There were powerful but contradictory psychological forces at work on the young, developing Soros. On the one hand, making money is critical for survival in hard times, and making more money is much better than making less. Given the role of trading and his strong association with his father in saving people during the war, this became an obsessive drive, only partly delayed by his abortive, but also compulsive, foray into philosophy.

On the other hand, his father was adamant that money shouldn't be made for its own sake. For Soros, approval from his father and from the people he helped during the war came from making as much money as possible and then giving it away.

Soros is great at making money. He is a natural trader, he can't help himself. But when Soros began making money he became conflicted and anxious. He couldn't help making money and needed to because he was programmed that way, but he hated having the money. The anxiety of making money could only be allayed by giving it away to people who needed to be rescued. Hence Soros became at once one of the richest men in the world and one of its greatest philanthropists.

References:

Kaufman, MT 2002, *Soros*, Random House, New York.

Slater, R 1996, *Soros: the Unauthorized Biography, the Life, Times and Trading Secrets of the World's Greatest Investor*, McGraw-Hill, New York.

Chapter 9

Steve Jobs

Forbes information 2007
Rank: 132
Citizenship: United States
Wealth: US$5.7 billion
Industry: computing

Steve Jobs was the unreliable market visionary for the start-up Apple Corporation. He recognised the potential of computers and was behind many of Apple's signature features and successes. As a young entrepreneur he was an arrogant outsider with one nearly fatal flaw—he placed no value on the opinion of others. This led to Jobs being responsible for some of Apple's early failures. Jobs delivered to consumers what he wanted, not what they wanted. After being fired by the company he helped found, and possibly having learned from his early marketing mistakes, he came back to lead Apple to huge market success with the fashionable iMac and the even more fashionable iPod and iPhone.

Achievement

In 1976 Steve Jobs and Steve Wozniak started Apple Computers. The under-funded start-up company was born in the bedrooms and garage of the Jobs family's home in San Francisco. The name was inspired by apple orchards, where Jobs had a holiday job.

Wozniak and Jobs belonged to a loose fraternity of 'wireheads' that had been put together following the seminal edition of *Popular Electronics* in 1975 (the issue with the rudimentary computer on the cover). They both thought that computers were the future and they set about finding a market edge.

Because their strongest influences were in electronics rather than programming, they took a slightly different and more traditional route than Gates and Allen—they decided to make their own computers. Consequently they developed an operating system for their creation, thus inextricably linking their hardware and software. Gates, on the other hand, was interested in the software side and only built hardware when it was necessary. Gates's business model was not dependent on any one hardware manufacturer, so he was able to play one manufacturer off against the other. Apple, in the mould of IBM, was really only interested in software to the extent that it supported hardware sales, therefore, Apple had more trouble expanding than Microsoft did.

Wozniak designed the computers, Jobs did the buying and marketing, and a (temporary) partner created the graphic art and manual. Jobs made a sale of fifty Apple 1 computers to the Byte shop (a local, pioneering computer store) and the three partners went into a frantic round of design and construction, pressing family members into production and turning Jobs's home into a factory.

The Apple 1 computers were crude and eventually only 200 were sold to the Byte shop. Of the 200, only 150 were actually sold to the public.

Wozniak came up with the idea for the Apple 2 computer, which included much-needed features, such as a keyboard and a screen connection, as well as Wozniak's newly invented floppy disk drive. They took the new computer to a trade show but were given a bad location. This, coupled with amateurish displays and sales material, meant that sales were slow. The pair tried to raise capital by selling the company, but were turned down because two kids producing computers in a garage didn't look serious enough.

Jobs kept trying to find a backer and eventually located a venture capitalist, who, in return for 30 per cent of the company, provided much-needed capital, credibility, a new location to work out of and some discipline. Their task was to get ready for the next trade show.

At this time Jobs began reverting to type by showing characteristics that would eventually get him fired from Apple. He was hard to please, seeing himself as an artist and visionary more than a businessman. Jobs would make lots of changes during projects, which often made it difficult for Apple to meet deadlines and sometimes led to technical problems.

With Wozniak in charge of the technology, Jobs was in charge of parts supply, aesthetics and marketing. He was brilliant at supply, able to negotiate parts on credit. He was a problem in the aesthetic department because he insisted that computers look and operate exactly as he wanted them to without reference to users. Throughout the early life of Apple Computers while Jobs was there, there were costly aesthetic and user interface mistakes. With some models the cases were too small, so they overheated. Also, screens remained too small for too long, and there were arbitrary changes in interface protocols so that new computers were not compatible with existing software or hardware, forcing comsumers to completely change everything when they bought a new machine. And, as most product managers know, this increases the chance of customers switching to other products, which they did.

This problem of Jobs foisting his opinion on the market without checking has plagued him right up until recent times. He now seems more willing to take advice or, maybe, he has had a fortuitous but random alignment of his tastes with that of the public's.

Despite these problems, computers were ready on time for the trade show and sold well.

Following the show it became obvious that Apple needed a president and an external appointment was made, since it was evident to all but Jobs that he was unsuitable. His artistic orientation, perfectionist demands and general lack of social skills were inconsistent with running any organisation, let alone a profit-making company on a rapid growth trajectory. The new president **Jobs became both an annoyance and a source of considerable inspiration within Apple.** had to fight Jobs for control, because Jobs liked to make the decisions. Jobs ended up with the position of vice chairman.

Jobs became both an annoyance and a source of considerable inspiration within Apple. The president would complain that Jobs was not able to manage people. With no clearly defined role in the business, Jobs would interfere.

By the end of 1977, more than 2500 Apple 2 computers had been sold and the two dozen employees were working in a space the size of an average home. It had something of a camp atmosphere. In 1978 they moved to bigger premises. Jobs did his rounds. He continued to anger staff because he was so difficult to please; 'behind his back they called him "The Rejecter"' (Wilson 2001). Sales of computers rose to 8000 in 1978 and 35 000 in 1979. Apple was about to go public and Jobs's name wasn't on any list of employees—he had no official position in the newly listed company. He was furious!

The company went public in 1980 and, at twenty-five, Jobs became one of the youngest super rich, with more than $200 million in Apple shares. Jobs bought a new house and moved in, but, in his typically eccentric style, did not furnish it—repeating his pattern of previous houses.

On a trip to the Xerox labs, Jobs saw the prototype of what was to become Apple's on-screen look—overlapping windows with pop-up menus controlled by a mouse. Indeed, it was to be the look of all contemporary personal computing. Xerox had little interest in it, but Jobs saw the potential and immediately set a group of Apple engineers to work creating a similar product.

In 1980 Apple 3 was shipped, but Jobs's interference with the design meant that it overheated. It eventually made a loss of $60 million. Jobs was not given a role in the development of the next generation of computers, of which the Lisa was to be the flagship product and the Macintosh more experimental.

Jobs somehow managed to secure a role as head of development of the Macintosh range of computers and went into competition with the Lisa project. He installed his small team off site and instilled a sense of camaraderie. They had perks such as a masseur on call, expensive lease cars and food laid on. People wanted to join his team. Jobs had taken his development team back to the early days of Apple, of pioneering work. It was them against the world. Unfortunately, the world they were against was the greater Apple organisation. The group named themselves, and became known as, the 'pirates', because they pirated the best employees from other Apple divisions and other companies. Outside their building they flew a flag with the skull and crossbones with apples for eyes. Jobs's staff were busy and worked hard for the time being.

Jobs and the president of Apple had been at constant war with each other. The president's effectiveness had been slipping because of personal problems. When he was out of town on leave, Apple executives sacked him and reshuffled the executive positions. Jobs became chairman of the $2 billion corporation. About this time, IBM entered the PC market and within two years exceeded Apple's sales—Apple's share of the market began to shrink dramatically.

Initially IBM's computers were unwieldy and Apple executives wrote them off as no threat. But IBM did something that Apple never did, it road tested its product and constantly improved it. IBM rapidly improved its product as well as its market share. Most importantly, its product was priced well below Apple's, so it became the default entry level computer of choice. Typically, Apple did not meet IBM in the market with an entry level computer, and so suffered for its oversight.

The Lisa computer was a commercial failure and Jobs had the Lisa division merged with the Macintosh division. Jobs launched the Macintosh in 1984 to an excited market, but sales disappointed. Once again Jobs had designed something the way *he* wanted it. The Macintosh had advanced graphics but a small screen with no colour. It had few programs and no printer, and it was not IBM compatible or, more to the point, it was not Microsoft compatible. IBM had conducted surveys to find out what people wanted when building its machines; Jobs and Apple had not.

By this time, IBM was beginning to learn the cost of its decision to not own its operating system. Microsoft had begun licensing other computer manufacturers with variations of the operating system and allowing large numbers of software developers access to the software development code. IBM compatible machines, as they were then known, began flooding the market, the amount of software available ballooned and prices of hardware and software tumbled.

Apple always maintained tighter control over both its operating system and its software developers. It only had a small range of high priced product with limited software available. Apple computers certainly grabbed a very strong niche market of dedicated supporters, particularly in the art, graphics and publishing market, but were completely swamped in the general and business markets.

Jobs lost his job six months after the launch of the Macintosh and was unceremoniously dumped from all operational responsibilities at Apple. A few months later he had to resign completely after trying to poach Apple executives for a new business he was putting together. He sold all but one share in Apple to finance his new venture, Pixar Animation Studios, ultimately responsible for the special effects in the *Star Wars* and *Jurassic Park* movies. He financed *Toy Story*, *A Bug's Life* and *Toy Story 2*. Unlike at Apple, Jobs left decisions to the qualified staff at Pixar and Pixar was a success.

Jobs's next computer project was called NeXT, aimed at the education market. This time Jobs asked people what they wanted. He invested his own money and brought in a partner, Ross Perot. He unveiled the computer in October 1988 to a great deal of interest. A Japanese company paid $100 million for a 16 per cent share in NeXT, again making Jobs one of the richest men in the world. NeXT was launched eleven months after the unveiling. Despite having good software and having done his research, NeXT failed because it did not deliver what educators wanted, was too expensive, was underpowered and had a non-standard disk drive. Jobs had listened then done what he wanted. He had again delivered what he wanted, not what the market wanted.

For such a bright young man, Jobs was an extraordinarily slow learner. Introspection was clearly not his strong suit.

Apple was struggling in the market and had been named the worst-run company of 1996. It needed new product so it bought the NeXT company and brought Jobs back as an adviser. Increasingly he became more influential, and this time his influence was aligned with Apple, whose fortunes began to improve. The iMac was launched as an internet Mac with multicoloured cases. The attractive machines were so popular that one was sold every fifteen seconds every day for the next twelve months. This was followed by the iBook and, most recently, the iPod and iPhone.

Jobs's highly personal method of product development had at long last worked—there was a spectacular alignment of Jobs's personal tastes with the market's tastes, and Apple's fortunes rose meteorically. He is also reported to be much humbled by his constant market and organisational failures and has learned his management lessons. To the public he remains a guru with an amazing following of acolytes; inside Apple he is reported to be much more a team player, allowing input from others, and by all appearances he actually consults the market from time to time on what it wants.

In 1999 a US university student invented a way to transfer music from compact discs and transform it into easily copied MP3 files. The electronic transfer of music had arrived and the music industry was in turmoil. Illegal downloads of music spread like wildfire. Apple had already bought a software product for its computers, SoundJam, and had turned it into iTunes, but because it only copied music off CDs to play on computers, it lacked market penetration.

By 2001 Jobs had spotted the trend of music being downloaded from the internet as having potential, so he set about the task of making a legal licensing arrangement for music downloads. At the same time, it was also recognised within Apple that the market was limited until downloaded music was able to be made portable. Apple found and bought a company that had a nearly fully developed MP3 player, Apple put on the Jobs design touches and the rest is history. iPod and iTunes had arrived!

Jobs's personal fortune has rocketed from $2.1 to $5.7 billion, on the back of both the iMac's and particularly the iPod's success. This is the biggest percentage rise of any billionaire in this book, his ranking in *Forbes* rose from 262 to 132 between 2004 and 2007.

Development

Steve Jobs was born on 24 February 1955 to a couple of unmarried academics. He was adopted by a childless working-class couple within weeks of his birth. The birth parents would ultimately marry, have other children and teach at a university. His biological sister would go on to become a novelist.

His adoptive father was a machinist and his adoptive mother an accountant working in stores and, early on, babysitting for extra money. That couple would also have a biological daughter.

Jobs was a bright, hyperactive child who required little sleep, so he must have been somewhat of a challenge to his adoptive parents. By all accounts, Jobs had a loving upbringing but he was a super-bright kid in an average working-class environment, so he would have always felt like a square peg in a round hole. His adoptive father loved cars and Jobs frequently went with him to jumble sales and other buying trips, bargaining for parts. It was during these forays that Jobs learnt about trading and negotiation.

Without question Jobs is very intelligent, and was much too intelligent for his school environment. Having been born of two bright parents and then raised in what was essentially a working-class environment with parents of average intelligence, he just did not fit. His family moved to a new suburb when he was six, after kindergarten and presumably after at least one year of school.

Steve joined a swimming club. He was results sensitive and would cry if he lost. Also, he was teased and flicked with wet towels by the other boys. He just was not a sportsman! Like Bill Gates, Jobs could never be 'one of the guys' and he would have become highly sensitised to failure at sport. He would only play if he could win.

He had learned to read before kindergarten and often found school boring. He refused to do anything he found irrelevant. Like bright, bored boys everywhere, he underperformed in class and played up. He and some others were expelled for letting snakes loose in the class and exploding bombs.

At the age of ten, Jobs befriended an engineer who worked for Hewlett Packard after the man showed him a microphone. Jobs was fascinated and the engineer enjoyed sharing his knowledge. This was a critical event in young Jobs's development — here was an adult he could admire and who showed a genuine interest in him.

Jobs was inspired to join the Hewlett Packard–sponsored Explorer's Club. Engineers demonstrated the latest products and acted as both inspiration and role models. The club had electronic projects and junior engineers made simple gadgets. Jobs liked to show off his gadgetry to classmates, but mostly they didn't understand it (or him). So low was his social standing in the school pecking order that they thought he was lying about making the gadgets and what the gadgets did.

In fourth grade, he found a friend in a teacher who recognised his brightness despite the fact that Jobs had poor grades. Through bribery, she motivated him to produce high-quality work. This fostered a love of both learning and money. Her efforts were so successful and Jobs so advanced that she recommended he jump two grades — something his adoptive parents finally agreed to. This caused further social dislocation when the much younger Jobs was moved into a class of older kids, which caused his grades to suffer, again.

As an adult, Jobs is tall. However, after being accelerated two grades he would have been short in relation to his classmates, emotionally immature and have appeared even more odd than he did in his own age group. Even before his acceleration his classmates were not his peers, and his acceleration would have made them even less so. Already a demonstrated failure at sport, he was now in a hopeless position. Any sporting activity guaranteed loss and humiliation.

By the seventh grade, Jobs was having real problems at school. He had been promoted away from his supportive teacher to more unsympathetic teaching. The school was rough and Jobs was in danger of becoming a juvenile delinquent. Showing considerable insight, he insisted his parents move him from the school.

Jobs's family moved again, to a neighbouring suburb so that Jobs could begin high school in an academic program for gifted students. Sport played a miniscule part in his life, especially after he was expelled from the water polo team for bad behaviour. He joined the marching band, which provided him with a kind of group to belong to.

Even though he had left the Explorer's Club behind, his interest in electronics continued apace. Through a friend he met his later partner in Apple, Steve Wozniak, who was a year ahead at school. Wozniak had built a computer for which he had won a prize at a local science fair, something that very much impressed the young Jobs. With Wozniak's encouragement, he enrolled in an electronics class at school.

Jobs, always the inventive thinker, approached problems differently to others. Once, when short of an electronics part, he convinced an out-of-town supplier to provide the part free and even to pay reverse charges for the call. Jobs and Wozniak became 'wireheads', different from and much better than 'nerds' because wireheads made things. Unlike his friend, Jobs did not continue electronics classes after the first year; he had other interests such as literature and classical music. Obviously he was mainly interested in electronics for the friendship and involvement it gave him. His electronics teacher pegged him as a loner with a different way of looking at things.

Despite dropping the electronics lessons, Jobs and Wozniak kept up with the electronics together. Jobs also made items such as laser lights for rock music from parts his father brought home, a product he and Wozniak later adapted for a local jazz band. To earn some money, Jobs used his negotiation skills at flea markets to buy electronic parts and sold them to an electronics store. He was offered and accepted a part-time job at a huge electronics store after he was noticed spending so much time there. He made enough money to buy a car, which helped him with his girlfriend. Jobs stands out as a rare male billionaire to have had a steady girlfriend while at school.

In his final year at school he studied literature and, since his English and writing skills were so advanced, he sat in on classes at Stanford University. It was the time of flower power and hippies. While affecting the external appearance of the hippies, he was too intellectual for them. He had the brain power of a nerd, but he wasn't nerdy. He never fitted into either group; in fact, he never fitted into any group. He was his own man, an outsider.

Jobs, ever on the lookout for money-making schemes, found some hints from a magazine about a device for getting free trunk calls from phones by imitating the tones the phone made. With poor judgement, typical of young men everywhere, Wozniak and Jobs built some of these illegal 'blue boxes' and went into business selling them. They made $6000 out of the venture but stopped when it became obvious that their business was vulnerable because of the illegal nature of the product. The next money-making venture was playing *Alice in Wonderland* characters at the local mall for $3 an hour with his girlfriend and Wozniak.

All the time, Jobs was becoming more and more eccentric. He grew tall and thin. He experimented with sleep deprivation and various diets. He convinced his parents to pay for an expensive, out-of-town but eccentric university — Reed, a place for 'loners and freaks'. He became even more eccentric, the king of the loners and freaks. His hair was long and unwashed, and he rarely showered or wore shoes.

Jobs had few social skills and hadn't carried any existing friendships forward into this out of town university. Just like Gates, he undoubtedly suffered social failure rather than intellectual failure. The college was too expensive for Jobs's parents, so they stopped sending him money. Jobs got a job maintaining electronic equipment in a psychology department and was reported to be very good at it, even though he had no formal training.

Reed was a demanding college and Jobs, while being bright, dropped out after the first semester because his restless nature made university education feel irrelevant to him. Or so he says. In fact, the wildly eccentric Jobs was just too eccentric, even for such an unconventional institution. He was lonely and isolated.

Jobs experimented with food, including extreme fasting and eating only specific foods (such as carrots) for several weeks. He began to follow eastern religions such as Buddhism and he wanted to go on a pilgrimage to India. But while his head had dropped out of college, his body hadn't. He continued to live in the dormitory, moving from room to room as one came free, living out the whole college year without paying, but finally he had to leave.

Upon leaving Reed he moved back home and got a job fine-tuning computer chips with Atari, the computer game company. Atari had a flexible employment policy and because he smelled so bad from strange diets and not bathing Jobs chose to work at night. He was the only employee to work at night time. During this period he became reunited with Wozniak, who used to come in at night to play games and give Jobs occasional technical help.

Jobs went on a pilgrimage to India and on returning negotiated an engineering job at Atari. He was again asked to work nights so he would not upset other employees, either with his unusual personal hygiene habits or his lack of formal training. Again, Wozniak helped at nights.

Inspired by the 1975 *Popular Electronics* magazine with the computer on the cover, Wozniak began building hobby computers. He also attended computer hobbyist meetings with Jobs. Jobs saw the market potential in what they were doing, and he talked 'Woz' into starting a business. They have later claimed that their aim was for every home, school and business to have a computer.

It was around this time that Jobs paid a private investigator to find his natural parents. For Jobs, family ties are important and, unusually for a billionaire, he had girlfriends through high school and college. He is now married with children.

Interpretation

Jobs was born of very bright parents and adopted to parents of normal intelligence. The super-bright Jobs was always a handful for his parents and did not fit very well into his family, his early neighbourhoods and his schools when growing up. He must have felt like he was from another planet.

It is not clear when he found out about his adoption but this obviously caused in him feelings of abandonment, because he hired a private detective to find his parents as soon as he had his own money and well before he was rich.

He appears to have got on well with his adoptive parents, both of whom worked. His father was a car enthusiast and Jobs often went with him to markets for car parts — it was there that Jobs learnt to bargain, a skill he has used effectively throughout his life.

Bargaining obviously gave Jobs considerable emotional rewards. First he spent time doing this with his adoptive father and this was probably one of the few activities they could connect on. Second, he managed some unusual deals, purchasing parts for his school electronics club for which he received rare admiration from teachers and peers, and also for buying electronics parts that he sold to an electronics store.

Jobs was unaccustomed to being admired and the praise would have been emotional gold to him. Bargaining and social reward would have become inextricably linked to the approval-starved Jobs. Procuring supplies at bargain prices was ultimately to be one of Jobs's key roles in the early Apple Corp. It was also Jobs, the dealer, who persisted in finding Apple's first venture capitalist backer and who recognised the business potential of computers.

When he was growing up, Jobs was always a square peg in a round hole. He was obviously too bright and naturally unconventional for his parents and most of the kids around him at his working-class school. Already a social misfit with no aptitude for sport or tolerance of failure, he was advanced two grades at school. He was immature and short compared with his new classmates, guaranteeing sporting failure and humiliation; something that would have further isolated him from them, isolation that was exacerbated by moving schools a number of times.

Jobs has a major strength — his big vision. His Achilles heel is that he always knows best. Sometimes he did and sometimes he didn't know best, but he always saw things differently.

Despite taking on the role of visionary at Apple, Jobs's record in new product development has been patchy, until recently. Always the outsider, he rarely found the opinion of others worth listening to when growing up and as an adult he felt the same. He didn't change that even when he was developing products to sell to a mass market. Unfortunately what he delivered was what he wanted, which was sometimes quite different from what the public wanted. When he got it right, he got it very, very right, when he got it wrong, it was a disaster. At the moment he seems to be doing everything right, so he may have learned that lesson or, more likely, he has had an unusually beneficial lining up of his vision with the wants of the market.

Jobs was lucky to have met the Hewlett Packard engineer when he was ten. He found an adult who approved of him and could extend him intellectually. He was also lucky to have been able to join the Explorers Club and to play with electronics. This helped him find a community that shared similar interests and which ultimately led to his association with Wozniak, a person of considerable technical talent. Belonging to this group and his friendship with Wozniak grounded him sufficiently so that he did not go completely off the rails in late adolescence and early adulthood. It also gave him a safe haven to return to after his social failure at Reed.

By studying electronics and joining a club of wireheads Jobs had found a fraternity of outsiders to belong to. Jobs, however, was not a true wirehead; he had broader intellectual interests and dropped school electronics as a subject. He maintained his involvement in the club, especially with Wozniak, almost certainly because that group was probably the only group where he could belong. If he had been less of an outsider he probably wouldn't have continued in electronics at all, instead choosing to concentrate on his main interests, which were arts and literature.

Social failure at Reed must have been a seminal experience for him. Humbled, he came back home and took up again with Wozniak. Jobs was bright enough to do almost anything he wanted, but he had such a strong desire to belong that he got re-involved in what Wozniak was interested in.

Having started a venture with Wozniak, Jobs needed to have a role. Wozniak was the technical wizard, so Jobs took over other functions such as procurement, aesthetic design and business development. It was in business development that Jobs excelled and made the critical connection with a venture capitalist. Having done this deal, Jobs became increasingly redundant in the start-up Apple Corp. He was not really technical, his management was appalling and his vision was too personal and idiosyncratic—too much product failed in the market. He was fired.

His most successful other venture prior to returning to Apple, Pixar, fared better than others because he stayed out of it, while his other start-up company, NeXT, benefited from his money but suffered from his involvement. When hired back to Apple, Apple became increasingly successful. It is not possible to know if this success is a result of random alignment of Jobs's vision and market demands or whether Jobs has tempered his outsider ways and actually started taking the market into account.

It is interesting to compare and contrast Jobs and Gates at this point. Of all the self-made billionaires in this book, these two are the only two that are directly comparable. Both have a brain the size of a planet, both are in the same industry and both were there at the beginning of the personal computer revolution when *Popular Electronics* published its seminal issue in 1975. They have been in the same race but have taken different routes and ended up with different financial outcomes.

Jobs is more the heroic, wild-eyed inventor. Gates has never been this. He has allowed the media to paint him as such and gone along with it for the sake of image, but he has always been the calculating, game-playing businessman. Gates has been criticised for making derivative product but this has actually been one of his key strengths rather than a weakness. Unlike Jobs, who has always wanted to be the design hero, Gates rarely develops product from first thought. He allows the army of heroic, wild-eyed inventors to do that and take all the early risk on market failure. He then picks off what works in the market, pays the inventor only as much as he has to and takes the development and marketing from there. Gates lets others take the development risk.

The young Jobs and Gates were very similar. Both hated team sport, both were accelerated at school, both were outsiders at school, both had social rather than intellectual failures in their first year at college and both heard the pistol shot that signified the beginning of the personal computer race.

Gates had very sharply defined positive experiences associated with game playing. For him, computing led to belonging to a boys' club and the need to bring in deals to remain not only in but at the head of that club. Gates needed to control it all to belong.

Jobs's school experiences were much more diffuse. He roamed around picking up bits and pieces of experience here and there. He learned trading from his father, he became interested in electronics because of its social nature, but he never really 'owned' the clubs he belonged to. He stayed in the clubs but it wasn't his responsibility to keep them going. He was rewarded for being the inventor and unorthodox supplier of parts. His relationship with Wozniak was different to that of Gates and Allen. Jobs drifted back to Wozniak after other things failed, and became involved with electronics because that is what Wozniak was doing. Gates, on the other hand, drove the relationship between himself and Allen.

There is a sense with Jobs that he was less obsessively tied into computing and business. His need is for personal recognition so he wanted to be the lone hero at the centre of the computing industry. This explains why, in addition to incredibly poor socialisation, the young Jobs interfered so destructively at Apple and why it took him so long to learn that he often didn't know what the market wanted.

He shares with Gates and Ellison the need for self-aggrandisement, and all three take on guru personas in public. Jobs in particular has a large personal following—FOJ, or 'Friends of Jobs' as it is called. There is no similar organisation for Gates—in fact there seems to be a much greater but informal group that think he is the devil incarnate.

It is interesting that Apple's most recent phenomenal success with iPod and iTunes has come about by Jobs dropping the wild-eyed inventor part of his persona. Both these products are derivative, they were brought in from outside, but developed at Apple. Ellison and Oracle have also done this. Both Jobs and Ellison have advanced much more rapidly up the billionaire league table since taking a leaf out of the Gates book and dropping their heroic inventor stance.

Mind you, Jobs won't entirely drop the hero stance, and while sharing some of the credit with others he still over-claims responsibility for Apple's products.

References:

Wilson, S 2001, *Steve Jobs: Wizard of Apple Computer*, Enslow Publishers Inc, New Jersey.

Young, JS and Simon, WL 2005, *iCon: Steve Jobs, the Greatest Second Act in the History of Business*, John Wiley & Sons, New Jersey.

Chapter 10

Charles Schwab

Forbes information 2007
Rank: 155
Citizenship: United States
Wealth: US$5.2 billion
Industry: stockbroking

Charles Schwab developed his stockbroking business isolated from the big players on Wall Street. Having developed his business from first principles, he made the unprecedented move of actually understanding what the mum and dad share traders wanted and giving it to them. Rather than gouging them with high fees and bombarding them with information that was stacked against them, Schwab gave them low fees and no information. They loved it and loved him. Discount broking was born and is now a thriving industry.

Achievement

In 1974 a Stanford buddy came to Schwab with the idea of starting a discount brokerage business. Schwab loved the idea. As luck would have it, Schwab caught the seismic shift in the US securities industry when, on 1 May 1975, deregulation commenced. This shift loosened the stranglehold that conventional broking firms had on share trading, and it was broken by abolishing fixed brokerage commissions.

Prior to this, conventional wisdom among the brokers—who had (illegally) colluded in their response to deregulation—was to put up the rates to small investors while cutting rates to large investors. Schwab, the broking outsider, went counter to the market trend and lowered rates across the board, which helped him pick up a large number of small investors.

Up until that point Schwab's career as an entrepreneur had been up and down. This was about to change dramatically. In adopting discount broking and later electronic trading, he completely changed the broking service model. Schwab did not tout for business in the same way that the major brokers did, by cold calling investors with hot tips. Both of these 'services' were subject to very large biases against clients, as brokers boosted their favourite companies or overpromised benefits in order to gain commissions from the companies whose shares they were selling. The largest commissions were gained for selling the riskiest investments.

> In adopting discount broking and later electronic trading, he completely changed the broking service model.

Schwab rightly considered these common industry practices to be a swindle. His firm did not give advice as other brokers did and he put his staff on salary rather than commissions. His business was to carry out the trades and only to carry out the trades. This meant that he could control the cost of executing trades and by so doing could lower the cost to consumers. Not only did customers benefit from the reduced cost of trades, they didn't have to carry the costs of 'advice' that was inevitably biased against them. They didn't lose money by making investments on the basis of that advice. Certainly they were on their own, but they didn't have to contend with biased information.

Schwab was unencumbered by the industry way of doing things. He put small, no-nonsense ads in *The Wall Street Journal* introducing the company and offering discounts of up to 80 per cent off the usual fixed commissions. Calls came in from all over the country on the new toll-free telephone numbers and Charles Schwab & Co was in business. Charles Schwab & Co was one of the first discount brokerages. Initially his company was too small to attract Wall Street's attention, so Schwab could push ahead, gaining size without picking up competition or resistance.

The public liked Schwab as a personality, so the company's brand came to revolve around Schwab. By 1977 he was so well regarded that he was the first person to have his photograph on the front of *The Wall Street Journal*, but even then he was still pitching in when the load of orders in the phone room became too great.

The business developed by trial and error. This led to interesting developments such as adopting new computerised methods of trade fulfilment and then allowing customers direct access—the precursor to internet trading. Naturally, trial and error development can also lead to some very expensive and potentially catastrophic problems. One such problem was the back office error rate at Charles Schwab & Co. All financial institutions need to record each transaction accurately. Accurate recording means that money goes where it should and shares purchased end up belonging to whom they should belong to. The greater the number of errors, the more time is required to fix them. The cause of the high error rate in the early Schwab company was inferior administrative practices. Schwab was not one for administrative detail and had already demonstrated this fatal flaw with the collapse of a previous brokerage company.

The company risked its total revenue (underpinned, as Schwab expected, by growth) on computerising the back office. Schwab's brokers were the first in the industry to have computer terminals to buy and sell shares. The benefits were colossal. Broker throughput went up, transaction accuracy increased, executions happened immediately and the error rate plummeted. The system became more automated—customers could bypass traders by direct personal computer access via telephone and much later the internet. Schwab could offer twenty-four hour service.

Schwab's trading volumes increased rapidly during the market bull run of the early 1980s. This caused other brokers to start paying attention. In a typical response from entrenched cartels, they tried to stop him with the old-tech rules of broking, but they failed. They also began half-heartedly adopting the technology, but Schwab's early lead and single focus kept his growth ahead of the rest.

In those early discount broking days, Schwab's branch network had an unforeseen advantage. Discount investors were most strongly attracted to Schwab's company for the psychological comfort that those branches gave them, even though they hardly ever traded through the branches. In other words, it was important for them to know that they could interact face to face if they wanted to. The fact that they had this option gave investors so much comfort that they rarely actually visited, except for opening accounts.

Growth continued apace, but this had its problems, the largest being that the regulator required a certain level of capital in the company at any one time. The problem of meeting the capital requirements was so great that Schwab decided to raise capital by listing on the stock exchange.

Unfortunately, and despite a previous lift in administrative accuracy thanks to computerisation, the error rate was still such a problem that in 1980 Schwab failed in his attempt to float the company on the stock market. He tried without success to pass the error rate off as simply a result of the company's growth. His inclination was to break through with charisma. But sometimes even huge dollops of charm aren't enough to deflect attention from real problems and eventually the company had to get Schwab out of the way and fix the problem.

The failure to float led Schwab to sell the company to the Bank of America for $53 million. By that time the company had 500 000 customers. Schwab was to regret this decision almost immediately.

Schwab stayed with the company and in 1987 executed a management -led buyback for $280 million. This was not without problems for Schwab as the stockbroking bubble burst around that time.

Like many company founders, Schwab had to be kicked upstairs so that the increasingly complex operation of running the business could be carried out without interference. As had been shown on several occasions in Schwab's business career, he was a liability to have around any administrative system.

By the time the internet boom began in the early 1990s, Schwab was positioned with a strong retail, or what is pejoratively called 'mum and dad', base of shareholders trading through his company. Schwab had a mid-tech direct trading system with customers dialling directly into the Schwab system. The company was moderately mature and, as with all mature companies, it had sunk psychological and systems costs into the old way of doing things. Schwab was resistant to change and required strong persuasion to enter the internet trading market, but when he eventually did, the company experienced another growth spurt.

Paradoxically, having branches again gave Schwab's new internet investors security during their transition from physical share trading to internet trading. As in the past, new share trading customers liked some sort of physical contact when starting something as important as investment and, as luck would have it, Schwab still had a strong physical presence due to a well-established branch structure left over as a legacy of his early business operations. As in the early discount broking days, a strong branch presence gave Schwab's company an important market edge over the early internet start-up companies. They were sufficiently old school to give comfort, but nimble enough to keep up with the changing market needs.

Schwab also had the advantage of working out of San Francisco while the major brokers worked out of New York. This helped him to stay under their radar. Operating out of California had the added advantage in that the population is inherently more likely to adopt new ways of doing things.

The Schwab model could have been copied by any of the very large broking houses at any time. But the big Wall Street traders had become so rich and complacent that they did not want to change the system that had benefited them for so long. They fought every inch of the way to keep the old methods, and by the time they entered the market had a long way to catch up.

While not the first in the market, Charles Schwab & Co was able to capitalise on its existing brand and a network of branches to become the market leader. Strong growth continued, and by 1998 Charles Schwab & Co passed Merrill Lynch in stock market capitalisation.

Development

Charles Schwab was born in 1937 to a second-generation lawyer. Schwab's father was an attorney in Sacramento, later a district attorney. He left the public service in 1946 and moved his family to California in 1949; his profession there is unrecorded, but he probably worked as a lawyer in private practice. Schwab's mother's occupation is unrecorded. There is nothing written about his relationship with his parents. His uncle was a successful manufacturer who leant Charles money from time to time for both his broking business and for other unsuccessful ventures that Schwab started prior to broking.

His parents allowed him to develop businesses through his teenage years. Obviously his father knew that young Charles was bright but he had a reading handicap, dyslexia. Following his father into law was obviously out of the question as the reading demands were just too great.

Schwab was allowed and probably encouraged to develop along lines that were appropriate for his abilities and skills. He and his father shared an interest in investing and Charles showed a great fascination with investment patterns.

Born in Sacramento, Schwab then moved to nearby Woodland where he started school. The family moved to Santa Barbara when he was twelve. Schwab went to at least three schools in two cities. No comments have been made about the disruption this caused to young Charles, but it is significant to note that his business activity started around the time of his last move.

Shortness coupled with dyslexia meant real status problems at school, where he had a very difficult time. As with many dyslexics, he often considered himself to be dumb. He compensated by developing a strong, likeable personality. He also started businesses that enabled him to achieve out of school.

Schwab is not recorded as playing any of the mainstream boys' team sports, so it is safe to assume that either he didn't or if he did he was hopeless at it.

He took up golf while at school and it still plays a big part in his life. He received great satisfaction playing golf and became very good at it. This led to him being named captain of the school golf team.

With his quadruple handicap of dyslexia, shortness, serial uprooting and lack of mainstream sport, Schwab was an outsider. So, he did what he could do — business. He had a walnut-harvesting business and he ran chickens. Other children thought he was odd spending his time on these agricultural pursuits. He was beginning to develop his maverick personality. He also enlisted some other children to help, undoubtedly outsiders like himself. He became the boss of a little band of outsiders bound together by a common business purpose.

> He became the boss of a little band of outsiders bound together by a common business purpose.

He also started earning an income as a caddy. He charmed the professional golfers that taught him, he charmed his caddying clients and most of all he charmed his way into Stanford. He had developed charisma and was receiving the benefits. Some of the money he earnt from his business ventures he invested in shares.

Unfortunately his reading difficulties caused him to fail some subjects in his first year at university, though he did well at economics. But Schwab learned to compensate. He later said he thought he often bluffed his way through. He worked hard and had a bright personality, and says he used it to charm his teachers into giving him beneficial treatment.

Schwab had learned to compensate for a lack of attention to detail, brought on by his dyslexia, by being a charismatic leader. However, in an industry where all the back-end processes require detail, charm will only go so far. Settling accounts, reconciliation and compliance requires a detailed mind. Several early business failures and later close calls can be attributed to this shortcoming.

While still studying for his MBA, Schwab began as an analyst for a brokerage firm, and by the age of twenty-three was a vice president. He was highly successful, but his youthful ambition and feelings of invulnerability led to dissatisfaction and he moved on.

In 1963, with partners, he started an investment newsletter. The circulation high point of the newsletter was when it reached 3000 customers, with a subscription costing $84 per year. Schwab was the junior partner because he came in without financial backing. He felt overworked and underappreciated, which, given his ambition, troubled him. The newsletter's growth in the eight years of Schwab's involvement was incremental rather than meteoric, and Schwab rankled at the lack of progress.

The company leveraged off the success of the newsletter 'and launched one of the first no-load mutual funds in the country' (Kador 2002). It was soon to become one of the largest mutual funds in California. But Schwab's disdain for administration, regulation and regulators was a fatal flaw in the business, which resulted in Schwab making a terminal error in the way the business was run. The company ran foul of the regulators, losing everything and ending up $100 000 in debt. It was 1972, Schwab was thirty-five and he was in disrepute.

Schwab then tried a variety of ventures that failed, including a theme park and running a rock concert (with no knowledge of the contemporary music market). He lost heavily when his associates quit the enterprises and left him to cover the losses. Nevertheless he remained optimistic that things would go his way.

Schwab's first marriage brought three children, but it ended in divorce during the strained early years of business. Schwab then married the daughter of a Texas oil magnate, and had a further two children. While his wife's family is rich, it would appear that there was no money coming to Schwab from that direction.

Interpretation

There is nothing written about Schwab's relationship with his parents, except that his father obviously provided formative approval from a relatively young age for an interest in shares and for doing business. He also gained considerable formative approval and much reward through his charisma, both at school and in his early business ventures, particularly caddying. Obviously the emotional rewards for succeeding in these early businesses were very great, resulting in him largely ignoring school as a means of connecting with people and receiving approval.

Schwab was happy-go-lucky, which is not a trait of a traumatised boy—or is it? Schwab had reason for trauma—he had undiagnosed dyslexia, he was short, he was from somewhere else and he wasn't connected at school through mainstream sport. A short, 'dumb' outsider is always in danger of falling to the bottom of the pecking order—a very painful place to be. Schwab used the time-honoured method of developing a positive personality to ingratiate himself into a system that was stacked against him.

He was never going to be a sporting success at the dominant male sports in school because he was too short. It is very likely that he was teased or bullied until he developed strategies to deflect these punishments and gain approval for himself. Obviously becoming good at golf and then becoming captain of the golf team gave him some standing at school. On the way he probably developed his happy-go-lucky personality to deflect scorn and this would later gain him customers and approval. Charm and humour are always a handy set of skills for the otherwise low-status kids to develop to gain some status and deflect derision. It is also a trait that Richard Branson used, but Schwab is not a prankster like Branson.

Golf was a perfect outsider sport for Schwab. It can be learnt and practised out of sight of others. If proficiency is not achieved then no-one need know. It relies on accuracy and patience, not on speed and strength. It also has a transactional society around the pro shop, which an outsider can fit into. An enthusiastic boy with a happy disposition can become a caddy and earn money and appreciation by hauling golf bags.

Schwab obviously became proficient at the game and became golf captain. This is probably as high in the status stakes an outsider like him could expect to rise at school. Compared to, say, being on the elite football, basketball or baseball teams, it is a bit better than being a mascot, but is it definitely off centre and low, but not bottom, of the pecking order.

Business gave young Schwab a way of succeeding outside the normal school-based social system. He developed a sense for what customers wanted. He harvested walnuts and ran chickens from which he sold eggs, meat and fertiliser. He had partners (he was the charismatic leader) and he sold out when the time was right. As with his caddying, his relationships were held together by financial transactions. This was friends by doing business!

He reportedly runs his operations in an easygoing way, but he has zero tolerance for unethical behaviour. If an employee violates any regulations or does something illegal, then that person is gone immediately.

Schwab had a solicitor, share-trading father and an entrepreneur uncle, so trading was not only familiar to him but also encouraged. His father and uncle strongly reinforced Schwab's interests and this encouragement would have been sweet for a small boy struggling both socially and academically. It would have conditioned him and set him on his path, ever searching for money-making ventures. Schwab's early transactions with golf ball sales and other small business ventures would have reinforced any inherited trading tendencies. He was well aware of his limited opportunities in occupations that required reading and so he was open to occupations that used trading and charisma instead.

Schwab had already experienced belonging through friendships based around transactions, so it was natural for him to go into a field of endeavour that bound people together by transactions. He settled on a career in business and the emotional associations and familiarity with shares made stockbroking an obvious way ahead for him.

Schwab was convinced that he would succeed despite a string of failures in the early years. At least two of those failures came about because he departed from his very early adherence to the principle of giving customers what they wanted.

Highly aggressive, Schwab was motivated by the need for professional respect and wealth. But like many charismatic leaders, he was flawed. He was a strong leader but a poor manager. His business systems were chaotic. He demanded fierce loyalty and if that wasn't forthcoming, execution was swift and ruthless. He punished mavericks severely. To question the great leader or the myths surrounding him was to court instant dismissal.

Charisma and an apparently easygoing nature is a personality cloak he adopted as he was growing up. Underneath that is a driven man. Transactional relationships always gave him his place in the world and shares gave him his comfort. What better way to live your life than owning a stockbroking company?

References:

Kador, J 2002, *Charles Schwab: How One Company Beat Wall Street and Reinvented the Brokerage Industry*, John Wiley & Sons, New Jersey.

Chapter 11

Ralph Lauren

Forbes information 2007
Rank: 158
Citizenship: United States
Wealth: US$5.0 billion
Industry: fashion

Ralph Lauren, a Jewish wannabe WASP (white anglo saxon Protestant) performed a minor fashion miracle by reinventing WASP fashion and selling it back to them. Always enamoured with the horsey style of the English and classic fashion of Hollywood, Lauren invented the near timeless styles that have since become a trademark of his now international Polo brand. These styles have huge appeal to men who need to change their clothes but don't want to think about fashion. What better way than to have a stylish brand with lines that barely change?

Achievement

Lauren was in heaven when he landed his first job as a buyer with Brooks Brothers department store on Madison Avenue. He was just out of school and in love with WASP fashion, fashion that quietly exuded overtones of belonging to the upper white classes not more than a few miles away, but a million miles distant from the immigrant ghetto he grew up in. All his life he could see the promised land over the imaginary walls, as projected by Hollywood and Cary Grant movies in particular. For Lauren, the clothes said it all.

His honeymoon with fashion was interrupted by a short stint in the Army. Back in New York, Lauren found a job as a glove salesman charged with the responsibility of extending the product range. He became excited when he sold to an equestrian store on Madison Avenue—he loved fashions for riding and polo. This was true style! It was just about as far removed as he could get from the late 1950s buzz cut and Oldsmobile or slicked back and hot rod male fashions in America at the time. Lauren was attracted to the fashion of traditional England, or at least the fashion as interpreted by Hollywood. He even owned a rare English sports car.

Lauren extended his range to include ties, and won his first write-up in the trade papers. Lauren had been putting much of his meagre earnings into having his own clothes tailored, full of detailing a man on his income could not afford. But the financial stretch to appear super elegant paid off!

Lauren had no formal training in tailoring, so he watched his tailors closely, and learned rapidly from the people who worked on his clothes. He was constantly studying style from the movies—especially movies with Cary Grant in them—and having his tailors mimic, modify and extend the celluloid-based fashions.

In the 1960s, eccentric fashion became the norm, even the straights had weird get-ups. Lauren spotted a trend to wider ties and wanted to put them into his range but he couldn't get his boss to commit to more than a few, so he quit and joined another company. He started his own line, innovating on fabrics and style. He even cut up sofa fabric to make ties. While wide ties were not his idea, he did make them his own.

> Lauren had no formal training in tailoring, so he watched his tailors closely, and learnt rapidly from the people who worked on his clothes.

He made them elegant—and costly. During this time, Lauren came up with the brand Polo. It was English, equestrian and upper class, all summed up in four letters.

He worked frantically to build the business. He knew style, and picked and helped shape the fashion trends. The business grew slowly and Lauren got himself into financial trouble because of a trait he would exhibit over and over again—he loved clothing perfection more than profit. He landed Bloomingdales flagship store as a major account—the ties were so successful they almost walked out of the store by themselves.

Bloomingdales ran a huge advertisement, featuring a naked model draped in ties. Sales soared and so did Lauren's image.

It was 1969 and Lauren began opening stores for his employer. He was starting to make a name for himself and build confidence in what he was doing. He was getting press. He was designing an ever widening product range. In 1970, he won his first Coty award, the designer's equivalent of the Academy Award. A journalist wrote that the 'Lauren Look' had arrived and Lauren recruited her to become his right-hand person. The polo player motif was designed and put on clothes. His clothing was increasingly in demand.

But Lauren, the perfectionist, was difficult to work with, and his perfectionist demands became too great, causing critical cost over-runs. Unlike Lauren, his boss was in business to make money, not fashion, so they agreed to part company. His boss was happy to let him go so long as he paid for excess inventory. In fact, he was so relieved to be rid of Lauren that he let him go with the Polo brand name. Lauren raised finance and a loan to start a new business. The cost to Lauren was that he had a partner with 50 per cent ownership of the business. The partner was bought out several years later.

Lauren had no formal training in fashion, he just knew what he liked. To a large extent, what he knew about clothing came about by getting clothes made for himself. He knew what he wanted and brow-beat tailors to modify clothing to suit. His lack of training became a problem, for while he knew what he wanted, he never had any formal way of expressing it. A great deal of Lauren's design team's effort was tied up in trying to interpret Lauren's unclear instructions, which were usually accompanied with tantrums and tears.

Because he was technically untrained, his design processes left a lot to be desired. He had a clear vision of what he wanted, but he could not articulate it to his designers. When the designers didn't come up with what he wanted because of his unhelpful directions, he would get extremely angry at them. But despite his problems with some staff, he surrounded himself with a string of extremely loyal sycophants.

Lauren could be pleasant to designers at the beginning, but it would often end in abuse. He had a need to show them who was boss, and would attack people's self-esteem.

On the plus side, however, because he was not formally of the industry, he was not inculcated with the industry culture and ways of doing things. Despite his trial and error design ways, his outsider vision had cut through the market and sales continued to grow.

Lauren was a demanding martinet with a vision and the right clothes for the times; this kept his business growing. But he was despised, and in turn despised others in the industry. One notable adversary was Calvin Klein, an old boy of Lauren's school, PS 80. He despised Klein as much for being everything that he, Lauren, wasn't—tall, handsome and gregarious, while Lauren was short, considered himself to be ugly and was extremely shy and awkward in public.

Lauren's business and brand growth was not all smooth. He continued to be extremely poor at the control aspects of business—he often carried too much inventory, missed deadlines, made too many last-minute changes and had too many returns. This nearly drove him to bankruptcy in 1971. This general process weakness again demonstrating that he was in business to make fashion, not in fashion to make business.

Lauren would push his staff relentlessly, often beyond the point of frustration. He was determined to make Polo a household name. This was part of his brilliance—he knew that he had to build a brand. The other part of his brilliance was to repackage some of the American dream in clothing.

> [He] took the 1959 L.L. Bean catalog … and turned it into
> the best part of a billion dollars … Lauren understands
> from the inside the yearning of people who didn't go to
> Ivy colleges. And his timing was exquisite. The old WASP
> hegemony was breaking up; retail in America was tired;
> and he saw the way to appropriate WASP culture and
> rebrand that image to his own (Gross 2003).

This is perhaps more cynically stated than it needs to be. However, Lauren's luck was that the way he wanted to dress coincided with the way millions of others wanted to dress, which was different to the way the contemporary fashions dictated. Going his own way paid off. His own deprivations and aspirations while growing up lined up with those of the market.

Lauren introduced and maintained a stable line of fashion for the everyman, that part of the market that isn't very interested in fashion—those who are pleased fashion remains more or less the same for years or even decades. As everyone in business knows, repeat business is always more valuable than new business, and Lauren had found a fashion formula to keep the customers coming back year in year out. He developed a near timeless range that remains stable year after year so his customers don't have to make much of a fashion choice.

Learning from Coco Chanel and others, Lauren adopted the concept of licensing, and it was onwards and upwards from there. He licensed his name to a fragrance, which remains a top seller. He licensed women's wear, bedding and homewares. The polo shirt kept on going and going.

In 1980, Polo began expanding again on the back of huge royalty income. This was despite Lauren being difficult to deal with and his perfectionism causing late deliveries.

Development

Ralph Lauren was born Ralph Lifshitz on 14 October 1939 in an immigrant enclave in New York. He was the youngest of four children and his family was poor. He grew up in a house where the children slept three to a room. He was the shortest in his class, and he had a lazy eye and a lisp. To compound the physical insult of his appearance, his older brothers were taller and more handsome. Always certain of unfavourable comparisons between himself and his brothers, appearances began to matter to young Lauren.

His mother was related to a Jewish dynasty with aristocratic heritage in Europe, including many important rabbis. The benefit of Lauren's mother's heritage did not extend to life in New York, consequently she felt the fall in circumstances acutely, particularly as Lauren's father's side of the family were nobodies and unable to help elevate her status or circumstances. Both sides of the family were extremely religious and steeped in orthodoxy.

Lauren's parents were reportedly very private—they hardly ever saw anyone inside their house. They kept to themselves and their English was limited. Lauren's mother was the force in the family; she was the boss. The family did as it was told.

Lauren was a sickly child, small and scrawny. He had sinus problems and a perpetually runny nose, a lazy eye and a lisp. Very uncertain of himself, ashamed of his ugliness and certainly teased about it, Lauren was aloof and kept himself from the games fellow children played, often sitting for hours on the step of the house watching the other children play but not joining in. He was a loner or outcast. Lauren dreamed of being Hopalong Cassidy, and other movie stars—an enduring influence on his fashion emphasis.

While there is no doubt that his mother loved Lauren, her influence was far from benign. Her fiercely held, unswerving aspiration for Lauren was for him to become a rabbi just as her noble ancestors were. Consequently, as Lauren moved more and more from that goal, she became fiercely disapproving of him.

Lauren's father, on the other hand, was a dreamer. He was a frustrated fine artist forced to work as a house painter in order to support his family. All the children were artistic and able to draw. They were poorer than average for the area, Norwood, a lower middle-class suburb of New York that was at that time a strong Jewish enclave. It is interesting to note that that area and ones adjacent to it have spawned a disproportionate number of very successful people. These people had experienced the Depression and the horrors of Europe during World War II. It created a group of people in search of recognition, success and stability.

Almost everyone in that area was guaranteed to be an outsider to mainstream US culture as soon as they moved beyond the enclave. It was tough being a young Jewish person at that time, with the conflicting environments of home and the outside world and it was even tougher if you were a small, ugly boy like Lauren.

Initially Lauren went to the local public school, PS 80, for two and a half years. He had a poor attendance record and achieved indifferent grades in all but music, art and shop. His mother transferred him to a fiercely orthodox Jewish school half way through the second grade because she wanted him to become a rabbi.

Lauren was disadvantaged at his new school because he didn't know Hebrew or Yiddish well. He often did not understand what was going on in class. Because of this and his poor academic record he was put in a class of younger boys — in other words, he was held back academically.

It was a very grim place. The school ran on fear and corporal punishment, with fierce rabbis who had lived through the Holocaust. Lauren's performance did not improve and he skipped nearly a third of the time — his grades were low in all but art. It is not recorded what he did when he skipped class.

There were two types of pupils at the school. One type fitted in, the other type rebelled actively. Lauren fitted into neither group. He was not popular, but he was cunning and managed to convince the rabbis that he knew what was going on.

With no attributes that he could use to break into the hierarchy, he opted for the time honoured solution used by powerless outsiders everywhere — he worked at making himself a small target or invisible, someone apparently inoffensive, someone who looked like they fitted in or, at least, someone who was not a threat.

While making himself a small target may have worked at school, it did not work as well going to and from school. Lauren walked through tough areas, where being visibly Jewish and obviously defenseless could easily lead to a bashing. He developed his own style to protect himself. He became 'preppy', and didn't wear 'ghetto' clothes. He looked fashionable and tidy, and would wear pastel colours, nice shirts and ties. Most of all he looked like he belonged outside the enclave and in WASP society. Again he had managed to pull on an invisibility cloak, ensuring him a modicum of safety in the danger zones outside the Jewish enclaves. He was learning invaluable lessons about fashion as camouflage.

Once he had learned the lessons of disguise through fashion, he began extending this technique. Since he couldn't fit in and he couldn't beat the others at their own games, he made his own game using style and cool. Lauren developed a strong love of clothes, and he had natural style and good taste. But most importantly, he also learned that dressing up made an impression and set him apart. Not only did his fashion sense save him from being beaten up, it also gave him status and friends. He started looking like someone who mattered and his status and self-confidence improved.

By fifth grade, Lauren's grades had improved. His mother had obviously temporarily given up on Lauren becoming a rabbi and he was moved back to PS 80, where he flourished. At first the boys made fun of him, but he eventually prevailed. Understanding that sport is the glue of male culture, he worked hard at sports, especially basketball. He was far from being a natural because of his small stature. However, he made the team as a reserve, but he hardly ever got a game. He was adopted as a kind of a mascot, but at least he was close to the heart of boy power. Lauren was an energetic but indifferent sportsman. He looked good but didn't actually do much else.

Being cool has a way of attracting people, and Lauren developed a small circle of acolytes. He enjoyed the attention, and surrounded himself with people who wanted his advice on fashion and how to look good. His style and cool became so convincing that some people wanted to look like him. But Lauren was aloof, and maintained an attitude that he was above everybody else. As a small, slightly dull boy with a lisp, Lauren had found acceptance and a way to excel. He had found an important way to survive and flourish in his harsh world, the way that would lead him on to become a billionaire. It centred on style and manipulating those around him to believe he was more than he actually was so that they would want to be with him.

Just when things were going well for Lauren, his mother sent him back to the Jewish school to finish his high school. He had to leave his friends, followers and a girlfriend. It reportedly drove him crazy. This time, however, Lauren flourished. He was magnetic, and was elected class vice president. The lessons in social survival through image had paid off! He graduated without any particular distinctions.

During school, Lauren went to holiday camps and mixed with real WASPs—here he honed his style skills by both fitting in and standing out thanks to the clothes he wore. He wanted to out-WASP the WASPs.

Lauren went to a public college in New York. For a time he went to college during the day but later switched to night classes while working in a variety of clothing related businesses. He dropped out of college at the end of his third year.

He continued his makeover by changing his name to Lauren when he was nineteen and having his lazy eye fixed.

Lauren married in 1964 to the receptionist at the medical centre where he had his lazy eye fixed. While Lauren has been married to the same woman since the 1960s, he is believed to have had several mistresses. Only one mistress, Kim Nye, ever made it into the press. Very little is said about his marriage, but it appears that he is at home as he is at work, a martinet. He is a control freak who likes to intimidate people, and he doesn't like it when others disagree with him.

Despite his international business and fashion success, Lauren remains insecure. Success made him less secure rather than more secure. He worries excessively about how he looks. Work at Polo routinely grinds to a halt while Lauren spends time fussing about his appearance and seeking affirmations from everyone. He is also domineering, and once threatened to fire an employee because he didn't like her boyfriend.

Lauren commands fierce loyalty, creating an atmosphere akin to a cult. He is the hero leader and style god, and everyone else his followers. The culture maintains Lauren as the cult leader; anyone who doesn't believe this doesn't get in, and if employees dare forget this during their time they are quickly out the door.

But it is not too hard to maintain Lauren as hero. Fashion is a glamour industry and people flock to it. There are beautiful clothes and beautiful colours and beautiful people. Lauren and Polo are no different—there was a buzz about the place and people want to be part of that.

In 1987, Lauren had a tumour removed from his brain. His behaviour is reported to have become worse. He developed hypochondria and became more combative. It is reported that his need to belittle others and instil fear increased.

Interpretation

In his early years, Lauren lived in a world completely outside his control. His mother, as the custodian of a distinguished rabbinical tradition, obviously confused what was for Lauren's good with what was for her own good. She arbitrarily moved him from school to school and bullied him in a futile attempt to turn him into something he was never going to be, a rabbi. She was intrusive, demanding and arbitrary.

In addition, Lauren was short, puny, had a lisp and a lazy eye, and was shy and unable to find a place with the other children. Worse, he was teased and bullied for his afflictions by other children and compared unfavourably with his handsome sporting brothers by teachers. Sitting on the step watching the other children at play was as close as Lauren could safely get to the action. He vicariously shared in the play without putting himself in physical or emotional danger.

His outsider standing would have been amplified by the fact that his mother, and family, was isolated from the community—the Laurens rarely, if ever, invited others into their house and nobody invited the Laurens. Consequently, if Lauren was going to make any friends he had to make them without assistance from his family.

Like many isolated and powerless children, Lauren escaped into fantasy. He had seen innumerable Hollywood movies, possibly when he was playing truant. In particular he admired Cary Grant's style. His fantasy was to be like Cary Grant, who lived the good life in the style of a wealthy and powerful Ivy League WASP. Like any child, Lauren dressed up. Interestingly he did not dress in cowboy clothes like his early hero, Hopalong Cassidy, but as close as he could to Ivy League.

Lauren initially changed his style to protect himself while passing through hostile territory—to make himself invisible with fashion camouflage. A secondary and totally unexpected benefit was that his fashion camouflage also enhanced his status back on his semi-hostile home ground. He gained approval, friendship and admiration. He developed a facade of style and charisma that allowed him to charm people and control his environment.

> Lauren initially changed his style to protect himself while passing through hostile territory—to make himself invisible with fashion camouflage.

He gained safety in the first instance by avoiding bashings for being Jewish. As he became more and more established in his fashion, he became popular, even to the extent of having a girlfriend and being included in male company.

Lauren's brain became hard-wired with the belief that 'clothes maketh the man'. Lauren knew what he was doing, and he also knew that it was a facade. At any moment someone might see through his deception and expose him. His facade had to be maintained at all times. Unable and unwilling to reveal the real Ralph Lauren, he was insecure and anxious.

Insecurity has dogged him his whole life. Underneath all his success, Lauren essentially lacks the confidence that the inner Lauren does not measure up to the outer Lauren. He fears he may be found out at any time. Now, as then, he must obsessively maintain this style because only then can he be safe and wield power over people.

At school he could only influence people through his style and charm. He would seduce them into being his friends. But he had to keep his anxieties in check and he couldn't exert too much unreasonable power over people. Friendships are voluntary and can be lost very easily. Lauren had to behave!

Bosses do not have to behave however. As an employer, Lauren is reported to seduce new employees into working for him. But true personality is only revealed by observing how people behave when they have others in their power. Once he had people in his power, his insecurities ran rife in the workplace and there was nothing anyone could do about it. He could rant and rave with impunity. He could hold up professionals while he obsessed about his looks. He could make arbitrary decisions any time he liked, and he is reported to do these things frequently.

It is also logical that he should hate Calvin Klein and other people in the industry. His style solution was hard-wired into his brain when he was in the schoolyard. School is a very small style market with no room for competition. Any person with competing style was a potential catastrophic threat to Lauren's standing and must be dealt with immediately and with venom.

Lauren's anxiety and attacks on other stylists were transferred to the world of fashion, even though logically the world has much more capacity to absorb competing styles than the schoolyard ever did.

As a child at school, Lauren was constantly dressing up. He was obsessed with clothes. He would talk of nothing else because that was the sole source of his safety and power. This also explains why he has been obsessed by the style side of the business and is a perfectionist. Despite this, his style solution has found a broad and lucrative market. That and his obsessive drive, fuelled by anxiety, has made him a billionaire.

Lauren's family do not obviously have a trading background but he reportedly came from distinguished lineage in Europe, including highly regarded rabbis. There could well have been successful traders among his ancestors.

Lauren's luck and brilliance was in his dealing with a hostile world in those early years with an image that could be turned into a business. He feared and hated the environment he grew up in, he hated himself and needed to escape persecution and isolation. Style was his solution and his obsession. This was his luck—to develop an obsession that lined up with the market.

He didn't like what he was or his origins, and wanted to change his style to be more traditional than traditional—a super WASP.

References:

Gross, M 2003, *Genuine Authentic: the Real Life of Ralph Lauren*, HarperCollins, New York.

Trachtenberg, JA 1988, *Ralph Lauren: the Man Behind the Mystique*, Little, Brown & Co., Boston.

Chapter 12

David Geffen

Forbes information 2007
Rank: 167
Citizenship: United States
Wealth: US$4.7 billion
Industry: media/entertainment

David Geffen turned an early fascination with shows into a fortune in show business by obsessively scheming to own more and more by takeover. He has used his personality as a weapon, employing abuse and invective to wear down all who stand in his path. He attained the coveted, but informal, title 'the most powerful man in Hollywood', and accumulated wealth and power, but this has ultimately brought him no satisfaction as he now cuts a lonely figure, constantly in therapy, able to make piles of money but not true friends.

Achievement

At only twenty-five years of age, and only a short time into a new talent agency job, David Geffen became bored, and obsessed with starting his own record label. This he did, calling it Asylum Records. Asylum Records was to become the most successful start-up record label ever.

Geffen has a prodigious work ethic and determination to succeed. His strength is in planning and seeing a path to success where others don't, combined with an unfailing hunger and the unorthodox, frightening behaviour necessary to carry it off.

Past loyalties mean nothing to Geffen if the person stands between him and the money. It matters equally as little if the person has been a mentor or is just a casual acquaintance. Getting between Geffen and the money is always a very dangerous place to be.

In an industry that sells talent, he is a deal doer and he relies on others with 'talent' to carry out the creative parts of his business. Unconventionally conceived and ferociously executed business deals are Geffen's forte, not talent scouting. For example, he has a gift for finding and working with the best talent scouts, a strategy that he has used right through his career. Geffen, with little contemporary taste of his own, relies exclusively on his trusted scouts. In the 1970s, using his talent scouts as spotters, he signed superstars Joni Mitchell and Crosby, Stills, Nash and Young to Asylum Records. He 'found' Jackson Browne and groomed him for success. Jackson Browne in turn found him the Eagles, destined to be Geffen's biggest group at that time. All through this, Geffen had no idea whether the work the artists were producing was good or not.

As early as the 1970s, Joni Mitchell and Don Henley of the Eagles were well aware that Geffen was becoming more rich and famous than they were. Good dealmakers usually end up richer than the talent because they can constantly put deals together. Artists can only produce so much before the market is either unable or unwilling to absorb more or because they simply can't produce fast enough. Dealmakers can spin a deal a minute and take a piece of every one. The bigger the deal the bigger the return and showbiz deals are big, so Geffen became richer and more famous in Hollywood than many of the stars.

He met Cher at a club while dining with Bob Dylan. She was breaking up with her husband, Sonny Bono, so Geffen weighed in—he won out for Cher and then tried to take control of her life (by attempting to marry her) and her career. This only worked for a short time as Cher was unwilling to submit to Geffen.

He had spent considerable energy wooing Bob Dylan, only to spoil it in a fit of jealous pique when Dylan failed to acknowledge his contribution at a concert. Dylan defected and only released one poor-selling album with Geffen.

Geffen sold Asylum Records to Warner Communications, despite promising his artists that he wouldn't. He made millions of dollars from the deal, but typically he was not happy with the outcome. Nevertheless he stayed on in various roles at the record company and at Warner Bros.

Geffen had always wanted to run a movie studio. At thirty-three, he got his way through general bad behaviour. Geffen's strengths are not management nor are they related to movie content. He has no idea what makes a good movie or a bad movie or, more importantly, a commercially successful movie. He failed at running Warner Bros. movie studios and, following a series of blunders, he was fired in less than a year. He sat out the next three years on full salary, refusing to return to the record business. By this stage Geffen had grown his $5 million from the sale of Asylum to $20 million through real estate investments.

He met Calvin Klein and partied hard with him and his friends, at the infamous Studio 54 among other places. Geffen helped Klein when his business got into trouble.

Geffen returned to work with Warner Bros., cutting himself a brilliant deal to start Geffen Records, and eventually setting himself up to be one of the richest men in Hollywood. Such is the power of Geffen's 'negotiating' techniques that Warner Bros. put up all the money yet split the profit fifty–fifty with Geffen.

While at Geffen Records, he signed John Lennon just prior to his assassination. The assassination helped Lennon's record sales but predictably only for a short time. Other faded stars he signed were not so successful. Geffen Records struggled for some time until eventually one of his talent scouts found and signed Guns N' Roses, a group that went on to be one of the of the most successful groups of the 1980s and 1990s.

> While at Geffen Records, he signed John Lennon just prior to his assassination.

Around this time, Geffen began producing movies and put money into stage shows, most notably *Cats*.

Despite the obvious value of Geffen Records to Warner Bros., Geffen carried out a hectoring campaign for more ownership and was given nearly 100 per cent of the company. He then auctioned if off to MCA for nearly $550 million in stock, chiselling some minority shareholders along the way. The company was taken over by Japanese investors and its cash value rose to over $650 million. Geffen had reached his goal of becoming one of the richest men in the US, but he 'continued to take petty and vindictive potshots at the people who for decades had been his allies' (King 2000).

He is compulsively driven to make more money and bigger deals. But with all his money, Geffen was unhappy and bored. He was in therapy continually and never succeeded in finding a permanent partner. Part of the reason for this was that while he was homosexual, he fought against it for a long time, refusing to acknowledge it even while having homosexual affairs. His attempts at marriage to women were part of this denial and not successful for obvious reasons

As Geffen became richer, he began to take a more high-profile role in public campaigns. He became a most effective AIDs fundraiser and assisted in raising funds for the Democrats to get Bill Clinton elected president. It was at one of the AIDs fundraisers that Geffen came out and admitted publicly that he was homosexual.

He has since gone on to form a major film company—DreamWorks SKG. The 'S' stands for Steven Speilberg, 'K' is Jeffrey Katzenberg and the 'G' is Geffen.

Development

David Geffen was born in 1943 in a lower working-class suburb of New York, Borough Park. He was a spoilt second child.

His father was an unassuming telegram delivery boy when he met his wife in Tel Aviv. She was the daughter of a well-to-do, stern Jewish landowner and a pharmacist mother in the Ukraine. She was separated from her parents by the communists while getting educated abroad and had to live by her wits, eventually going to Israel. While not reported, this separation must have caused her considerable anxiety and explains some of her bizarre behaviour and later emotional breakdown. Arriving in New York in the midst of the Depression, Geffen's mother became the breadwinner of the family by starting a small enterprise to manufacture women's underwear. The Geffens were an unconventional Jewish family, with the wife the breadwinner and matriarch, while the husband was a man who liked to read and spend time alone.

Geffen's mother was extremely controlling and combative with everybody. She was aggressive and would verbally assault people, leaving them shaken; something her boy would later do, too. She wore Geffen's father down until he was virtually a shadow around the place, unemployed and deeply depressed. She berated him more than anybody else, and would not leave him alone. Family life was tense and unhappy, friends were few and company rare.

Geffen was the second born of two boys. He was his mother's pride and joy and she was determined to give him everything that she had missed out on in life. Any amount of bad behaviour was tolerated from Geffen. In other words, she encouraged him to be a brat—she defended every action no matter how offensive. And Geffen, unchecked by his mother—or maybe even cheered on by her—and unable to be checked by his father, took on many of his mother's combative ways of communication, ways that were guaranteed to win him money but cause problems with relationships. Even as a pre-school child Geffen was not popular.

When Geffen was six his mother had an emotional breakdown brought on by, among other things, learning that her parents had died in the Holocaust. Her eccentric behaviour made Geffen even more of a social outcast. She was hospitalised for almost six months. This, along with his unemployed father, made him a subject of derision. Not surprisingly, Geffen began having emotional problems at school. In discussing his 'nervous' behaviour, the nurse diagnosed him with emotional problems, saying he craved attention and talked constantly. He was often late for school.

When his mother returned, after what was a traumatic separation for Geffen, they spent time going to see movies in Manhattan. Later she let Geffen go to Manhattan by himself when he was only ten.

His mother continued to be a tough-minded businesswoman and she taught Geffen well. But she was incredibly lax with his moral education. He did not develop a sense of right and wrong because she allowed him to get away with almost anything. He simply did anything to get what he wanted, even if that included cheating or lying. His mother never reprimanded him for such behaviour.

Geffen's high school was tough and overcrowded, and he struggled both socially and academically. His behaviour was disruptive and his grades were poor. He went there with the stigma that his parents were not 'normal' and Geffen's unruly personality, combined with his lack of involvement in sports, isolated him.

At high school, he decided to excel in organising a school theatre revue. He campaigned and won the male chair for the juniors, a position he shared with a female chair, who reportedly saw him as a liar, cheat and someone who obsessively hogged the credit.

Previously unnoticed, Geffen finally got some attention. He had honed his political skills and campaigned furiously. Against all precedent, the juniors put on the winning act. When the results were announced, the auditorium erupted. His mother jumped and screamed. It was the best moment of Geffen's school life, and helped determine his path.

Geffen tried to repeat his initial success in organising school theatre, but he did not get the result he was after. Ongoing battles with the co-chair forced him to leave the theatre project, putting an end to the only involvement at school that was rewarding for him.

Even though Geffen grew to be ashamed of his strange, poor mother, he remained loyal and brought her out to Hollywood in her old age, every now and then showing off his showbiz friends to her.

While at school, Geffen was obsessed with the business of show business. He bought seats to all the best musicals on Broadway. He loved show business and it stimulated the businessman in him. He turned into a successful ticket scalper, and at a young age was showing an insatiable desire to make money. He even used tickets to bribe teachers.

Geffen found he was confusingly attracted to boys, not girls, at a time and age when this was highly undesirable. Already dubbed a sissy for being short and non-sporting, and seen as a compulsive liar, with broken-down, unbalanced parents, he did not want to face further humiliation if his secret got out. This only added to his insecurities and unhappiness and led to him denying his desires.

He finished school ranked about the middle of his year. When he left he did not even bother to pick up his diploma.

He applied to go to college and was accepted by the University of Texas in Austin. He began but again Geffen was an outcast, and he received a traumatic hazing from his fraternity. He left without completing a term or any examinations.

On leaving school he headed straight for the business side of show business. His most significant early job was as a mailroom boy for the William Morris Agency, a premier booking agency in New York. At that time, being a mail boy was the obligatory entry point into the agency, if not the industry — it was the starting point of all careers. Geffen lied about his qualifications to get in and then, using his position in the mailroom, located the reference check letter that would have exposed him as not having graduated from university. He reportedly forged a letter from UCLA in response to the reference check by his employer — in essence, he committed credential fraud. It was a sign of where Geffen's morals lay when he was trying to get something he wanted — unconstrained by manners and feelings of fair play, all behaviour was acceptable if it led to Geffen winning.

While in this agency job, he adopted a strategy that he used repeatedly throughout his rise to riches. It was a plan he developed early in life with the encouragement of his mother. The strategy was to develop a powerful mentor (originally his mother) who found him cute or, in the case of businesspeople, cute and useful. While he treated his mentor well, he behaved appallingly towards those around him. When people complained to Geffen's mentor about his behaviour, he would be protected by the incredulous mentor. This is because the mentor had not seen what had happened and either did not believe that Geffen could do such things or found it useful to have such divisive behaviour in the ranks.

In one early episode, while still in the agency mailroom, Geffen read every memo he could get his hands on and used the information to his advantage. When found out, Geffen was fired by his immediate boss, but he was reinstated by the top boss. Geffen had made some enemies, but was friends with the one person who really mattered—the big boss. Later, he did as he would frequently do in the future—he turned on his mentor.

In those early years he made friends such as Barry Diller, another Jewish kid, who would become one of Geffen's closest friends and a fellow Hollywood powerbroker.

Geffen was promoted out of the mailroom to become an agency assistant. He worked hard and his commitment to his clients was so complete that he was promoted to become a full agent. He knew how to caress the right egos to get what he wanted. Geffen began accumulating clients.

Geffen also began to accrue mentors, such as Clive Davis, the head of CBS Records. Importantly, Geffen swung good deals for his clients. Aside from this he also had a stake in a music publishing company, which was in direct contravention of the music governing body's rules.

At twenty-five, he was headhunted out of the Morris Agency to another agency. He continued to work hard and make deals frantically. He would dote on potential clients and make promises he had no intention of keeping to get them on board.

Geffen's core behaviour was self-centred and neurotic. He was completely unable to see anyone else's point of view. His abrasive personality meant he was often offside with people, but he always claimed to be in the right. If friends or colleagues were perceived to have crossed Geffen in some way then they often became the subject of vendettas. There are several famous vendettas Geffen carried out in Hollywood. These could carry on for years. Even when he made deals that were extremely generous to himself, he was either resentful or at best ungrateful because he came away believing that not only could he have made more, but that he deserved more.

Without a second thought he would do almost anything to advance his own cause.

Being so self-centred gave him an orientation that others didn't have. Without a second thought he would do almost anything to advance his own cause. He was extremely dogged and hard working. He almost never gave up and always demanded more. He would use any trick to get his way. He would schmooze or abuse, yell and most effectively scream. Any relationship between what he promised and what happened often appeared to be purely coincidental.

Geffen was far from loyal. He would turn on anyone and use any behaviour he felt necessary to get his way. He was determined to succeed, and was always manoeuvring to get something for himself. It proved successful.

Paradoxically, while he achieved huge financial success, it did not bolster him very much emotionally. His moods would go from euphoria to depression, while some of the biggest deals he pulled off sent him into an existentialistic funk. Even when Geffen was riding high he felt insecure. He was never satisfied. No matter how much money Geffen had, he hungered for more. He also hungered for more recognition. He lobbied the editors of *Forbes* to make sure he got on its list of richest Americans as soon as he could.

Despite his tough business practices, he was loyal to some friends. He bailed out Calvin Klein when his business was in trouble and helped Cher, Joni Mitchell and others. But a wrong word or misplaced phrase could bring huge vitriol down on the perpetrator. Having wooed Bob Dylan over a long period of time, Dylan's failure to publicly acknowledge Geffen at a concert started a feud that was ultimately self-destructive on Geffen's part. Dylan terminated his relationship with Geffen. Similarly, Geffen gratuitously interfered in Paul Simon's business and was cut off by Simon.

Geffen also held irrational grudges and sought revenge for any perceived slights. One unfortunate agent, who had the double problem of representing the best interests of his client against Geffen and being named 'the most powerful man in Hollywood', had his life turned into a living hell because Geffen coveted the title himself.

Geffen has been in psychoanalysis for most of his adult life. His ethos can be summed up by the following quote:

> If you maneuver enough, you can get away with anything,
> and winning is easy. It does not matter if you tell the truth,
> cheat on a test, or step on people on your way to the top.
> It only matters if you win (King 2000).

In essence, if a person is totally unconstrained by the normal rules of interpersonal interaction or ethical behaviour, and is driven and insecure, then almost any deal is possible. But the price is high—money and success do not guarantee happiness.

Despite being homosexual, Geffen had serial obsessions with women, including Joni Mitchell and Cher, but naturally these relationships didn't work out. He wanted marriage and a family, and pursued and dated women, but most of his sexual partners were men. He was tormented by his sexuality. With men, he could get plenty of sex but for all his wealth and power he could not sustain a meaningful partnership for long. He could get a meaningful relationship with women for a time, but no sex.

Despite being hugely rich Geffen is alone and isolated.

Interpretation

While Geffen's mother obviously loved him, she was emotionally unstable and incapable of giving him the type of love a child needs growing up. Her obsessive and intrusive behaviour would have constantly upset her infant. Geffen felt abandoned while his mother was confined to a mental institution for six months. Also, Geffen's mother was a model of bad behaviour, which encouraged Geffen's own bad behaviour. This would have had grave consequences for his emotional and social development. Geffen's father faded away and had literally been nagged to death, so did not provide any substantial foil for her influence.

By the time he got to school, Geffen's behaviour pattern was developed. In addition to having a difficult personality, he was small, with an unstable mother and a strange, disconnected father. Naturally he was bullied and terrorised at school. To top it off he was guilt ridden and confused about his sexuality. He was desperately insecure and frightened.

Geffen's mother was tiny and she compensated by having a booming voice and commanding presence, something Geffen also learned to do.

His early good times seem to have been largely associated with movies and theatre. He started going to the movies with his mother after her illness and it probably represented the only situation in his life where he could be near his mother, receiving proximity, love and not being harangued by her. They were both there watching a movie or show and talking was not permitted.

The only recognition he achieved at school was by co-organising a theatre event. Here he exhibited the curiously self-destructive characteristic of doing something that could win him admiration, but in which he actively destroyed that possibility by being insufferable. This is a pattern that he perpetuated right through his career with many stars.

He scalped tickets on Broadway and used tickets to smooth his way with teachers. Geffen had learnt to make money out of show business, and he liked it. In fact, he more than liked it, it was one of the very few things he did when he was young that ever brought him a reward. It was certain. He could get fleeting admiration from people by getting them something they couldn't get for themselves. He could get momentary admiration by transacting but he could not sustain the admiration. Never learning to socialise his trading, fleeting admiration gained by transacting was as close to friendship and admiration as he got and it became his obsession.

It has not been stated but it's almost certain that his mother would have given him approval for making money by scalping. She probably even turned a blind eye to his truanting in order to do it. Her ethos would have been that scalping is business and business is good.

With a combative, difficult personality shaped by his mother and virtually no moderating influences while growing up, combined with a few early positive associations with theatre, movies and ticket scalping, Geffen was on his way to a fortune in showbiz. Trading was obviously a family trait. Geffen inherited this trait from his mother's family, and he was bound to have been praised by his mother for it.

Geffen was very self-centred about his loyalties. While growing up, he had no experiences of enduring friendships and the mutual responsibilities and interdependencies they lead to. He only had instrumental arrangements — arrangements in which people were useful or not. A person was an ally, an enemy or irrelevant. If a person was of no further use they were abandoned. When Steve Ross, Geffen's mentor of many years, was dying, Geffen did not even visit him.

For Geffen, a fortune is not enough. While winning a big deal may bring praise, it is hardly the stuff that relationships are made from. Geffen never had any problem finding a lover, but the lovers were always more interested in his money than in him.

Despite deal doing being demonstrated as not leading to reliable relationships, Geffen has kept on and on. He had become addicted to the fleeting fix gained by closing a deal. He was always unsettled and always wanted more deals and more money. While making Geffen ever richer, the unfortunate emotional legacy of his mother condemned him to a life without a partner, to loneliness, constant self-doubt and anxiety.

References:

King, T 2000, *The Operator: David Geffen Builds, Buys and Sells the New Hollywood*, Broadway Books, New York.

Singular, S 1997, *The Rise and Rise of David Geffen*, Birch Lane Press, New Jersey.

Chapter 13

Frank Lowy

Forbes information 2007
Rank: 172
Citzenship: Australia
Wealth: US$4.6 billion
Industry: property

Frank Lowy brought a deep hunger and fear of failure with him from the dark days of World War II Budapest to Australia where he began his shopping-centre empire. Obsessively driven to expand, he reinvented the shopping-centre concept in the US using the Australian model. He now sits atop a global shopping-centre business but remains just as hungry.

Achievement

Lowy and his partner, John Saunders, made the unlikely transition from a migrant delicatessen and coffee bar established in 1955 to small-time housing developments to become a worldwide force in shopping centres. The Australian company took its name, Westfield, from the western Sydney fields the original developments started in. The company latched on to the new US idea of shopping centres in 1958, evolved its formula in Australia and, after a successful out-of-town experiment, burst onto the US shopping centre market in 1977 with a fresh take on the tiring concept. Under the relentlessly hungry stewardship of Frank Lowy, Westfield has gone on to become a world force in shopping centres.

In 1958, the fledgling Westfield property development partnership set up by two émigrés to Australia was beginning to show promise. The partners had begun very small time, first operating a delicatessen and coffee bar, then moving to small-scale home development and then on to building shops. Hungry for success, they latched on to the emerging shopping centre concept. This concept had been extraordinarily successful in the US and the partners wanted a piece of the action.

The scale planned was miniscule compared with present day mega malls. Nevertheless it was an ambitious plan in those days, doubly so given the embryonic nature of the partnership. The partners developed a centre around a square with twelve shops, a supermarket and a department store. While it was being built, Saunders went to the US to survey the scene. The concept was novel in Australia, and since the centre was immediately successful the partners were in demand. They and others could see that they were onto a good thing.

In September 1960, with four substantial projects on the books, Westfield Development Corporation was floated on the stock exchange. The original partners retained 21 per cent each, 20 per cent went to another partner and 38 per cent to the public. The roles of the original partners became more defined, and they were a good match. Saunders would look for new ventures, and he thoroughly researched business, architecture and engineering to help him identify good opportunities. Lowy became the expert in accounting, financial and legal matters, and would look after this side of the business. They further complemented each other because Saunders operated on instinct and was an opportunist, while Lowy was methodical. It proved to be a good combination for the rapidly expanding business.

After only eight years in Australia and not yet thirty, Lowy was beginning to attract media attention. A newspaper article stated that the 'movers and shakers' of the time were mostly immigrants. It was an exciting time in Australia with a structural change in retailing rapidly underway. Regional brands were going national. Westfield forged a strong business link with major retailer Melbourne's GJ Coles in Coles's national expansion program. Lowy took his first study tour to the US and was further excited by the developments there.

By the end of 1963, Westfield had completely abandoned residential development. It focused entirely on shopping centres. Westfield was also changing its business model, moving from a developer to an owner. It was starting to own a stake in the centres it was building. Through ups and downs, complications with purchasing and council planning, persistence was Westfield's catchcry. Lowy would later say:

> Never give up! People don't understand how persistent
> you have to be ... Unless you are very strong and
> convinced you can succeed, you will get swept away
> (Margo 2001).

Westfield expanded into the Australian states of Queensland and then Victoria. Westfield was not known in Queensland, and the task of filling the shops in its first Brisbane centre was difficult. Lowy spent six months pounding the pavement until eventually he had twenty or thirty tenants. Once the concept was sold and proved, momentum picked up and the centre was filled. Lowy never rested.

Lowy had almost obsessive control. He wanted to read every letter and every document that came into or out of the company. He monitored cash flow and, with Saunders, signed all cheques. Naturally enough, as the business grew, Lowy worked harder and longer, while activity and profits grew.

By 1970, Westfield was still relatively small. It had built nine shopping centres and was consistently profitable, so much so that in 1971, after it had announced its eleventh consecutive profit increase, it was wooed and won by Credit Suisse of Zurich to be a partner in shopping centres.

But it was not all plain sailing. They were involved in deals that made little money, they missed opportunities, such as an early entry of shopping centres into Israel, and had problems of selling residual house lots and credit squeezes.

Along the way, Lowy became more entrepreneurial and was inclined to propose opportunities that Saunders turned down. Rifts were now beginning to appear between the dominant partners.

In a classic move where an outsider takes a modified and improved product idea back to its originating market and makes money, Lowy took shopping-centre development back to its heartland—the US. In 1977, Westfield bought a mediocre shopping centre in a good area in Connecticut. This was the beginning of a new Westfield empire in America. Lowy and Westfield brought the techniques developed in Australia to the US. These techniques required them to squeeze every dollar out of a development and make every square centimetre count. Their Australian experience meant they knew how to capitalise on small sites with multi-storey buildings and rooftop or underground parking, and they knew how to redevelop a site to fit in the maximum number of stores.

But the US ventures drove a wedge between the partners. Lowy forged ahead in the US while Saunders stayed back in Australia minding the store. A further wedge was driven by Lowy's graduation into high finance. Westfield was no longer a small enterprise and it restructured its financial and ownership arrangements. The exercise gave Lowy a gratifying sense of wellbeing, because for the first time the company had cash. This sense of security was short lived as the Australian government changed the rules to close the tax loophole exploited by Westfield and others, causing considerable financial pain.

Lowy's eldest son joined Westfield in 1977, followed later by his other two sons. Not surprisingly, the founding partner, Saunders, found himself more and more on the outer. In 1984, Saunders finally decided to sell out of Westfield and he left.

In 1986, Westfield diversified by buying a regional media company. Very soon after Australian media rules were changed and the whole media landscape was up for sale. Westfield bought Channel Ten television and made it into a completely national network. Unfortunately things didn't go smoothly. Lowy said the stakes were high, he was in unfamiliar territory and dealing with difficult people. He had moved into an industry that he didn't know well. He was caught out, disproving the notion that success in one industry automatically ensures success in any other.

Ratings were a huge problem and Lowy was out of his depth negotiating programming. He thought his Jewish connections would help him negotiate with the Hollywood heavyweights. It helped him get a foot in the door, but he was taken for a ride anyway. He later admitted that he had been taken advantage of because of his inexperience in the industry. It also appears that Lowy had not proceeded with his usual caution.

Channel Ten went from bad to worse and, finally, in 1989, Lowy decided to quit. He could have walked away leaving banks and shareholders to take the loss, but instead he put $200 million back into the business before he left, despite having no obligation to do so. He was concerned about the shareholders and also wanted to protect his good reputation. He also was strongly influenced by his grandfather's ethos not to go bankrupt.

Lowy put his efforts back into shopping centres, expanding in Australia and the US. He now sticks to his main game, shopping-centre development and management, and has become a major global player. In

1990 he was named one of the six pioneers of modern shopping centres by the US-based International Council of Shopping Centres.

Development

Lowy was born in 1930 in Fil'akovo, a small town in Czechoslovakia, the youngest of four children. Lowy's mother was the daughter of shopkeepers and his father the son of a school teacher father and later a publican.

His father was happy-go-lucky and popular, but a poor businessman. He squandered the marriage dowry and eventually ended up as a not very successful travelling salesman for his wife's rich cousin.

Fridays were especially important to young Lowy, because that was the day his father came home and made a fuss of him and gave him food treats. According to his brother, Lowy was the darling of the family and adored by all. But his sister remembers him as pushy and bad tempered and used to getting his own way.

Times were hard, money was in short supply and arguments were plentiful between the parents. In a bid to improve the family's finances, Lowy's mother borrowed money from her brothers and went into business in a small grocery store. The family lived behind the store, and the children would sometimes serve the customers. This was a time of relative calm and prosperity compared with what was to come.

It wasn't only the Lowys that were finding the times hard. It was difficult in the 1930s in central Europe for just about everyone. Europe was living in the shadow of both World War I and the Great Depression. It was particularly hard for Jewish people with the Nazis on the rise in Germany and anti-Semitism on the rise throughout central Europe. Czech anti-Semitism was relatively mild until 1935, but from 1936 persecution of Jewish people increased.

Lowy's father began collecting information on emigration to Brazil and Palestine but failed to act. This lack of action would ultimately have fatal consequences for Lowy's father and grim consequences for the rest of the family. Life carried on fairly normally for the Lowys until 1938 when Nazis occupied up to the Czech border, and the area where the Lowys lived became Hungarian. Anti-Semitism increased further, and Lowy and his friends were harassed. Lowy found life both humiliating and dangerous.

Business and employment opportunities began shrinking for Jewish people. The cousin's business was in decline and Lowy's father lost his job as a salesman. Money was again in short supply and the shop and family home would have been repossessed if Lowy's uncles hadn't come to the rescue again.

Deportation of Jewish people began in neighbouring Slovakia and a number of relatives were lost. There was sadness, and the family and the community could sense the imminent danger. The decision was taken to move to Budapest where it was thought they would be safer.

Lowy was eleven when the shop and house were sold. Initially the Lowys moved in with friends in Budapest, and they soon had their own apartment. As Lowy's father couldn't find work, the major responsibility for earning a living fell on the children. Lowy's schooling was disrupted by the need to support the family. He was to get some primary school education only. Lowy supplemented the family income by scalping tickets for the theatre. His sister became a couturier, while his brother became a travelling salesman of metal kitchenware. Metal was scarce and orders could not be filled, but the brother, undaunted, discovered an artisan making pots out of black market iron, so he went into business selling these and made a handsome profit.

During this time, the Lowys were to experience a false sense of prosperity and freedom. With this money, the family thought it had left its troubles behind, and life began to improve. Lowy was experiencing the difference money can make.

The tranquillity was broken on 19 March 1944 when the Nazis finally invaded Hungary. The very next day, Lowy's father went to the railway station to investigate moving his family to the country. He was rounded up by the Nazis and deported, never to be seen by the family again. His eventual fate was unknown until many years after the war ended. The uncertain loss of their father caused the Lowys great distress, with twelve-year-old Frank spending many days searching for him and waiting in the rain hoping for his return.

Frank's brother took over as head of house but options for Jewish people were becoming very limited. Jewish people were required to wear yellow stars and were dispossessed — thrown out of their homes and places of work. Lowy's brother and sister took Christian identities and left the family group. Lowy and his mother were moved into a Jewish quarter. Life was a daily dice with death, a hunt to get food and protect self and loved ones.

Life became harder and harder. In an environment where a single mistake could be fatal, Lowy learnt to be extremely alert and to pay attention to detail. For Lowy and his mother it became a matter of simple survival. Lowy would spend his days simultaneously trying to find food and avoid capture. He became very resourceful.

The Jewish people in Budapest were forced to move into a ghetto. Some fast thinking on Lowy's part got himself and his mother a new apartment in a 'protected' area of safe houses elsewhere in Budapest. But even those in safe houses weren't safe for long. Once the Nazis had cleared the ghettos they began systematically killing people in the safe houses. Lowy and his mother were within days of being shot when they were saved by the Russian invasion of Budapest.

Lowy and his brother set out for Palestine separately. En route, both were interred by the British, Lowy for three months, his brother for over a year. Meanwhile, his sister emigrated to Australia with her husband and his mother remained behind.

In Palestine, Lowy went to a youth settlement. In the morning they worked and in the afternoon went to school, where he made up ground. Lowy was one of the top students in three of his classes.

He was perceived as more worldly, so he became a youth leader. It is reported that in avoiding capture by the Nazis he had avoided the concentration camps, therefore, he had been able to live by his wits to a much greater extent than those forced into terrified passivity in the camps. This made him more resourceful than his peers who had been interred in the camps. Also, Lowy was popular with the girls because he knew how to talk to them.

The Israeli War of Independence began on 30 November 1947 and Lowy fought with the Jewish Army, eventually belonging to an elite commando group fighting with guerrilla tactics. The group was disbanded in January 1949 and Lowy did a radio training course, during which time he realised that he was a fast learner. On discharge he took a job at the post office and then in a bank. But the need to reunite with his family was strong. So, in 1952, Lowy and his brother emigrated to Australia.

Australia was not kind to immigrants in the early 1950s and it was hard to find work, particularly for those with little English. Lowy eventually got a factory job and then a job as a storeman, all the while dreaming of being a travelling salesman or delivery driver.

Bored with being a storeman, he decided to move on. With the help of his sister-in-law, he got a job in a sandwich shop. He became passionately involved in the Jewish football club and taught Hebrew to enlarge his social circle. Through the latter, he was invited to a party and met his future wife, Shirley. Almost immediately after their honeymoon, Shirley became pregnant.

By this time, Lowy had found the job he had earlier dreamed of — a delivery truck driver for a small wage and commissions. The commission gave him the opportunity to earn more, and he developed new customers and increased sales. Lowy was enthusiastic and hard working. He started early, drove fast, and fitted several runs in a day. He clearly demonstrated his enduring hunger for earning. His wage was £9 a week plus 2 per cent commission, but his efforts meant that he usually brought home at least £100.

It was on his delivery run that he met his future partner John Saunders (Schwartz), a Hungarian Jew and survivor of the Nazi concentration camps. Saunders owned a delicatessen. Lowy impressed Saunders, and as Saunders was looking to expand he invited Lowy to be his partner. They struck a deal and went looking for a new shop. Eventually the partners settled on a location in Sydney's Blacktown, opposite the railway station. At that time, Blacktown was in the centre of a European migrant settlement with little ethnic variety in the shops. Saunders's hunch about the opportunities in Blacktown for a delicatessen specialising in European foods proved correct and the business was a great success.

The store next door became vacant and the partners expanded. They installed an espresso machine and their European-style coffee bar became an instant hit. The coffee bar and delicatessen became a thriving oasis of ethnic colour in the dull western suburbs of Sydney.

Sydney was inundated with migrants who needed a place to live. Seeing the opportunity, Lowy and Saunders went into land subdivision. They did an initial project for small but encouraging profits and decided to continue more seriously. Time spent running the espresso bar became onerous, so they sold it for a handsome profit and went into business as residential property developers. Lowy and Saunders would negotiate the purchases themselves, hire contractors to do the work, and then make the sales. The company Westfield was born, taking its name from a combination of western suburbs and fields, which was where their subdivisions were taking place.

Some new shops were built near their delicatessen and sold for a handsome profit, so the partners decided to move into commercial property development. Westfield built four new shops which it sold for a good profit. A clothing retailer was impressed with its development and asked it to build another for it, which Westfield did. This also proved to be very profitable for the fledgling development company. In 1958, they sold the delicatessen for a further profit and moved into property development full time.

Lowy exhibited the tendencies that were later to become his most famous characteristics. He worked 'like a machine', paying attention to every detail and squeezing every dollar out of Westfield's developments. But he also made time for his family in his busy life. It was reported to be a happy household and Lowy was living how he had always wanted. But he was also a strict disciplinarian—he was the boss and ruled the house, while his wife saw that they were all looked after.

Soccer was Lowy's personal obsession. His love for the sport was instilled as a young boy while watching the occasional game with his father prior to the war. Lowy was extremely competitive. A close friend would describe him as 'the worst loser he had ever met' (Margo 2001). He also played tennis, but it was never just social. Lowy played to win.

Lowy was very much involved in the administrative side of the Jewish soccer team in Sydney. Like his father before him, Lowy would take his children to games, and he encouraged their enthusiasm for the sport.

Lowy taught his boys the importance of success, or more importantly of avoiding failure, a lesson he learned at a time in his life when a slip-up could mean death. Lowy would encourage and support his children, but he abhorred laziness. If they had made a genuine attempt at something then he was happy, but he would be furious at a less than committed effort.

Today the Lowy family talks business all the time, and it is in constant communication. For the Lowys business never stops.

Interpretation

The key to Lowy's behaviour is his experiences during World War II in Budapest. With the disappearance of his father and when his older siblings moved out of the family group, Lowy was the man of the family, needing to feed and protect himself and his mother. Any false move could have killed young Lowy. He had to survive on his wits, and attention to detail was paramount—to miss one tiny detail may be fatal.

This experience engendered in him the feeling that he was never safe and could never have enough food or shelter. This constant terror forged his drive. These events caused a deep hunger in him, one that was never satisfied. He cannot rest, he has to have more and more.

Over a twenty-five year period, Westfield's share price increased 300 times over the initial list price. This pleased Lowy, but he didn't slow down one bit. No matter what he achieves, he always strives to do more, not necessarily for financial gain but because he is driven to give his all to everything he does.

> Over a twenty-five year period, Westfield's share price increased 300 times over the initial list price.

It is claimed Lowy was 'luckier' than the Jewish people sent to the concentration camps because he had some limited freedom to act. Having some control over what happened to him gave him increased vigilance and drive. His immediate reward was that he and his family stayed alive and out of the concentration camps. He is now fiercely protective of his family, and needs to be in touch with them constantly.

Probably hankering for the 'stable' times before his father was whisked away from the family, Lowy's start in Australia followed the family tradition of food and travelling sales. His absolute hunger for sales as a travelling salesman made him early money and sufficiently impressed his soon-to-be partner. Both he and his partner were hungry for success, and were the ones who introduced the new shopping technology (shopping centres) to Australia.

But the time before the Lowys moved to Budapest wasn't stable. Lowy's father was loving, but he was a hopeless provider and he wasted the initial capital the dowry provided. This caused considerable stress between Lowy's parents. His mother had fallen from grace and felt it terribly. She started a shop and this saved the family for a while and brought some peace. Lowy would have felt the need to provide a stable income for the family even before he began his wartime foraging for survival. Lowy's work since has been strongly influenced by both his mother and father. First there was travelling sales (after his father) that led to his involvement in shopkeeping. He moved off this base into subdivisions then shop building and shopping mall development and finally ownership.

Both Lowy and his partner were immigrants. In other words, outsiders. They weren't held back by the way things were done in Australia and they recognised that their fellow migrants weren't being adequately catered for by the retail outlets offered at the time. They knew there was another way to do things, a different set of produce that immigrants would buy, and so they set about providing these things.

Innovations began for Lowy as the salesman by providing a service that others didn't. Then Lowy and Saunders introduced a delicatessen and espresso bar—both novelties for Australians, but serving a well-known need for migrants. But Lowy wasn't just any migrant outsider. He was supercharged by a deeply hard-wired hunger. Almost inevitably, his early ventures were a success.

Like many successful innovations, Westfield's have been slightly ahead of the field rather than way ahead of the field. Ventures including introducing shopping centres into Australia and later importing the Australian concepts of shopping centres back into the shopping-centre heartland of the US were successful because they were only slightly ahead of their time.

Of his business success in America, in addition to hard work and entrepreneurial skill, there was a crucial difference between Lowy and the Americans. The American style was to create large, extravagant, spacious malls. But Lowy wanted to make the most money for Westfield, so he learnt how to squeeze the maximum return out of the available space.

He is absolutely focused on work. Speaking of a trip to the US, a colleague said that it was possible to sit next to Lowy on a twelve-hour flight and not have a single personal conversation. They would talk business the whole time, and there was no spare time for relaxation once they arrived.

This intense drive came at a personal cost that was often not obvious to others. Lowy worked very long hours, his body was tense and sore, he had stomach pains, and could often only sleep with the help of sleeping tablets. But he would still be up at 5 am to get back to work. He often cancelled holidays because of work demands. He has said that his achievements are due to effort and determination to reach his goals, rather than genius. He also expects maximum effort from those he works with.

Lowy has also acknowledged that his motivation is not for wealth but from a fear of failure. This was bred into him as a boy during the war, where even a small failure could mean death for him or a loved one. Failure, therefore, could not be contemplated, an attitude Lowy has carried with him ever since. Lowy has reportedly mellowed a little with age, but he is still highly motivated.

He is very determined to avoid failure, particularly in public. His failure with Channel Ten led to a very public humiliation, which he bought Westfield out of even though he could have let that particular entity go bankrupt and been financially better off for doing so.

Lowy's view is that for every problem there is a solution. His mantra is never give up, and since he never gives up he keeps going until he finds the solution. It may be a negotiated solution, or a financial restructure solution.

There is very little luck involved in Lowy's success. It is a consequence of huge effort, constant vigilance and attention to detail, and a deep, unsatisfiable hunger.

References:

Margo, J 2001, *Frank Lowy: Pushing the Limits*, HarperCollins, Sydney.

Moodie, A 1998, *Local Heroes: a Celebration of Success and Leadership in Australia*, Prentice Hall, Sydney.

Chapter 14

Richard Branson

Forbes information 2007
Rank: 230
Citizenship: United Kingdom
Wealth: US$3.8 billion
Industry: air travel and retail

In September 2004, Sir Richard Branson and 1008 Virgin employees set a world leapfrogging record. It was during a staff party at the billionaire's mansion and they smashed the record by over 150 people. Another day, another stunt, but most importantly another story in the media right around the world. High-energy, high-profile fun is his way of marketing the Branson brand by grabbing the headlines. In so doing, he has converted a lifetime of pranks into billions of dollars of free advertising and corporate desirability.

Branson's big cheeky schoolboy grin and adventuring antics are his brand and his marketing edge. His grin and exploits are known all around the world and continue to sell his autobiography long after other billionaire biographies are out of print. Branson is the Peter Pan billionaire, the one that never quite seems to grow up. And it works; he is ever popular with the media, the population and, critically, people with new deals to offer him.

Like many naughty schoolboys he is apparently anti-establishment, but he deceptively remains staunchly establishment. Branson calls foul constantly and uses litigious establishment weapons when it suits.

For more than thirty years his winning charm and childish exploits have deflected scrutiny from what his companies really are and how he makes his money. But, like every cheeky schoolboy, the grinning charm hides a dark side.

Achievement

After a few minor business ventures at school, Branson's first step in building his shambling empire was to start a national student newspaper that struggled to take off. He took on many student social causes (such as suicide and drug counselling) and fought a court case to be allowed to continue. During that time he cut his teeth as a budding entrepreneur. Unable to be involved in the detailed editorial side because of dyslexia, he looked after the revenue side of the newspaper — getting advertisers and paying bills — while his partner looked after editorial. At this time he inveigled a casual remark out of John Lennon's manager for a free promotional record. Lennon, caught up in his own problems, initially did not deliver and was issued a writ by Branson, the first indication of the real litigious establishment man behind the anti-establishment grin.

Branson started Virgin records when one of his friends noted that the large record retailers were not providing the right service for the swinging sixties youth-oriented market. Virgin's records were originally distributed by mail order. Later, Virgin set up a series of retail outlets, initially in the UK and then in Europe. The business was built up slowly but was always undercapitalised. Branson paid everyone, including himself (he claims), the same amount of money.

Along the way Branson got into a scrape with the law over sales taxes. He discovered, quite by 'accident', that if he took records out of the country and then brought them back in without declaring them to customs, he could avoid paying sales tax. He became very blatant in this activity — it was so common that the customs department mounted a large scale sting operation against him. Even so, he managed to wheedle his way out of a criminal conviction using considerable charm, some tears, and pressure from his establishment parents to convince the authorities that criminal charges shouldn't be laid.

The fledgling Virgin established a series of precedents that Branson used for much of his rise to wealth. First is that the business ideas came from others. Second, he claimed pay equality with his workers. Third, he claimed to represent the little person against big business, a kind of Robin Hood, while the benefits flowed to Branson. Fourth, schoolboy stunts and charm can keep him in the newspapers and friendly journalists can contribute not only spin but what could add up to billions of dollars in unpaid advertising. Fifth, otherwise hard-headed businesspeople are convinced by the constant spin in the media and come to him with deals that ultimately benefit Branson and reportedly all too often end in financial disaster for the other person. Sixth, if grinning charm fails, you can always intimidate people with prospective court action and win sympathy in court with tears. Seventh, keep company structures invisible and the contracts ambiguous, all the better for creative negotiations later with the possibility of moving cash from one company to another in a kind of financial shell game.

Branson moved into recording music in the early 1970s. He had lots of fun but struggled to keep going until Virgin Records signed Mike Oldfield with the huge hit *Tubular Bells*. Virgin survived off those royalties for years. They later signed the Sex Pistols and had some success in the reggae era with Peter Tosh and a string of minor bands. They were often living dangerously close to financial disaster, with no cash reserves. There were constant trips to the bank to extend loans.

Branson continued to diversify, into books with Virgin Books and films with Virgin Vision, which was sold as a share swap, and then lost the proceeds when the buying company failed.

By 1983, Virgin Records was making money and, against the wishes of his partners, Branson decided to have 'fun' and start an airline, Virgin Atlantic. In typical Branson style, Virgin Atlantic was born undercapitalised in 1984. Branson was inexperienced in running an airline but, as usual, was full of bravado. It succeeded by the pure determination of Branson and a lot of hard work by his hatchet men behind the scenes. He is reported to have constantly underpaid his staff but compensated by providing parties and fun, a ploy that gained him considerable goodwill in the early days but eventually palled.

While Virgin Atlantic was still a fledgling airline with only four planes, Branson committed the company to a humanitarian flight to extract British citizens from Iraq during the first Gulf War. His plane was the last commercial airliner into Iraq and Branson was on it. He gained a huge amount of favourable press coverage. He has been accused of using this mission as a publicity stunt.

He battled banks, authorities and—most of all—British Airways (BA), both in the market and through BA's so-called dirty-tricks campaign. Branson eventually sued and won a huge moral if not financial victory. But the battle Branson was fighting was mainly a media battle. The insignificant fledgling airline was represented as the battler against a predatory BA. This couldn't have been further from the truth. While Virgin was a battler, it was so insignificant at that point that BA did not yet care about competition from Virgin.

Branson's continual goading of BA executives in the media meant that eventually they retaliated in a clumsy way, leaving them open to further attack and later humiliation in the courts. Keeping the battle going gained Branson acres of column space and free press, to the benefit of himself and his airline, which enhanced his cheerful Robin Hood image.

In taking on British Airways, Branson was a bit like a tiny terrier yapping around a chained-up great dane. The public would see the great dane either as impotent if it did nothing or vicious if it responded. Journalists love a personalised fight and have a natural tendency to champion the underdog. Branson versus BA was an easy story with clear heroes and villains, and the press covered Branson's antics almost uncritically. The underdog made it particularly easy by being charming and providing the news in easy-to-understand, bite-sized bits. Branson controlled his media by freezing out journalists who gave him what he considered unfavourable press; this included any press that tried to be objective or balanced. Favoured journalists were rewarded with easy access to Branson and press junkets on Virgin planes.

Eventually Virgin Music was sold to keep Virgin Atlantic in the black. Selling Virgin Music allowed Branson to put money into the airline and keep it going rather than have it go bust. Branson, the tone-deaf entrepreneur, didn't care that much about the music, he only loved the money it made him. There was much more for him to love about owning an airline, including being surrounded by pretty, blond, busty flight attendants, the parties it allowed him to throw and the favours it allowed him to bestow.

On winning a court settlement from BA, Branson 'shared' the £500 000 damages with airline staff as part compensation for reduced salaries and cut bonuses. In reality, it was reported that it was not competition from BA that kept the incomes of his workers down, but Branson's own profit drive. At the same time he gave huge parties as a way of convincing people that they belonged to the Branson 'family'. Who questions income when attention is being deflected by parties? Nevertheless, the money from the litigation was known about so it had to be dealt with publicly.

Distraction deflected attention from poor pay and conditions for a while, but it was inevitable that the airline staff would catch on. Virgin employees bumped shoulders with staff from other airlines on a day-to-day basis and learned how poor their conditions really were. Morale in Virgin Atlantic was reported to have gone into decline in proportion to the decline in conditions. Virgin Atlantic stopped being fun to work for and Branson, the boss of parties, was no longer fun to work for. But Virgin Atlantic kept going.

Branson survived three recessions and always felt keenly that he was on the edge—a very thin line between success and failure—and often under threat from bankers wanting to call in their debt. After 1993, he was cashed up enough that he vowed that no bank would ever be able to dictate how he ran his businesses.

When asked to define his business philosophy, he generally refuses. He has been quoted as saying 'I don't believe it can be taught as if it were a recipe' (Branson 2002). He says there are no prescribed instructions for success.

Where Branson's businesses have been successful they have exploited cracks in existing markets. Initially, Virgin Records provided funky stores for the youth market, whereas existing retailers were stuffy and inflexible. There is a similar model for Virgin Atlantic, still youth oriented with an ordinary-people bias and party flavour in the advertising at least.

While Branson appears to start new businesses, the new businesses usually don't actually do anything particularly new. He's out in the world with his cheeky schoolboy grin keeping his particular personality brand with slightly anti-establishment overtones in the faces of the public. In fact, most of his major deals have had a schoolboy anti-establishment element to them.

Always relying on his charisma to pull in new opportunities, he was chagrined to have missed the tech boom. While the tech boom was a revolution that wasn't anti-establishment in the normal sense, Branson missed it, and continues to miss it. His investments in this area have been well behind the leading edge, 'very me' too and, therefore, not generally successful.

With the exception of Virgin Atlantic, Branson uses his personal brand, Virgin, as an umbrella for others to run their businesses under. In other words, he franchises the brand name. People come to Branson with deals. These deals generally involve Branson offering the use of his brand and his marketing expertise for a major stake in the business, with only a minor financial contribution from Branson. Many of these ventures have struggled because Branson's 'just do it and have fun' approach to business is too hit and miss in many markets. Marketing is more than stunts!

Branson's attempts at beating Coca-Cola with Virgin Cola were dismal, as were his clothing, cosmetics and finance ventures. His rail operations limp along, continually beleaguered by performance, labour and market problems. But Branson still makes money because it's usually not his money at stake. He always makes sure he gets his slice whether or not the venture is successful. Branson gains from his partners on the upside and usually doesn't share the downside.

Branson has never been able to deliver bad news himself. Longing to be loved, he has hatchet men who deliver bad news for him.

While there is business going on at Virgin, Branson's wealth is based on trading and self-promotion. Other people run his companies and do what business is required. His antics, self-promotion and compelling public image distract journalists, the public and potential investors from looking too closely at Virgin's accounts and true business performance.

Such perpetual media cleansing makes Branson look like a sure bet, and people don't subject sure bets to too much scrutiny. After all, if the media is saying nearly every day what a success Branson is, then he must be! If a joint venture fails, as too frequently seems to be the case, then the investors may privately complain but they don't challenge Branson publicly because they would be publicly humiliated. Business partners generally did not carry out the most basic of business checks on the way into their deals to understand the risks and benefits. Unlike public companies, private business can and does bury its failures far away from public scrutiny. No wonder Branson hates being part of public companies.

But if it doesn't always work out well for his partners, it certainly works well for Branson. His personal wealth has nearly doubled (from $2.2 billion to $3.8 billion) since 2004.

By now there must be an issue for the Virgin franchisees because the businesses are so dependent on Branson's image. Once he goes there may not be much left to leverage.

Branson is also well known for his headline-grabbing adventuring. He has been involved in a number of high-profile boating and ballooning adventures, any of which could have, and nearly did, claim his life. His autobiography and media coverage paint him as the big adventurer, but his collaborators tell the story somewhat differently. They claim he is only interested in the media attention he can gain. Far from enjoying the adventuring, he takes no interest in piloting his vehicles and is either terrified or bored by the experience.

Development

Richard Branson was born in 1950, the descendant of three generations of lawyers on his father's side, and the firstborn and only son of three children. His grandfather was Sir George Branson, a High Court judge, and his great-grandfather had been a publisher and lawyer in India. Unfortunately Branson's father had a mediocre career and this irked Branson's mother.

His mother is reported to have been a social-climbing small-time entrepreneur from a previously wealthy trading family. Having fallen from grace, she was desperate to return the family to the glory it enjoyed in past generations and constantly extolled her son to succeed from an early age, using his father's apparent failure as a goad.

To distract everyone from what she believed was her family's undeservedly low social situation, Branson's mother constantly bragged to families in her social orbit that the Bransons were flourishing. She would dress up and make herself an attraction at social events, instilling in her son the powers of self-promotion, the need for vigorous good times and a constant whirlwind of stunts to distract others from what is really going on. This is Branson's self-promotion model writ small!

Branson grew up in what appeared to be an apparently loving, if somewhat unconventional, family. Branson says his mother was always generating work for them, and was always thinking of different ways to make money in her attempts to elevate the family's status. Unlike the experiences of most other self-made billionaires, the core of his formative approval was not contradicted when he was embarking on his own life at the end of school. Not only did his mother believe in what he was doing, she appears to have been almost hysterically supportive.

Branson tells of a time when he was 'lovingly' abandoned at the age of four, as a bizarre lesson in independence and self-reliance. His mother stopped the car a few miles from home and made the young boy find his own way home. He was also forced to ride his bike to relatives fifty miles away before he turned twelve.

His parents were liberal and, aside from a status-hungry mother, morally non-prescriptive. The children talked openly with their parents and would discuss their father's work. Most importantly, young Richard came to understand the game playing that goes with the law and was later never frightened to take people to court. For Branson, the lawyer's son, it was just part of the air he breathed.

Branson's parents allowed him plenty of room to invent himself. Both parents encouraged Branson to carry out small businesses. Along the way he started businesses raising birds and growing Christmas trees.

Curiously enough Branson's parents sent him to boarding school when he was only eight — probably more because it was tradition rather than a considered decision. In England a good school is always the first step to a place in the establishment, and Branson's mother desperately wanted that for her son.

But Branson was never going to become a part of the establishment by conventional means, as he was burdened by two related disabilities. The first was dyslexia, and the second was a trial and error approach to learning. He can't easily read a body of written text or even detailed business analyses, which meant he developed a highly intuitive way of making business decisions. Branson relies on gut instinct rather than an analysis of numbers. In addition, he feels numbers can be manipulated to prove anything. Almost certainly, dyslexia makes written analysis so painful that he avoids it if he can.

Branson, like other people with learning difficulties, could not produce good results at school. He could solve real-life problems with numbers, but had difficulty with abstract mathematical problems in the classroom, as well as any other subject requiring reading and writing. Consequently, Branson had limited success at school and claims he suffered two expulsions, finally settling at Stowe, a big public school. He graduated with six bare passes and neither the scores nor the will to go to university.

At the age of eight Branson still couldn't read, and he was also short-sighted. People generally hadn't heard of dyslexia then and it was a while before anybody thought to check his eyesight, so his struggles meant he was perceived as lazy, stupid or both. He says that as a result he was beaten once or twice a week.

Branson claims he was very good at sport in his early school years. With his poor academic performance, sport was his only chance to gain approval. He became the captain of various sporting teams, which helped him enjoy some popularity and tolerance from his teachers.

He also claims that at ten, disaster struck while playing rugby — he permanently injured his knee. Without the aura of sporting success, he became an outcast and suffered much humiliation and punishment for failing to learn. After the age of ten, it is certain that Branson was an undistinguished outsider with few friends and poor support from teachers.

While he may have had problems at school and with fellow students, he claims he had no such problems with girls. He says that he was expelled from one school for sleeping with the headmaster's daughter. He gained parental approval for sleeping with the girl, but not for the expulsion. But there is no corroborating evidence for this, so it may just be another embellished adventure for public consumption. Branson's embroidered stories are always entertaining, if not always accurate. They always portray Branson as the flawed hero irrespective of the facts.

By the time he left school, Branson was well and truly an outsider. He had survived in a hostile schooling environment with a cheeky grin on his face. Because of his reading problems he knew that conventional professions weren't going to be for him. All his rewards had come from entrepreneurial activity. He had the idiosyncratic view of the world that comes from being born an outsider and then being forced to live as an outsider. He viewed the world differently from just about everyone else. And that, along with a robust self-promoting, pranking, grinning personality and love of making money, set the scene for his success.

While at school he set up small businesses with limited financial success. The businesses provided modest but good training opportunities. He was always given strong approval by his parents, particularly his mother. While he was not very good at maths, he says he really loved doing business plans. More likely this was conceptual planning rather than a true business plan. He set up a small bird breeding operation and a Christmas tree plantation, neither of which were successful. Towards the end of high school he decided to set up a school magazine. This seemed a little small to him, so he and his schoolboy partner decided to turn it into a national magazine. They attempted to sell advertising to major companies before the magazine even existed, a difficult proposition, especially for two fifteen year olds. Branson's school work suffered even more.

It seems a curious choice that a dyslexic school failure would choose to start a school magazine. But right from the beginning he worked to his strength — spruiking deals and grabbing headlines. He would spend his time on the phone chasing advertising, articles and interviews. His partner knew what they should put in the magazine and why; Branson was the one who would try to make the business of publication happen. They were a good team. Branson says he always tries to find business partners who complement his skills.

That was the start of his business and the model for how he runs businesses. He is the 'boss' but he surrounds himself with 'friends' who can compensate for his weaknesses. Arguably, partnering with friends with little real business experience slowed him down for some time, but then, becoming a businessman wasn't really a stated objective. He is a man who does deals. So long as some of the money can be captured on the way through, it usually doesn't matter if the business is successful or not. Being a deal junkie underpins his wealth!

In a typical bit of deflection, Branson says that he doesn't start businesses purely to make money: 'If that is the sole motive then I believe you are better off not doing it. A business has to be involving; it has to be fun, and it has to exercise your creative instincts' (Branson 2002). Fun maybe, but he must do deals. He admits to little market analysis. While he claims that his criteria is to have fun, and his outward behaviour would suggest this is so, mostly he is concerned with making money by limiting his losses and maximising his gains. He generally leaves it to others to take the real risks.

When the idea of starting a new airline came up, Virgin Records, then the core business, had gone from near disaster two years previously to strong profit. More cautious businesspeople would have wanted to consolidate their financial position, but not Branson. Branson addressed his dismayed and vehemently opposed business partners by saying that the risk was small and it would be fun. 'Fun' is one of his oft-stated reasons for starting a business.

Branson is compulsively outgoing and apparently fun loving. Unlike most billionaires, he is seen in the company of lots of glamorous women. Hardly a week goes by that Branson hasn't pushed some scantily clad model into the water. His legendary parties at Virgin Atlantic put him in the company of many attractive female employees. In the days of Virgin Records at its big country recording studio, while those around him were indulging in sex, drugs and rock'n'roll, tone-deaf Branson was much more the business and sex man, and much more the business than the sex.

Branson's public justification for business is that he likes to take on the big boys. He likes to enter markets where there are large, established corporations that are leaving gaps in the market. This leaves room for him. In the 1990s he launched Virgin Cola against Coca-Cola and Pepsi. Later it was life insurance, credit cards and cell phones. These business ventures have either reportedly failed or have had mediocre success at best. Branson himself and the Virgin group, however, did not fail because his business partners took most of downside risk while Branson reportedly benefited by 'legitimately' moving money for various other purposes.

He gives the appearance of being very honest and ethical. His public image is that of a man who fights for the battlers. For example, Virgin Records had been made a public company and the share price suffered in the stock market crash of 1988. Branson decided to buy the company back at the original buy-in price, rather than the stock market price of around half that amount. On the face of it, it was a very generous gesture to the original shareholders. But it was a very pragmatic move to protect his image. Tom Bower reports that in addition, what the public didn't know was that Branson was working on a deal to sell Virgin Records, a deal he closed after the share buyback. A deal that gave him a handsome profit, a profit he didn't have to declare publicly or share with previous shareholders.

His most audacious move, however, was beginning an airline against a heavily protective and protected national airline. Against the odds and claiming to be the champion of free enterprise, he charmed, browbeat, threatened and otherwise clawed Virgin Atlantic into existence. Posing as the champion of free enterprise, he inveigled politicians to give him access to air routes and numerous advantages. Today, Virgin Atlantic is one of Branson's few major business successes.

Owning a fledgling airline and using the media to bash British Airways led to his other large altruistic gesture—to fly the stranded British citizens out of Baghdad. But there were intended business spin-offs. Virgin had usurped British Airways and become a default national symbol. Branson had helped people in need, and made Virgin look like a major player. There were risks and there were benefits to others, but most of all there was a media coup to Branson in his dogged pursuit of British Airway's market share.

Interpretation

Branson was born with dyslexia. He was always going to struggle with formal learning, and once alone at boarding school he had very big problems.

His mother was obviously loving, but unconventional. She was obsessive about improving what she saw as being her undeserved low social status. She did this through minor entrepreneurial ventures and frantic social climbing. She set about disguising the Branson family's lack of standing with a barrage of disinformation.

Given young Branson's incapacity for conventional schooling, he was left with few choices. However, small-time business was something he could do. Small-time business isn't complicated and, like most start-up businesses, young Branson set about it in a trial-and-error fashion—some businesses worked and some didn't. This is still very much his way of doing things. As a minimum, his parents were probably relieved that he found something he could do that he found fun and that strongly reinforced what was probably an inherited trait for trading. But given his mother's social climbing and her need to make money, it is almost certain that the love she gave Branson was both intrusive and contingent on his business performance.

His mother made some very strange decisions in relation to young Branson. She sent the infant Branson off on character-building treks across the countryside. If this is true and not another of Branson's embellishments, then the kindest thing that can be said of her was that she lacked judgement. More seriously, her poor judgement continued when she sent her small, vulnerable, dyslexic eight year old to a series of what were virtually educational concentration camps. These were 'camps' in which her young son could never succeed and in which his constant failures were going to be severely punished. He could only escape humiliation and pain by expulsion and, if his reports are correct, this is what he did.

What is even more curious is that upon his being expelled from one boarding school his mother would pack him off to another. She must have been totally wedded to the notion that a good school is the cornerstone of social acceptance in England and a goal to be pursued irrespective of the damage it does.

In the early days there was a kind of natural progression in his businesses from newspaper to records. Both were youth oriented and anti-establishment and both were the idea of his partner. Then along came Branson's first original business idea—starting an airline from scratch.

Bear in mind the old joke, 'Question: How do you become a millionaire? Answer: You start as a billionaire and begin an airline'. It was a very peculiar move to begin such a high-risk venture when the base business, music, had only just become successful. Branson must have had a deep-seated reason—maybe he so loved his mother that he felt compelled to buy his ex-flight attendant mother an airline.

There is something slightly Oedipus-like about his choosing to found an airline. His mother provided young Branson with love that was contingent on financial success and achieving social standing. Consequently, Branson had a bigger incentive to own an airline than most other businesspeople. Not only was there ego and money at stake, but also owning a successful airline provided the extra benefit of access to flight attendant admiration. Like his mother's admiration, flight attendant admiration was contingent on business success, and the bigger the airline the more attendants it employed and the more approval he had access to. No wonder Branson was driven to make a success of the airline!

In addition, his mother laid several other foundations of Branson's formative business personality—aggressive partying and constant diversions to shift attention from the real circumstances.

He attributes much of what he became to the entrepreneurship he inherited from his mother's trading ancestors. While that is certain to be a strong element of his character, it considerably sells short his inheritance from his lawyer father—an inheritance he would use to stare down the bastions of establishment business in Britain by playing games of legal chicken with them.

There are three generations of lawyers on Branson's father's side. Discussions around the table were liberal, full and frank. A number of those discussions were about legal cases, so obviously Branson understood at an early age how the law works and how much of it is a game of tactics and brinkmanship. He also would have come to understand how deals were done and undone.

Undoubtedly, Branson suffered considerable adversity due to dyslexia and the strange decision of his parents to send a boy with learning difficulties away from the emotional support of home and into the hostile environment of boarding schools. Once sporting injuries made it impossible for Branson to gain approval by being good at sport, he claims he was treated appallingly. This is entirely consistent with what happened to other billionaires, so it is credible. It is incredible that he managed to survive boarding school at all without having severe psychological problems.

Through these dark times there were three things that gained him approval—his family loved him and rewarded him for carrying out small entrepreneurial activities; his big cheeky grin; and the ability to spin a tale, which undoubtedly deflected some punishment.

Given most of his love and happiness had been achieved through entrepreneurial activity and that his career opportunities were always going to be limited in the mainstream economy due to his lack of reading ability and school achievement, he was faced with limited choices. Branson realised he could only succeed in business without formal qualifications if he was his own boss.

It was probably at school that Branson developed his characteristic grin. He found that happy, charming, good-looking people can get away with more for less punishment than the dour, stubborn and ugly. Pranks are personally more rewarding than belligerence, gratuitous violence or vandalism, and can get applause from unpredictable places. A big cheeky grin and a whole lot of charisma can distract authorities from the scent. Even boarding school teachers have been known to be charmed by humour, hence the long British tradition of the brilliant but unstable comedians emanating from its boarding schools. Even if the teachers aren't amused, some of the pupils may be, so it was possible to elevate himself off the bottom of the pecking order.

A key during that time was a deep dislike and distrust of authority and the ability to keep going in the face of unreasonable punishment. He learned at school that the establishment was wrong and that it punished severely if you fell outside its rules and were caught. Branson used these lessons (along with his obviously natural abilities as negotiator, advocate and deflector) to beat the British establishment at its own games. Paradoxically, because of his mother's influence, he also longed to be part of the establishment and worked hard to become Sir Richard Branson. Branson eventually achieved knighthood in 2000. His knighthood was awarded for services to entrepreneurship, providing yet another diversion from the near bankruptcy of the Virgin businesses.

Like the naughty schoolboy that he remains, Branson hates scrutiny. He has a confusing array of companies and will only venture into publicly owned companies if he is desperate.

Trading obviously is a part of his family background, particularly on his mother's side, but also features strongly on his father's side. Growing up with a solicitor father would have given Branson a keen sense of how negotiable the world was, how far the system could be gamed and how to stare down adversaries. Parental approval would have been extra sweet, and incredibly formative, for a boy who was always having difficulty at school.

While he did not thrive at school, he did learn that he was on his own. He also learned that there was no place in the establishment for him. Despite being Sir Branson, he stands outside the establishment in the company of rock stars, actors and other semi-establishment figures. Branson started as an outsider and remains an outsider. He just had to learn to adapt or face going under. He adapted and converted his subversion and grin into money.

References:

Bower, T 2000, *Branson*, Fourth Estate, London.

Branson, R 2002, *Losing My Virginity*, Random House, Australia.

Chapter 15

George Lucas

Forbes information 2007
Rank: 243
Citizenship: United States
Wealth: US$3.6 billion
Industry: media/entertainment

George Lucas is the creator and owner of some of the biggest film franchises produced in the latter half of the twentieth century. He is most famous for his work on the *Star Wars* and *Indiana Jones* films. Lucas has worked mainly as a producer and a screenwriter. He is least at ease as a director as he finds dealing with on-set artistic types most uncomfortable. He gives the directing role to others as often as he can.

Lucas has made a fortune by reinventing his childhood escapist fantasies and putting them into film, and adding to his fortune by playing to his first calling—as a toy maker. This toy maker has almost single-handedly changed the landscape of movie franchising.

Achievement

Lucas desperately wanted to get out of small-town California and escape having to take over his father's office supply business. His choices of university were limited because of his poor school grades. He was especially poor at English, probably because he had learning difficulties.

Following his near failure at high school, Lucas gained admission to the University of Southern California (USC) film school at a time when studying film was unfashionable. The school was underfunded and housed in crumby temporary buildings at the back of the university. At that time, the film school was a tiny, unfashionable, isolated faculty, which engendered an us-against-them mentality. Adversity bound the students together and their feelings of unjustified alienation helped to create a film revolution.

Film school fitted Lucas's technical talents. He had already made stop-motion films at home and was very technically competent, not only behind the camera but also because he was extremely good with his hands, having made toys, props and worked on cars.

He was able to keep the shoddy equipment running where others failed. Lucas's mechanical skills were in demand, and often he was the only one that could fix temperamental equipment. Lucas honed both his technical and filmmaking skills and won student awards. He helped others and stayed focused on developing his craft. His commitment at film school was incredible. He was utterly focused. There were no parties, no sex, just work.

By the end of film school Lucas was thinking bigger than and differently from his peers, or anyone else in the film industry for that matter. His awkwardness with people led to a disinclination to use actors, and his talent with technology meant he made different films compared with other students. Lucas's films generally had higher production values. Most of the other students had artistic or political motivations, or they simply wanted get a girl naked in front of the camera and into bed later. Lucas, the outsider, was unencumbered with any such film ambitions. He was not artistic in any conventional filmmaking sense; he was, essentially, a creative technician.

> By the end of film school Lucas was thinking bigger than and differently from his peers, or anyone else in the film industry for that matter.

Lucas wanted to make films about technical subjects because that was what he knew and loved. Also, he was most comfortable with technical people, people who got the job done without any need to express their creativity. Since he was very familiar with planes, cars and cameras he was comfortable using all in his movies. If he was making a picture about cars, he would hire a plane to do aerial shots and bolt the camera onto the car, calling in favours from racing car drivers and pilots alike. It was quite a step up from student movie making of the day.

On graduating, he went on to tutor at USC. His students were mainly navy cameramen doing refresher courses. Ever the opportunist, he used his position as tutor of navy personnel to direct and produce a number of short films. Because Lucas had a more technical than artistic or political orientation, the navy personnel liked and respected him. They worked with him and that gave him a team of willing and compliant workers as well as film stock. Lucas had many more resources at his command than others in his position. He learnt how to organise large technical teams, although it is notable that he has never been comfortable managing creative people, especially actors.

It is interesting that he was successful at managing sailors several years his senior, but he has always had difficulties managing film crews and actors, professing that he hated dealing with their volatility. The sailors had few artistic aspirations, they just got on with the job, whereas the same could rarely be said of many people in the film industry.

His most notable student film of the time was *THX 1138 4EB*, a short science fiction movie. This gained him notice, and through dogged persistence, gained him a scholarship to Warner Bros. film studio. During that time he gained some minor filmmaking jobs, such as filming the credits for the movie *Grand Prix*, and worked with noted director Francis Ford Coppola, who became a notable mentor to him.

Coppola organised finance for *THX 1138 4EB* to be remade as a feature-length film with the modified title, *THX 1138*. During the making of this film Lucas honed his filmmaking, particularly his skills producing special effects. Lucas introduced his toy-making skills to his craft. Lucas says his strength is in visuals, and that he might have been a toy maker if he wasn't a filmmaker. The bigger budget *THX 1138* had some minor success on the art house circuit, received some acclaim at the Cannes Film Festival and gained sufficient critical praise to warrant a two-page article in *Newsweek*.

In keeping with Lucas's orientation, *THX 1138* had great technical merit but failed to grab people emotionally. He was advised to produce something warm as *THX 1138* was seen as cold and humourless.

Taking the advice to heart, Lucas's next film was *American Graffiti*, which was essentially a romanticised look at Lucas's high school days. It was made on a low budget, including director's fees, but with 20 per cent of profits returning to Lucas. Filming was fraught for Lucas. He had so much trouble with actors and technicians that the rumours put out by the cast and crew pointed to the movie being a flop.

American Graffiti was released on 1 August 1973. Lucas, afraid of a bad reception, went on a holiday in Hawaii to escape any critical backlash. He needn't have feared. It was a smash hit! By being different to the prevailing styles of the time and breaking out of the dark political mould engendered by resistance to the Vietnam War, Lucas had mined a nostalgic vein the movie-going public was yearning for. Being the outsider and out of step paid big dividends for Lucas.

By the 1990s, *American Graffiti* had grossed more than $200 million, which is claimed to be one of the largest returns on an investment for a film ever. Suffice to say that the studios were very happy with the profits they made and were hungry for Lucas to do a reprise act.

With *American Graffiti* a hit, Lucas took himself off into isolation and came up with the idea for *Star Wars*. He always struggled with English, which made the writing process a torturous one. The story owes much of its flavour to science fiction serials and comics from the time Lucas was growing up. Unlike the science fiction films of the 1970s, *Star Wars* was optimistic and fun, and great emphasis was placed on action and special effects. Science was good again and it could save the world, which would have appealed to all those who loved sci-fi. Like *American Graffiti*, it had no political or allegorical aspirations. *Star Wars* was only ever intended as good, nostalgic entertainment.

There is nothing like a box office success to loosen a movie studio's purse strings. Even so, sci-fi movies were out of favour with studios and filmmakers. They were still concentrating on heavy, meaningful, political or relationship movies. Audiences couldn't even escape meaningfulness in comedies.

In his negotiations to get *Star Wars* made, Lucas began to stand apart from his fellow directors. By taking on more of the production and box office risk himself, Lucas accepted a lower than usual return for directing, writing and producing, but negotiated a bigger proportion of the profit (40 per cent of profit plus low fees) in return for 60 per cent of the merchandising rights, growing to 100 per cent in two years.

This was visionary on Lucas's part. Through this film, Lucas is credited with creating the modern film-merchandising business, by finding a massive demand from children for movie action figures. By 1981, *Star Wars* merchandising was worth more than $1 billion, with Lucasfilms gaining a substantial share. Lucas says that he is really a toy maker, and that the film was designed around toys.

Lucas had huge difficulties in making *Star Wars*, not least because he disliked interacting with the artistic types he found in the film industry and they with him. Unlike the people he preferred working with, technical and service people (transactional people who got the job done), artistic people have a point of view that is not always able to be reconciled with getting the job done. Or maybe artistic people just speak a different language that technical people can't decode.

In any event Lucas had particular troubles with the special effects teams in California and on the sound stages in England. These people were unable to see or visualise the filmed effects, being exposed only to what appeared to be shoddy models and fragments of banal dialogue. Lucas was breaking new ground and naturally these people had no experience of Lucas's outputs to base their opinions on. Lucas, constantly under attack from the crew, became more withdrawn and less inclined to tell people what was going on. Naturally this exacerbated his communication problems.

The general view among people on the team was that *Star Wars* was going to be a failure. This view was held by most involved right up to release time, and since bad news travels, its poor reputation had become legendary around Hollywood. The film's reputation was so bad that on final release few cinemas would take it.

As had happened with *American Graffiti*, Lucas was so lacking in confidence he again fled to Hawaii to avoid the embarrassment of failure. Despite the general gloom surrounding the making of Star Wars, it was a wild success. *Star Wars*, like *American Graffiti*, was a circuit breaker of the cinematic 'worthy' gloom cycle of the early 1970s.

Star Wars is essentially a return to the innocent and fun movie serials Lucas enjoyed when he was growing up in a small town in the US. He had lived on a diet of comics, adventure serials and science fiction. The small numbers of cinemas showing *Star Wars* were swamped on the first weekend and so the run was extended. The film was made available in more cinemas and its success spread like wildfire around the globe.

Lucas made a fortune. He was not entirely unmoved by the politics of the day nor the idealism of youth. He was feeling slightly socialist for the last time in his life and ultimately gave away 25 per cent of his share of the profits from *Star Wars* to actors, producers and other contributors.

But the experience of directing *Star Wars* had taken its toll on the socially awkward Lucas. He decided never to direct movies again. His solution was to become a producer and hire directors. The next two films in the *Star Wars* series were directed by others, and of his next hugely successful franchise, *Indiana Jones*, all three of the films were directed by Steven Spielberg. Lucas would only direct four feature films in almost thirty years.

Lucas had money and lots of it following the initial success of *Star Wars*. He bought a farm outside of San Franciso and proposed, somewhat grandly, that it become the filmmaking centre of the US, moving the emphasis away from Hollywood. He may have thought this would work, but its only effect was to move Lucas away from people. As time went on and his fame grew, he became more like a Howard Hughes figure, isolating himself and worrying about the negative effect human contact was having on him. On the farm he could control who got in and where they got to. Over the years the security and video surveillance grew until Lucas eventually needed a major control room to run it all.

> Over the years the security and video surveillance grew until Lucas eventually needed a major control room to run it all.

He appointed people to manage his growing empire, but would interfere gratuitously and then not be available when required. With increasing amounts of money going into the farm and seemingly arbitrary investment decisions, Lucas's income did not produce a burgeoning investment portfolio. In 1986, *The Wall Street Journal* depicted Lucas as 'an unbusinesslike businessman, remote from the reality of profit and loss' (Baxter 2000). But why should he care? He never made movies to be a businessman. He had also insulated himself from criticism since his biggest breakthrough successes had attracted huge criticism from industry insiders. His empire was based on income from films and merchandise rights, not investment. His position on the *Forbes* world's billionaires list remained static for years.

As he has grown older, his home on the farm, Skywalker Ranch, has become more like a fortress and Lucas has become increasingly isolated and imperial. It is reported that at one of his parties for friends in the industry, paths were roped off for Lucas to walk down. There was no informality; it was like an appearance of a guru or royalty among loyal but distant subjects. There was no touching, not even handshakes.

Lucas, Steven Spielberg and Oprah Winfrey are unlike the other billionaires in this book. While they make highly successful deals around their work, they are not essentially dealers. They personally make things and are intimately involved in the production process. They are highly successful doers in an industry that pays huge dividends for success.

Development

George Lucas was born in 1944 in Modesto, California. He did all his growing up in this small inland Californian town.

He was the first son and third child of four. His mother was the daughter of a notable local businessman and Lucas's father was a successful small businessman, owning and running a local stationery store. The Lucas family were big fish in a small pond. Business was all around as the boy grew up. Lucas was familiar with being able to use money to mobilise resources, something many of his filmmaking peers at USC did not have.

Lucas's father was a very religious Calvanist, with deep beliefs in God and hard work. He was a pillar of the community. Lucas's father was stern and abided by the Calvinist beliefs of hard work, frugality and not spoiling children with too much love. Calvinists can be stern and inflexible and Lucas's father was no exception to this rule. Lucas was regularly humiliated by his father, particularly by the annual lice-preventing head shavings he subjected Lucas to—a haircut guaranteed to accentuate Lucas's ears, which stuck out.

His father had typical small town, small businessman ambitions for Lucas. He wanted young Lucas to settle down in the home town, get married, raise a family and take over the family business.

Lucas's mother became ill very soon after his birth. His very loving mother was in and out of hospital at unpredictable intervals and the children were left to the care of their severe father and housekeeper. During the unpredictable and lengthy absences of their mother, Lucas and his sisters were brought up by a stern housekeeper with similar Calvanist ideals as Lucas Senior.

The way Lucas was treated changed radically between the times his mother was away and when she was home. His mother was doting and loving while his father and the housekeeper were stern and unloving. Lucas would have suffered a double wrench when his mother went to hospital—separation anxiety at the loss of his mother, loss of her love and uncertainty about her ever returning on the one hand and the austere treatment by his father and the housekeeper on the other. Lucas became a very anxious child.

Lucas's maternal grandfather provided an emotional bright spot in Lucas's early anxiety-ridden life. His grandfather came around to the house every Saturday and doted on Lucas. In addition, he was an amateur filmmaker, compulsively recording his grandkids with his 16mm movie camera. No wonder Lucas was drawn to movie making—the person who was one of his most constant sources of emotional warmth made movies.

Lucas experienced a deep period of existential angst that started at the age of six when he began questioning the existence of God and the nature of reality. He became a seeker trying to understand what was happening to him. Since his loving mother was repeatedly snatched away and replaced with advocates of a stern religion, Lucas could not believe in a benevolent God. More than that, he couldn't accept the world as given—all was not as it seemed. Such irreconcilable forces in his world turned him into a seeker and any technical seeker will almost inevitably be led to develop an interest in science fiction. His sense of powerlessness also led to needing stories with big adventure themes and heroes taking on the forces of darkness.

Lucas was not very literate, but he devoured comic books and TV. These were strong influences on Lucas's most successful movies—the *Star Wars* and *Indiana Jones* series.

Despite Lucas's mediocrity at school, this reflection at such a young age indicates high intelligence. To have such profound intellectual doubts about the world at such a young age as opposed to straight anxiety, or violent and disruptive behaviour, denotes a good level of control, abstract thinking and disassociation from mainstream thought—he was a thoughtful outsider. Like his later heroes in *Star Wars*, he avoided going over to the 'dark side'.

Lucas struggled at school. He was a bare C and D pass student. He was regularly late handing in assignments, so he either procrastinated or has an undiagnosed learning difficulty; probably both. Certainly he was bored, and he has said that the biggest problem he had at school was that he didn't want to learn what was being taught. Like Branson, he made the typical justification of a person who failed at school work, making the claim that it isn't needed. Perhaps they are right; both found future careers that worked around school achievement problems and that suited them very well.

At school Lucas was constantly helped by his sister, who reportedly rose at 5 am to help correct his English. Lucas undoubtedly suffered humiliation at school due to his disabilities in written work, but this seems not to have been a great concern to him, probably because he did not change schools so remained with his peer group. He did not have to suffer the added indignity of being a 'dummy' trying to break into a new peer group. Due to being short (five feet six inches) and having no interest in sport, Lucas had his place low in the social pecking order; he knew where it was and so did everyone else.

Even though Lucas did not do well at formal studies, he had an aptitude for art. Despite the discouragement from his father and teachers who wanted him to be serious, Lucas did as much art as he could. He couldn't get serious on their terms since he was always going to fail. As is typical of bright people with disabilities, he worked around the problem. He developed other, compensating, skills, in this case, talents associated with art. He found he had a talent for construction and toy making. He made dolls' houses, chess sets, toy cars to push around and toy forts. He would build elaborate forts with toy soldiers and vehicles, and had a model train running through his garden.

Lucas turned a neighbour's garage into a haunted house, and he and a friend charged people admission. It was very popular. He also made his first ever special effects film, a stop-motion film of plates stacking themselves up and then unstacking again. It was a heady combination of approval from his friends for creativity, toy making, filming, independent enterprise and approval from his father for making money.

In 1955, he and a friend also started a newspaper but it folded soon after for lack of news.

Television came to Modesto, and Lucas claims that his greatest influence was this rather than movies. He sat for hours, firstly at a neighbour's house, and then his own, watching serials such as *Flash Gordon Conquers the Universe*. He would never forget this experience.

He had a close friend whose father gave Lucas unsold comic books—Lucas ended up with a huge collection and was the envy of the other boys.

The film *American Graffiti* is a romanticised version of Lucas's growing up. Like the main character in the film, Lucas was a peripheral player, always around but never at the centre of things, never quite belonging. He would stave off humiliation by moving on before being rejected or hurt. His sister reports that he was often bullied by bigger peers. Lucas wanted to be in the bad boys' club, but never quite made it. He never managed to have a girlfriend either.

At fifteen, Lucas's family moved out of town to the countryside. Lucas was isolated from his peers, a virtual prisoner until he could drive. He became obsessed with owning a car and racing. He hung around with some of the local car gangs but he was never quite accepted. His father bought him a little Fiat, which embarrassed Lucas, so he and a friend hotted it up and together they went racing. Lucas developed confidence in his technical prowess and won the odd race. He also met race drivers who were to be of use in his student films. One fateful day in 1962, Lucas made a turn into his drive when he was hit by a car attempting to pass. Lucas was lucky to survive. He spent most of that summer in bed. This was his last year of school and it is believed that he probably only graduated from high school because of sympathy gained from being in hospital for most of his final year.

Lucas graduated from Modesto Junior College and achieved a modest C average—enough to get him into college. He wanted both to leave home and to stay close to home. Lucas was inspired by some new trends in filming brought on by improving technology—filming that was about things not people. His interest in cars shifted from driving to filming. At a loss about what to do, he enrolled at USC as a film major.

Interpretation

Lucas was a nervous child. Clearly the random and extended absences of his sick, loving mother meant he suffered separation anxiety that was never compensated for by his father and housekeeper. Lucas was often depressed and unhappy. He was often frightened of monsters under the bed. Also, he suffered the constant trauma of separation, perhaps more so than what a single, final separation would have caused.

Lucas's mother was admitted to hospital without warning or explanation and Lucas would just have to deal with it. Good Calvinists believe in being stern and uncommunicative with everyone, children particularly. It was probably represented as God's will. Since Lucas could not predict when it would happen or if she would return, he must have gone through a whole series of unresolved grief and anxiety periods. It is not surprising he was anxious through most of his growing up.

School was a torment. He couldn't do what was required of him, he was short and funny looking, something his father seemed determined to exacerbate, and he didn't play much sport. He was bright, but was considered dumb. The only positive was that he was good with his hands. He could draw, make toys and fix things. He was technical more than artistic but had come to art technique simply because he couldn't flourish in the course work that would be laid out in physics, chemistry and maths. No doubt he would have been smart enough had he been able to read properly, but this path was denied. By the time he left school he was still a comic book reader, not a novel reader.

As *American Graffiti* indicates, growing up in Lucas's hometown wasn't all bad. There appeared to be genuine feelings of warmth—the sort of feelings outsiders would have if they grew up in and were tolerated by a community. Not quite in but not quite out either, generally a tolerated peripheral character.

Craft-based activities gave Lucas obvious pleasure, with the added bonus of praise from his sisters and friends. But he didn't do it for their praise alone. Father was an extremely tough nut to crack. Praise was not a natural part of his Calvinist soul and would only be given to things that fitted his protestant work ethic. Young Lucas's activities would be seen as frivolous unless they made money or led to an obvious mainstream career. So Lucas made money from it and won grudging praise, but only for the business side of the enterprise. But this approval would be all the sweeter because it was so rare and would have given Lucas an almost addictive need to repeat it. Suddenly money making was intimately connected with toys and filmmaking—Lucas was primed!

Like Spielberg, Lucas set his movies according to his experiences. In casting *Star Wars*, there is the stern father, the loving but distant mother, and the decent but slightly lost boy who had things to worry about other than women.

But maybe there was more to it than that. Lucas didn't appear to be interested in women. There is no record of him having a high school sweetheart. He married once, to a beautiful film editor, Marcia, when just out of film school. But he was uncomfortable around women. He and his wife did not usually eat together.

> Like Spielberg, Lucas set his movies according to his experiences.

Lucas actively eschewed the casting couch. Despite his powerful position in movies, he tended to be indifferent to the charms of potential leading ladies. While this was good news for his wife, Lucas's increasing need for isolation and lack of interest in enjoying his wealth finally worked against their marriage. They divorced in 1982. Lucas has had few relationships since and he has remained single.

Lucas is ambivalent about the women in his childhood. His first and most important love, his mother, couldn't be relied on—she would disappear at random intervals. His sisters were helpers and his housekeeper was someone to stay away from.

His mother's absences were medically based. Fear of infection would have been rife. This probably explains why Lucas has isolated himself on his farm for so long and shuns physical contact. This could also explain why he has never used the casting couch. There are definite parallels here with the older Howard Hughes, who also isolated himself and feared infection. Lucas doesn't have long-term relationships with women, probably because his experience with his mother means he doesn't trust any women that he loves to stay around.

He is not only uncomfortable with women, he is uncomfortable with most people, particularly the artsy folks in movie making. Lucas says he doesn't enjoy directing because he hates dealing with volatile people.

Lucas is a technical person. Generally, technical people don't muck around with feelings and interpretation, they just get the job done. In movie making, Lucas was most comfortable with the navy cameramen and they with him. These men were transactional, used to just getting on with the job and doing what was expected. Certainly they were used to taking orders, but in their own work in the navy they also had a great deal of autonomy. They weren't grunts. They worked under the conditions as they found them. This is not the usual way for artists or even the artistic technicians on film sets. Everybody wants a say, everybody knows best and everybody wants credits. Filming is the only industry in the world in which the workers get their names boringly paraded in front of the public. Imagine if car makers did that.

Lucas, also, was used to dealing with racing drivers. Again, these were transactional people who just went about their business. No wonder Lucas, the technical outsider, had trouble with the artists. Lucas just wanted to get the job done, they wanted their say. He wanted to transact, they wanted to be loved!

Their constant carping on set made Lucas lose his confidence to such an extent that he sought refuge in Hawaii for the release of both *American Graffiti* and *Star Wars*. Fortunately he was so used to going it alone that the crew's complaints didn't make him lose his nerve during the making of both these movies. He toughed it out, but the wear and tear on his emotions made him determined to avoid directing.

Lucas is an outsider, someone close to the centre of things but not quite there. Given his obvious difficulty with reading and other school subjects, he compensated by developing considerable technical skills, which he honed while at film school. This gave him the edge over the artsy film students at the time. While the other students eschewed technical expertise to produce movies based on the European existentialist film movement, Lucas was counter trend, working to produce films of the highest technical quality about technical subjects. He also had the advantage of being a hard worker and understanding business, something he gained from his Methodist father's background. He knew how to mobilise resources and strike a deal.

The critical acclaim and box office failure of *THX 1138* showed Lucas that if he was to succeed he would have to move out of his technical comfort zone and warm up his technical edge. *American Graffiti* was both easy and hard. Easy because the material was familiar but hard because it was essentially not a technical film and Lucas had to cross over into screenwriting and dealing with people on set.

Lucas is principally a nostalgic artisan. He has stated that if he hadn't been a filmmaker, he would have been a toy maker. To an extent this is true. He has made a fortune from toy merchandising for which the film was the advertising.

He is different and his difference just happened to be what the market wanted. In the early days, Lucas went against conventional wisdom to make *Star Wars*. Conventional wisdom said that science fiction did not sell. Now his wisdom is mainstream, and he has spawned a series of imitators.

Lucas had business influences on both sides of the family. His father was a prominent businessman in a small town and would have rewarded any signs of business in Lucas. In addition, his maternal grandfather was also in local business. Lucas worked at odd jobs while growing up. His father thought Lucas was born for commerce and would have reinforced every money-making activity.

As much as Lucas has talent, there are millions of people with talent not making much money. Being in the film industry was important for the size of the deals being carried out. A successful filmmaker with a head for business can strike deals and make considerable money, while a successful mechanic has to work that much harder. If you want to get rich, you have to get close to the money!

Growing up, Lucas was good with his hands. He made dolls' houses for his sisters, toy forts for his friends and elaborate special-effects constructions. He did what he was good at and, luckily, that gained him rare and much needed approval.

When he was very young, his loving grandfather came over most weekends and made movies of the kids. Movie making and love became intimately associated. Drawn to movie making from that early experience, he later made stop-motion movies; peers paid to see both them and Lucas's special-effects constructions. He would certainly have gained approval from his father, a dedicated businessman, by selling admission.

Luck played a significant part in Lucas's success. He was lucky to have landed in the film industry at the time he did. Hollywood had had some success with break-away films, such as *Easy Rider*, and was looking for new talent.

Lucas came up with the right formula for the time. There was a hole in the market for Lucas's films. Most importantly, he was lucky to have been born and brought up with a curious mix of anxieties, motivations and abilities. The outsider Lucas was perfectly out of step with the world of movie making and perfectly in step with the movie-going public at just the right time.

References:

Baxter, J 1999, *George Lucas: a Biography*, HarperCollins, London.

Pollock, D 1999, *Skywalking: the Life and Films of George Lucas*, Da Capo Press, New York.

Chapter 16

Bernie Ecclestone

Forbes information 2007
Rank: 243
Citizenship: United Kingdom
Wealth: US$3.6 billion
Industry: motor sport/gambling/leisure

Bernie Ecclestone, a small man with no documented sporting ability, is one of the wealthiest sporting entrepreneurs in the world. He used his superb and ruthless talents as a negotiator and his obsessive drive to find the best deal, making Formula One motor racing the dominant motor racing sport in the world (outside the US) and Ecclestone a billionaire in the process. The cornerstone of Ecclestone's billions are the TV rights to Formula One racing.

Achievement

In the 1950s Ecclestone wanted to be a motor racing driver, but despite his enthusiasm he proved to be indifferent. At that time Formula One was essentially an Englishman's and continental gentleman's club sport.

It was poorly funded by car companies and many of the drivers and constructors competed for trivial prizes, which were only just enough to fund the next week's race. Through concerted trading, constant brinkmanship, driven self-interest and relentless hunger, Ecclestone almost single-handedly turned this gentleman's sport into a multi-billion dollar industry. This success is a monument to pure trading.

While it really didn't matter what the product was, Ecclestone, the compulsive trader, was going to use whatever vehicle was at his disposal to make money. For Ecclestone, motor racing seemed to have a special pull. It was the only sport that he could compete in where his particular talent, making money, ensured him a place as a competitor on the starting grid.

> For Ecclestone, motor racing seemed to have a special pull.

From those early beginnings in motor racing, Ecclestone came to control almost every aspect of Formula One—its branding, its look and feel, and most importantly its media. Like any highly competitive brand manager and product champion, he also had strong negative effects on competing products—in this case, other types of motor racing. He reportedly indulged in anti-competitive behaviour for the benefit of Formula One. This was mainly through his influence on the media, starving the other forms of racing media coverage, therefore denying them of TV dollars.

Through a series of tough negotiations and 'sharp dealings', he went from small-time motorcycle salesman just after the end of World War II, to car salesman, to property speculator and owner of a car dealership. He built up his dealerships and was involved in hire purchase and property dealing. Around that time, Ecclestone became keen to be a racing driver, but unfortunately his talent did not match his enthusiasm.

Formula One racing was terribly under-funded with drivers often doubling as their own mechanics—this was the case for Australian Jack Brabham, the only man to win a world Formula One championship in a car he built.

By the 1970s, the Brabham Motor racing team, along with Jack, had faded from its former glory. Ecclestone bought it and continued to run it, but he was not a racer, mechanic or conventional manager, so the Brabham team continued its decline. But Ecclestone was a wheeler and dealer, and by winning increased fees from track owners and promoters to race on their circuits he made himself better off and, incidentally, made the other constructors better off too.

The constructors, a loose band of mechanics and engineers with little interest in the business side of racing, were relieved to have an enthusiastic dealer on their side and delegated major appearance and competition negotiations to Ecclestone. He became the head of the Formula One constructors association, which put him in the driving seat.

By the time Ecclestone took over the Brabham team he had already begun making a fortune in property and motor vehicle dealerships. Why he moved on to such an unlikely vehicle for wealth creation has never been explained. Certainly he doesn't claim any vision for making Formula One racing into the global entertainment franchise it is now. The only answer is that it gave Ecclestone something he needed at the time that was better than money—it gave him a place to belong.

Motor sport is a turbo-charged, high-octane money guzzler. The constructors were constantly running out of money. The need to stump up funds interfered with their first love—cars and racing—but to not raise funds meant no racing. So along came Ecclestone to solve some of their problems.

Over time, the constructors and Ecclestone developed a self-interest co-dependency that Ecclestone simultaneously exploited brilliantly and depended on. Having got into motor racing and proved indifferent both as a driver and a team owner, Ecclestone had found his niche. He could do something that gave him his place and he could do it with dignity. The constructors needed him and he needed them. Also, the rules of membership were clear, so all parties could control their interactions. Membership was ultimately dependent on transactions and money. If enough money came in everyone was happy, if not the whole thing would fall apart.

By regularly negotiating for the constructors, and mostly giving them more in return than they could possibly have achieved by themselves, Ecclestone maintained their loyalty while all the time gaining more and more money and, critically, more and more of the rights. Ecclestone always made sure his slice of any deal was substantial, and the constructors didn't care because the money came in and they could concentrate on cars and racing. Ecclestone may have been a bastard, but he was their bastard!

If there were winners and losers in negotiations, Ecclestone was rarely the loser, and even if he lost a particular battle, he never gave up—he would keep going until he won the war. Ecclestone maintained ownership of his racing team for a while but ultimately lost interest and sold it off.

His practices were always sharp and ruthless. A typical example of this occurred after he had negotiated a contract for the Japanese Grand Prix. Ecclestone called the race organisers just four days before the race demanding extra fees for transportation costs and safety requirements. The race organisers inevitably caved in to the demands because they had passed the point of financial no-return. They had spent money on advertising, had sold tickets, entered into contracts for cleaning, catering and security. In any event, the Formula One race was likely to be the biggest cash earner for the year, so they didn't want to lose the income. This 'negotiating' tactic is pure Ecclestone. In almost all cases he has been successful. His tactic of threatening to abandon the race was very effective.

It was just another race for the constructors. While they loved to race, a lay-off can always be used to prepare for later races or rest, and besides it costs them money to race. There are benefits to cancelling out the occasional race, which are more than adequately compensated for by the certainty of earning more money. They could risk not racing, but the race organisers could not afford for them to stay away. Ecclestone had a negotiation weapon with almost no downside and considerable chance of increasing the upside.

Time and time again Ecclestone has employed this method. The threat of withdrawal worked on the premier Formula One race at Monaco, when he played chicken with organisers by refusing to allow cars to enter the track until his terms were met. They were met. Ecclestone has a constant campaign of extracting more dollars out of TV rights, track operators and anyone else involved in Formula One. In 2007 there was the very public threat to (yet again) exclude Formula One racing from the UK's Silverstone racetrack and to drop Melbourne from the race calendar. It's likely that there will be more in years to come.

In the world of racing, many of the organising bodies were 'gentlemen' more interested in the prestige than the money. But Ecclestone was after money and power, and this, along with his business skills, gave him the edge. He was indifferent to fame and public criticism. He will not be shamed into behaving like a gentleman, or a good sport for that matter.

Ecclestone made sure that he benefited through his tough negotiation. Once the costs of the race were covered and the constructors' share distributed, whatever remained was his profit. And profit he did, at every opportunity for as much as he could get.

Like many traders, Ecclestone takes an entirely amoral stance to his dealings—it is just business and anything is fair in business. Aside from cases brought against him for anti-competitive behaviour, there is no evidence that what he has done is illegal. Negotiations are tough, maybe outside the spirit of the contract, but if it is not proven to be illegal, then it is just business as far as Ecclestone is concerned. Ecclestone is typically slippery when justifying his actions. He has been accused of unscrupulous conduct, but when asked about this on one occasion he said, "'What, my friend, does unscrupulous mean? I don't understand the word". He seized the opportunity to portray himself as a much misunderstood man' (Lovell 2004).

Ecclestone is an obsessive deal maker. His first partner, the car dealer, simply couldn't keep up with Ecclestone's pace nor did he approve of his methods. This partner simply faded away and was bought out.

Ecclestone's obsession extends well beyond winning deals. He has to be in control of everything. He is obsessively clean and neat, which has become one of his hallmarks. In the early days he had spotless showrooms and workshops. In later years he applied his standards to Formula One circuits. Ecclestone was known to fly up in a helicopter to inspect the pattern of parking spaces, demanding changes on pain of withdrawal of the racing teams. While this idiosyncrasy may have driven circuit owners to distraction, it had a beneficial side. Ecclestone almost single-handedly imposed the standards that transformed Formula One from a greasy gentleman mechanics' sport to the glamorous international sport it is today.

The need for order led in part to his insisting that Formula One signage come under a company that could arrange the signs in an appealing way—with a cut to Ecclestone, of course.

Ecclestone is reportedly a tyrant as a boss, with a need to control everything. He calls employees in the middle of the night and expects them to be on the ball. Lack of cleanliness and order is guaranteed to infuriate him. He gets upset at the smallest thing, such as a splash of mud on a car. He runs his business with fear and conflict, and has been known to fire people for small transgressions.

His need for total control at work became a problem because it was too much for one person, which resulted in work being delayed. This isn't just inside his organisation; it includes everything substantial to do with Formula One and, in some other cases, other motor sports. In Formula One racing, to move without Ecclestone's patronage borders on financial suicide.

On the upside, Ecclestone's obsessive need for control worked well for him and Formula One. He came, via myriad dealings, to control the rights for broadcast of almost all the motor sports in Europe. Having achieved the rights it is reported he systematically went about killing off all opposition motor sports to Formula One. In this he met little resistance because he could intimidate most of the organisers.

He once met opposition from a small-time TV producer from one of the other motor sports. Intimidation and attempts at buying off failed and the producer brought an anti-competitive lawsuit against Ecclestone.

The case went before the Directorate-General for Competition, who identified several serious breaches of the competition rules. The judge was later quoted in *The Wall Street Journal*, saying he 'had rarely seen a case where there had been so many breaches of competition rules' (Lovell 2004). This whole episode caused Ecclestone some immediate problems, but he just kept going and became even richer.

Much of Ecclestone's control and power comes from not disclosing the level of his dealings with others. This is a very useful tactic, naturally, as the different parties can be played off against each other and it is often not clear where Ecclestone's real interests lie or how much money is being made from whom. While such non-disclosure dealings are extremely useful for a private operator, they cause slippery entrepreneurs considerable trouble when they try to capitalise their business via a stock market float or a bonds issue. Money men demand transparency and Ecclestone's business ventures were anything but transparent. Ecclestone failed two attempts at floating his businesses on the stock market because there was insufficient disclosure in his dealings to make the floats work.

From a man who has as much money as anyone could rationally want, he still works incredibly hard. In part this is to protect his empire, because he is convinced that if he slows down there are others who will take it all from him.

In his dealings, he is unusual in not worrying unduly about his reputation. He has an outcome that he wants and that is all that matters. He is only concerned when it interferes with his control and his ability to make money, as the adverse publicity around the float of his company did.

Development

Born in 1930, Ecclestone came from a tough working-class background outside London. His father was a fisherman and then a crane driver and his mother had part-time work.

Nothing much is known about the treatment Ecclestone received from his parents. Despite describing his parents as very caring and interested in his welfare, it appears that Ecclestone was never very attached to his parents or family. Once he left home, he hardly ever returned to visit. He has a strongly negative view of conventional family events, such as Christmas, birthdays, marriages and deaths. Family events obviously were unpleasant for him. As an adult he went to his father's funeral, but he did not enter the church. This lack of attachment would suggest the relationship between Ecclestone and his parents was neutral at best.

It is unlikely that the family provided much formative approval beyond general praise for looking after his own financial needs. Ecclestone needed to fend for himself, and calls himself an 'independent bastard'. He has made his way forward through his own efforts and hates being dependent on others.

Ecclestone has been married twice. His second wife is a Croatian model he met during a Formula One race, and who he actively pursued. Once won, she has very much taken a back seat. Ecclestone took half a day off to be married at a registry office. He plucked a stranger off the street to be a witness—there were no pictures, party or honeymoon. Ecclestone went back to the office and she had to go home. His wife still complains about the indignity of their wedding. She is angry, but not so angry that she would leave him.

He works extremely long hours—sixteen hours a day, seven days a week. He says that he attempts to spend half a day a week with his family.

It was tough times in England when Ecclestone was growing up. England had won the First World War but was in crippling debt, there was the Great Depression and in the 1930s work was not easy to find for the working class.

When Ecclestone was five, the family moved from a sleepy fishing village to a grim working-class suburb on the outskirts of London. The family moved again when Ecclestone was eight. Ecclestone was reported to be somewhat of a difficult isolate even before he left the fishing village. He always wanted his own way, and would throw tantrums when things didn't go his way.

One of his earliest reported business enterprises was when he was eleven, during the dark days of World War II, a time of deprivation and rationing. Ecclestone would buy buns from the baker and sell them in the schoolyard with a profit margin. He is reported to have never eaten any because that was his profit. Critically, as he was small, he paid a gang of bigger boys to protect him and his profits. He also says his paid protection prevented him from being bullied.

Ecclestone went on to other activities. He had two newspaper rounds, picked vegetables during school holidays and sold fountain pens in London's East End. He needed the money to buy safety.

Ecclestone is obviously intelligent because the arcane business structures and deals he set up required considerable mental capacity. He is also reported as having a prodigious memory. Nothing is forgotten. There is, however, considerable doubt about his education. He claims to have a degree in chemical engineering, but this is considered fanciful.

He left school in December 1946 without academic distinction. He got a job in the laboratory of the regional gas board with the hope of becoming a chemist. He has a very quick mind and is very good with numbers, giving him an advantage in the business environment.

Ecclestone's poor academic record, his phenomenal memory and the fact that he absolutely refuses to go to subtitled movies suggests that he has a reading dysfunction, possibly dyslexia. Despite his lack of formal qualifications he is reported as having a lightning-fast brain when it comes to calculations and understanding deals.

Ecclestone was obviously a loner and outsider. He paid cash for whatever admiration and protection he needed. He was moved around when he was young — movements that guaranteed social dislocation for a small, low-status 'dumb' child in hard times.

Just out of school, Ecclestone's first business break came when he convinced a local car dealer to allow him space to sell second-hand motor cycles. Soon Ecclestone's business was greater than the dealer's. By the time he was twenty-one, he went on to partner the dealer, then buy him out. Eventually he owned multiple dealerships and traded in property before moving on to motor racing.

Interpretation

From the time Ecclestone was in primary school, he was a trader. He stumbled onto it as a way to provide money to buy protection from bullying. Almost certainly, he was born with a predisposition to trade, and the discovery of the huge personal benefits of having money would have built this into a full-blown obsession.

While he has transactional allegiances, he is always his own man. If you are on his side and he can benefit from you, then things are fine. Otherwise you either don't matter or are an enemy. It is Ecclestone against the world. Anything that he can get away with is fine.

While some of the causes of Ecclestone's behaviour are obvious, many of the details regarding his early background are sketchy. He was a small, socially disconnected boy moved into a hostile environment. Despite being bright he obviously had learning difficulties; undoubtedly he was considered 'dumb' by both teachers and students. He could not defend himself with physical strength, sport or any other conventional means.

Even before he moved out of his fishing village he was a fractious loner, suggesting that he had a poor early relationship with his mother.

Despite saying he had warm feelings towards his family, he turned his back on them and had virtually nothing to do with them after he left home.

After leaving school, Ecclestone traded in property, motorcycles and cars. The last two were very important growth markets immediately after World War II. Motor racing was glamorous and many young men were drawn to it. Ecclestone had an advantage over most young men—he could produce what was most needed to be an active member in the sport, cash. Motor racing is a very transactional sport. If you have money, you can participate in one way or another. Ecclestone could buy a place, just like he did at school. It was a very familiar situation for him, money guaranteed belonging. Ecclestone may also have hankered after a bit of sporting glory, something he had missed out on at school.

Ecclestone was not sufficiently good at racing to achieve glory. But by doing deals for the constructors, he had found another place to belong. Right at the dawn of the present Formula One sport, it was not obvious that it could be grown into such a large franchise. Ecclestone could have easily put his efforts elsewhere and probably would have become richer than he is. He was already a consummate property dealer and car trader, and didn't need to muck around with motor racing. Ecclestone did it because he wanted to. It gave him a place to belong.

Ecclestone's belonging increased once he graduated from racing to representing the constructors. This loose club of 'friendly' competitors, tied together with a need for money, was a natural home for Ecclestone. They needed him and they gave him approval for doing the deals and getting them more than they could get for themselves. They probably didn't care much if Ecclestone was getting rich, they just needed someone to do the business for them because they couldn't or wouldn't or simply weren't interested. Money was just the fuel they needed to keep their show on the road—they weren't interested in it for its own sake. They were engineers and racers, not traders. Machinery and racing fascinated them, trading bored them.

This was the type of belonging Ecclestone understood and was comfortable with. He experienced this belonging at school—it was transactional. In this type of club it doesn't matter all that much whether people like each other, it only matters that they continue to perform as expected. Ecclestone had a place if he continued to bring in the money. The others only had a place if they had money and delivered racing to the market. It was a marriage made in heaven. Everyone knew the rules. Everyone was co-dependent. Individuals fell out, individuals came and went, the system grew and transformed but the essence of the transactional system remained intact.

Having business co-dependants was also better for Ecclestone than having employees because, unlike employees, the constructors acted as semi-independent people, almost as real friends might. They didn't need to be supervised and their incomes weren't coming out of Ecclestone's pocket, so he could relax his obsessive vigilance somewhat. It is obvious that Ecclestone is an outsider, and it is almost certain that all the constructors are too. They understand each other and the system they belong to. They interact to the extent they need to. Some are firm friends, some are deadly enemies, most simply transact in a mutually beneficial system.

For most of the time Ecclestone was increasing his control of Formula One and its size, most of the governing bodies, as well as track ownership, were in the hands of gentlemanly committees with a club ethos, not business. Ecclestone is no gentleman, and he played by completely different rules, using brinkmanship and ungentlemanly behaviour, dividing the opposition and winning considerable advantage.

Ecclestone has always been an outsider on the outer edge. His lack of observance of normal unwritten rules of 'gentlemanly' behaviour gives him considerable business advantage. Normal rules never served Ecclestone when he was growing up. While at school, being small, isolated, not involved in sport and academically poor, he was in a system that was at best indifferent to such a student and most times downright hostile. He had to fend for himself. Rules worked against him, never for him — they didn't protect him and they didn't give him friends, so Ecclestone made his own rules. He obeyed the rules that suited, but he also used the rules against others.

Like Icahn, when out of school, Ecclestone knew that others were bound by rules of good behaviour, and if he went against those rules he had an advantage.

One of the most powerful and implicit rules in many societies is related to public honour and the shame of having one's name held in disrepute. It acts as a brake for many powerful people and is an even bigger deterrent for less-powerful people. Worrying about what others think is one of the forces that lock people in place, preventing them from changing. For many, public humiliation is the worst punishment of all.

Having been exposed to considerable verbal abuse while growing up, Ecclestone doesn't mind his name being muddied in public. He doesn't seem to care about manners, he doesn't get humiliated, he simply keeps going and making money. The prospect of public pillaring doesn't stop him and negative publicity doesn't stall him. He doesn't mind being unpopular and disliked; that is how it has been for him his whole life.

He only belongs if he has money — approval and popularity have never been a factor.

Given this indifference to criticism, Ecclestone plays his brinkmanship games out in the open. He doesn't mind if the world sees him intimidating yet another racing circuit owner in exactly the same way that he has always done. And as he makes more money, he gains more credibility. The media continues to lionise him and fails to analyse his behaviour.

In addition, Ecclestone has something against churches. He travelled across the world to Brazil to the funeral of a close friend, driver Ayrton Senna, but did not attend the church service. Nor did he attend the church service for his father's funeral — he waited in the church yard. He didn't attend his mother's funeral at all. And he had a registry wedding. This suggests that he has more against churches than being bored while young, or not believing in God.

He discovered at school that if he had money he could trade that for safety and a sense of, if not exactly belonging, control. It wasn't as good as true friendship but it was a whole lot better than the terror of being bullied daily. The more Ecclestone had to trade, the better off he was in terms of safety and control.

Money began to equal safety and control. Having protectors around at least gave some companionship, even if it was not as good as true friendship. This early pattern became crystallised in his behaviour to such an extent that it made him a billionaire. But since Ecclestone bought his protectors' loyalty, he knew it wasn't a permanent thing that he could rely on. It would go away when the money dried up. Emotionally, he cannot let the money dry up. He developed a hunger for money that would never go away.

Ecclestone is compulsive. The world is a dangerous place for him and he can never have enough control. Control has to be bought; therefore, Ecclestone can't have enough money. He learnt early on that money could buy him safety, control and order, and obviously more money buys him more of those things. Having people on his 'payroll' is a way to control them.

Conversely, if there are people who are not on the payroll, then their loyalty cannot be guaranteed. Everyone is potentially a foe and Ecclestone would much rather attack than wait to find out just how much of a foe that person is.

In an interview Ecclestone is quoted as saying, 'You cross me and sooner or later I'll get you' (Lovell 2004). This shows that, despite his enormous wealth and success, Ecclestone still has a need to throw his weight around and to be feared.

Growing up was tough for Ecclestone. He was small and bright, but educationally challenged. Compounding this he had no sporting ability. He grew up in the rough and economically and socially depressed world of working-class England before, during and after World War II. This would have been a challenge for anyone, let alone an unprotected little Jewish boy coming from another place at a time when people did not move much. The dislocation caused by two moves in his formative years would have been socially and emotionally catastrophic.

While growing up, Ecclestone learnt many important lessons, but in particular he learnt that the world was a hostile place and that there are three types of people—those that are for him, those that are against him, or those that are irrelevant. Safety can only be achieved if it is bought.

Certainly, something very powerful disturbed the young Ecclestone. Whatever monsters chased Ecclestone out of working class England, they are still chasing him. He just cannot be safe enough.

References:

Henry, A 2003, *The Power Brokers: the Battle for F1's Billions*, Motor Books International, Minnesota.

Lovell, T 2004, *Bernie's Game: Inside the Formula One World of Bernie Ecclestone*, Metro Publishing Ltd, London.

Chapter 17

Steven Spielberg

Forbes information 2007
Rank: 287
Citizenship: United States
Wealth: US$3.0 billion
Industry: media/entertainment

Steven Spielberg is another filmmaker who emerged during the 1970s. Like Lucas, Spielberg became a filmmaker while still at school. It was an activity that overcame adolescent boredom and anxiety, gained him protection from bullies and increased his social standing. For him, filmmaking became a beacon of achievement in the gloom of academic, social and sporting failure. It was one of the few things Spielberg ever excelled at and, for all we know, it may actually be the only thing he ever excelled at!

Achievement

As Spielberg grew up, he made more elaborate movies. After hustling his demonstration films for a number of years, he made the movie *Amblin*, with the backing of a rich friend. This movie was sufficiently noteworthy for Spielberg to be offered work in TV production.

After landing a contract to work at Universal Studios, Spielberg laboured for years on a series of vanilla TV shows, all the time developing his craft and slowly rising in the ranks. By 1971 he was a senior journeyman director and Universal Studios gave him carriage of *Duel*, his first feature and international success. *Duel* was made as a TV film. It is about a trucker repeatedly trying to push a car off the road during a long desert chase. Spielberg planned the filming meticulously and brought the film in within two days of the planned schedule. The film was a success and Spielberg's credibility rose, both within Universal and outside. Other companies asked for Spielberg but were turned down by Universal. They wanted to use him on the plodding TV shows they produced.

Universal added nine minutes to *Duel* and released it in the cinemas. It gained critical acclaim at the Cannes Film Festival and elsewhere in Europe. Spielberg gained stature and powerful friends. He now had access to more of the emerging scriptwriters, composers and other bankable talent around Hollywood.

He moved away from TV work and into movies, both directing and producing them. *Sugarland Express* was released to great critical acclaim, but was a box office failure. In 1975 he made *Jaws* for an initial budget of $2.25 million. Spielberg, himself frightened of sharks and other sea monsters, conceived the film as an aquatic version of *Duel*, full of hidden menace. It eventually went on to gross in excess of $400 million, for which Spielberg earned $50 000 plus 3 per cent of profits. Spielberg was on his way!

His notable successes in the early years were with escapist movies, especially those based around his own nostalgia and experiences. For example, *Back to the Future* featured a young man who was a victim of bullying and who went back in time to try to fix up his parents' failing marriage. This is something the bullied Spielberg would have loved to have done when he was growing up. *Close Encounters of the Third Kind* drew on many experiences he had with his father, such as driving out to see a meteor storm and his father obsessively building a model mountain.

He was employed by George Lucas for the *Indiana Jones* trilogy. Other films of note that he was involved with are *ET*, *Hook*, *Who Framed Roger Rabbit* and *Jurassic Park*. Spielberg's movies are frequently derided by the critics as escapist pap. He has had forays into more serious themes with *Schindler's List* and *Saving Private Ryan*, and he cast Oprah Winfrey in *The Color Purple*. But whether it be escapist nostalgia or serious fare, Spielberg's sense of what will appeal to the market is usually very accurate and lucrative.

As Spielberg became even more bankable, he was able to negotiate better deals. He makes films for everybody and is unencumbered with artistic pretensions.

> He makes films for everybody and is unencumbered with artistic pretensions.

He is now partners with David Geffen and Jeffrey Katzenberg in the Hollywood hit factory DreamWorks SKG. These three are reported to be the most hated men in Hollywood, a triumvirate of greed. Even David Geffen, a man known for greed and ruthlessness, is reported as saying of Spielberg that he is 'selfish, self-centred, egomaniacal, and worst of all—greedy' (Baxter 1996).

Undoubtedly a talented movie maker with huge mass appeal, Spielberg's billionaire status comes in part from being in an industry that rewards its talent well. Even more than Lucas and unlike most of the billionaires in this book, Spielberg is a billionaire because he is a talent, rather than because he is a dedicated businessperson. This is not to trivialise his business ability, but that is not at the core of his achievement.

Development

Spielberg was born into a not particularly orthodox Jewish family in Cincinnati on 18 December 1947, the eldest child of four, and the only boy.

His mother was a former concert pianist who exerted considerable influence on his life. She was loving and playful; for example, they loved (non-kosher) lobster and when a rabbi came to visit, Spielberg hid the live creatures under his bed until the rabbi was gone. This engendered feelings of both terror and mischief, which are often present in Spielberg's films. It also explains the appeal of naughty boys, with mother being something like Wendy to Spielberg's Peter Pan.

She made life fun for Spielberg. On one occasion she cooked something with berries in it in her pressure cooker until it exploded, so that Spielberg could film the kitchen covered in the red mess.

But all was not well at home between Spielberg's parents. Spielberg senior was a workaholic. He was an electrical engineer who was involved with building the first computers. His job required the family to move around the country. His father was eccentric and would be enthusiastic about obscure events. On one particular occasion, he hauled the kids around the country to look at a meteor storm. This event was included in the filming of *Close Encounters of the Third Kind* and the obsessive father of the film was loosely modelled on Spielberg's own father.

While there was no doubt that Spielberg's parents were loving parents, his mother and father fought constantly, and their clashes grew worse as Spielberg grew up. There was a clash between the way the free-thinking and creative mother thought and the way the obsessive workaholic engineer thought. Spielberg used to put towels under the door jambs to keep out the sound of their fights.

He was sensitive and spent a great deal of time experiencing feelings of panic and dread. He was fearful at movies, even finding Disney's *Snow White* terrifying when he saw it at the age of eight. More than most children he was scared of the dark and often hid under the bed.

Spielberg's world was constantly under threat of unravelling. At different times one or the other of his parents would threaten to leave and take the kids, or make other similarly disturbing threats. The children heard these threats, and while not actually suffering from separation anxiety, would have come close to it on an almost daily basis. Tension between their parents made the children anxious and frightened.

The personality clashes between his parents grew wilder during Spielberg's adolescence. To top off Spielberg's instability, the family was continually on the move. Spielberg spent most of his developing years in Haddonfield, New Jersey; Scottsdale, Arizona; and California, where his parents separated and divorced. As the estrangement between his father and mother increased, his father was increasingly away from home.

Because of his father's absences, Spielberg grew up surrounded by females. As a testimony to his comfort working with women, he now surrounds himself with women, and says that he works better with them and has more faith in them. In his fantasy films the females are usually strong and independent and the men tend to be blunderers or stiff and unsympathetic. There is no record of Spielberg having girlfriends at school. He married actress Amy Irving, with whom he had a son. They divorced in 1985. He later married actress Kate Capshore.

Spielberg is slightly below average height at five foot eight, but at school he was short and unattractive. He hated school. Moving from town to town exacted a huge toll on the already sensitive boy. He would be thrown into a new environment just as he was starting to settle in.

Like George Lucas, his sometime collaborator, he may be an undiagnosed dyslexic. At best he suffered from the particularly male affliction of poor literacy skills and low interest in reading. He admits to a lack of book reading in his background, claiming a more visual education from a diet of TV, movies and comic books.

Spielberg describes himself as 'the weird skinny kid with acne. I was a wimp' (Taylor 1999). He was hopeless at games and he was never in a place long enough to fit in. At one school he was nicknamed 'the retard', not just because of his ineptness at sports but because, presumably, of learning difficulties. He was always the last boy to be picked for team sports, if he was picked at all. In biology, he was the only boy to throw up during the dissection of a frog. He just couldn't fit in with the macho boy culture. He was an academic, social and sporting failure, which led to him being bullied, vilified, lonely, anxious and bored.

When he was twelve, his father bought an 8 mm movie camera. Spielberg used it to gain his photographic merit badge at Scouts. Joining Scouts was a seminal event for Spielberg—it connected him with kids his own age and gave him the idea for and the reason to make movies. During his time alone at home he had spent a lot of time watching TV, absorbing its form, and this was put to good use at Scouts. This is probably the first achievement Spielberg had ever made outside home that was rewarded with praise, and that praise was sweet. He had done something good and it had been acknowledged.

From there he made short movies. When he needed an actor, he cleverly cast the biggest bully at the school as the hero in one of his films and showed it at the local cinema—it was his first box office success. It had other benefits also. The biggest bully was now his best friend and protector, so no more bullying. He gained peer approval and physical safety in one move. His father hired the local cinema to show the film, which was Spielberg's first box office success—he made a profit of $100. He was also admitted to the boys' secret honour society, 'The Order of the Arrow'. What powerful motivation to make movies!

Spielberg's family moved to California, and at seventeen he visited Universal Studios. Through nerve and persistence he gained the opportunity to show his films, but that led nowhere as he discovered that the industry was very much controlled and operated by middle-aged men operating on a middle-aged formula making movies for middle-aged audiences.

Spielberg persisted in trying to break into the film industry. He enrolled at California State University to study English because his high school grades were not good enough to get him into a major film school. He wasn't particularly interested in studying English, and kept going to cinemas and hustling movie-making executives. And hustle he did. The nondescript Spielberg drifted into the studios looking harmlessly like someone's nephew on work experience. He hung around film sets and pestered people to look at his films. He was highly ambitious and, having nothing else that he either wanted to or was qualified to do, he just kept plugging away.

Unable to gain entry into film school, Spielberg's only work experience was his own films and a voracious adolescent diet of comics, films and TV. Spielberg drifted around the movie and TV production scene between 1966 and 1969, connecting with people here and there and carrying out bits and pieces of work. This is a time that Spielberg is extremely vague about. He obviously worked on projects that went nowhere or simply filled in time. Maybe he even studied a little but he did not graduate from university. During this time, Spielberg gained experience in the craft and the business. With no other career options and no social networks, Spielberg, the outsider, had nothing to lose and everything to gain from being in place.

He was given advice to film in a larger format. He persuaded a rich fellow student to fund his first film using the new format, *Amblin* — a slick little movie designed to establish that he could make a professional-looking movie. It worked! At twenty-one, he was made an offer to work in television — not quite the movies but in the business for pay at least. Spielberg immediately dropped out of college. *Forbes* records him as having a bachelor of arts/science from the University of California, so presumably he was given an honorary degree at some later stage, because there is no record of him returning to study.

Spielberg's contract held him as a virtual slave to Universal Studios for a pittance without guaranteeing him any work nor any choice in what was offered. After cooling his heals for a while, Spielberg pleaded for work and gained a directing role for a sci-fi pilot starring the ageing actress Joan Crawford. Humiliation by Crawford and compromise to please her led to much of Spielberg's work being left on the cutting room floor. In shame Spielberg offered to resign but instead was given a year's leave without pay.

Spielberg lasted four months outside Universal as his attempts to broker other deals failed. Back at Universal, he pleaded for other work and was given journeyman directing roles on long-running TV shows, such as *Marcus Welby MD*. The pace was frantic, directing five days a week and jumping from show to show. Any failure to deliver on time was rewarded with firing.

At the time, long-run TV series were on the decline and the networks were demanding more features. Spielberg landed the directing role for a ninety-minute sci-fi feature, which had some success. It gained Spielberg some standing and he addressed a sci-fi conference, alerting him to the market for this genre.

Not long after came the opportunity to film the script of *Duel* for television. Spielberg made such a success of it that it was made into a movie for art house cinema release. Spielberg became a cinematic juggernaut almost overnight.

Interpretation

Spielberg was a very anxious child and teenager. His parents were constantly fighting and seemingly on the verge of divorce. Because of this, Spielberg would have suffered a sort of suspended separation anxiety, never certain whether his world was going to collapse. By itself this would have been bad enough, but because the family constantly moved around the country, Spielberg didn't have a social network to fall back on. Worse, he was such an outsider that the moves caused considerable stress all on their own. Adding the two together was emotionally catastrophic to the young Spielberg, resulting in periodic emotional meltdown.

Spielberg, the serial outsider, the sad, anxious, ugly little boy with almost no redeeming academic or social skills, was well rewarded for making his early movies. The first reward was possibly his first public approval ever and was gained for making a film at Scouts. The second was achieved by casting the bully as lead actor, instantly converting the bully to protector and ally and solving Spielberg's greatest school problem. Both of these events provided colossal, addictive emotional rewards. Safety, approval and friendship were achieved in one neat filmmaking package. From then it was onward and upward, with increasing acclaim from his school buddies for his movies.

Unlike many people, he had few, if any, obvious career choices, so he chose filmmaking. Unburdened by excessive career choice, he persisted through years of adversity and humiliation as a junior 'slave' in the Hollywood studio system. He wasn't driven by art, he was driven by necessity and the emotional trace of past rewards.

Inevitably, Spielberg inherited his mother's characteristics—artistic and playful—and, from his father he received his technically creative and curious traits. It was his father's camera that became the focus of his obsession and provided the solution to his emotional problems.

There is no obvious trading in Spielberg's background, but trading is clearly an intelligence he possesses. Some filmmakers and entertainers become merely rich. Some, like Lucas's famous mentor Coppola, never make much money at all, concentrating on worthy projects and failing to deliver the necessary box office receipts to cover the cost of production, let alone the huge production overruns.

Little is said of the cost of Spielberg's productions, so presumably this means that he consistently delivers on time and on budget. He also constantly delivers good-to-great box office returns with few real failures. Unburdened with artistic, intellectual or political pretensions he has an almost unwavering sense of what the public wants to watch. Mostly it fits very comfortably into good escapist fare involving an action-packed, adrenaline-soaked, nostalgic roller-coaster ride with little intellectual content. Certainly there are some intellectual and moral moments, particularly in his later work, but most of his early work was gut reaction movies that jump straight from the screen into the primitive reptilian centres of the brain, completely missing the intellectual processing part on the way through.

This and his finely developed film craft guaranteed box office success, and this, after all, is what showbiz is all about. The showbiz winners get to continue playing with bigger budgets. It's not the critic's vote that counts, the public votes with its money. Spielberg regularly wins these votes by massive landslides.

It is interesting that some of his most famous movies involve primitive animals. Films involving a huge shark and dinosaurs—what could be more primitive than those fears? Like Lucas and Oprah Winfrey, he has taken an admittedly high starting income from an outrageously highly paid industry and turned it into a personal fortune. While he is undoubtedly less of a deal maker than his partner Geffen, alone Spielberg was doing very well, but combined within DreamWorks SKG his increasing fortune is inevitable.

He may not be as consummate a trader as his partners, but his basic insecurity and neediness led him to continue to succeed—after all, in business the score is kept with money. And if money is approval, then Spielberg is going for as much of this type of approval as possible. This extends back to his school days when he hired the local cinema. The box office was as much a measure of his acceptance as the movie's worth and it still is.

Spielberg's insecurities led him to make movies that were nostalgic. While conventional filmmakers were making dark political movies, he and his sometime collaborator George Lucas were making escapist, nostalgic and childlike movies. He relived, edited and reorganised his pain and his hopes into a commercial product.

Luckily for Spielberg, his longing for the past as represented by Hollywood of the 1950s and 1960s, and the nostalgia for the childhood he never had cross-linked with bizarre renditions of his own unhappy childhood, hit a nerve with the film-going public. There is enough pain and suffering during childhood to go around and, even if that wasn't the problem, there is nothing like an action-packed ride full of lurking menace to get the public in. The scared, strange little boy found success beyond his wild imaginings.

He relived, edited and reorganised his pain and his hopes into a commercial product.

References:

Baxter, J 1996, *Steven Spielberg: the Unauthorised Biography*, HarperCollins, London.

Taylor, P 1999, *Steven Spielberg: the Man, His Movies, and Their Meaning*, Continuum, New York.

Chapter 18

Oprah Winfrey

Forbes information 2007
Rank: 664
Citizenship: United States
Wealth: US$1.5 billion
Industry: media/entertainment

Dubbed the 'Preacher Woman' while at school, Oprah Winfrey founded a media empire based on her compulsive need to communicate. Her program has huge appeal to women as she actively discusses women's business out in the open. Having been denied such an opportunity when she was suffering through abandonment and rape as a teenager, she has been evangelical in illuminating the issues of women and children in day-to-day life. She pioneered this style of program in the late 1970s and has since had innumerable imitators.

Achievement

While still at high school, Winfrey's extraordinary public speaking patter gave her an edge over the other beauties to be Nashville's Miss

Fire Prevention of 1971. She won the contest and was noticed by a local radio station, auditioned, and given a part-time announcing job. In 1973, while at college and still announcing, a local CBS TV station heard her and offered her a job. Winfrey worked on her style in front of the camera, learning how to come across as warm and engaging.

In 1976 she was offered a better job at a TV station in Baltimore. Once there, the station considered her news reporting style to be too down to earth for the station. She also adlibbed somewhat and often refused to interview people who were grieving. She was demoted to a five-minute magazine slot that aired at 5.30 am. During her time in broadcast purgatory, she kept to her style and honed her skills. She did not remain unnoticed. In 1978, she was given a co-host role on a morning talk show. After the first show she thought that she had found what she should be doing. She was a natural and described it as being 'like breathing' for her (Krohn 2000).

Her show was in the same timeslot as the nationally broadcast program *The Phil Donahue Show*. Winfrey's talk show soon gained a bigger local audience and she was especially loved by women.

> Winfrey's talk show soon gained a bigger local audience and she was especially loved by women.

After co-hosting the talk show for six years, she was offered a bigger job in Chicago. Her very personal, genuine style was extremely appealing. Unlike Donahue, Winfrey would get personal on her show, sharing her own feelings, secrets and problems. She began sharing her weight problem on air.

She was noticed by the movie producer and musician Quincy Jones. Through him she was approached by Steven Spielberg to play a major role in the movie *The Color Purple*, for which she earned an Oscar nomination.

Winfrey's show continued to receive top ratings. In 1986, she signed a deal to syndicate her show nationally, increasing her income to nearly $125 million a year. She created her own production company, bought the rights to literary works, started a book club and a magazine.

Now she hosts one of the most famous and lucrative TV shows on earth.

Development

Oprah Winfrey was born on 29 January 1954 in Kosciusko, a rural town in Mississippi, the illegitimate daughter of an eighteen-year-old girl and an army private who was stationed nearby. The mother and the father never lived together. The family was poor, times were hard and when Winfrey was four years old her mother moved away to work in Milwaukee, leaving Winfrey behind with her grandmother.

Winfrey's grandmother was very religious and wanted Winfrey to be the same. She began to teach Winfrey to read when she was only three, so that she could read the Bible. Winfrey began to memorise biblical passages.

Winfrey was isolated from other children. She only had her grandmother, and her grandmother gave tough love! Any love she gave was contingent on Winfrey pleasing her. Winfrey, the intelligent little girl, not only obliged but was driven to oblige as this was the only source of love she could get since experiencing what would have felt like being abandoned by her mother. She was encouraged to give recitations at church, which she did frequently and, in the process, gained a reputation, confidence, presentation skills, and most valuable of all to Winfrey, approval. In addition to approval from her grandmother, the whole congregation fussed over her!

But there was a downside to living with a grandmother who:

> ... believed in the Bible phrase, 'Spare the rod and spoil the child.' In other words, she felt that children who did not receive physical punishment would grow up to be spoiled and disrespectful. Oprah, lively and full of spirit, was strictly disciplined (Krohn 2002).

She was under-loved for all but her reading and preaching.

Grandmother fell ill when Winfrey was in first grade and Winfrey went to live with her mother in Milwaukee. Her mother discouraged Oprah's reading. By that time, her mother had another child. The baby received most of the attention, leaving Winfrey out in the emotional cold.

Her mother couldn't cope with raising two children, so she sent Winfrey to stay with her father. He lived in Nashville, in his own house, and worked two jobs as a janitor. He had married again. The father and stepmother welcomed Winfrey to the household with great joy. Winfrey was an only child there as they were unable to have children of their own. Like Winfrey's grandmother, they were lovingly strict and set on pushing her school skills, because they understood the value of education.

Winfrey got a library card and was required to write reports on the books she read. She enjoyed reading and studying, and also the attention her father and stepmother paid her for academic success.

Encouraged by her father and stepmother, Winfrey was again on the church speaking circuit, going all over Nashville. This made her truly happy. She was basking in the love and approval of her new parents and the congregation. Her talents grew so much that she became known as 'the speaker'. She would go on to speak at banquets, church functions and other events. Naturally Winfrey loved the attention and praise she received for this speaking. It made up in part for the continued neglect and lack of attention from her real mother.

Eight-year-old Winfrey went back to stay with her mother for the summer. Her mother had moved into a two-room apartment and had had another baby. Winfrey spent much of the summer looking after her two half-siblings while her mother worked long hours. So strong was the emotional need to be with her mother that she decided to stay with her.

To seriously compound her problems, she was raped at eight by her nineteen-year-old cousin while he was babysitting the children. From the age of ten, Winfrey was:

> … sexually abused by a family friend and then by an uncle.
> For several years, Oprah endured repeated sexual abuse.
> 'It was just an ongoing, continuous thing … so much so,
> that I started to think, you know, "This is the way life
> is" … every time I had a stomach ache, I thought I was
> pregnant' (Krohn 2000).

Oprah lost herself in books to forget her troubles.

As Winfrey grew she became unhappier. She was starved of affection from her mother and continued to suffer sexual abuse. Her behaviour deteriorated and she became wilder. She ran way from home, missed school and stole money from her mother. Her mother did not know about the abuse and didn't know what to do about the bad behaviour. She tried to put Winfrey into a detention home for troubled youth but it was full, so Winfrey went back to her father and stepmother in Nashville.

Winfrey was glad to be back with her father, even though he was strict and did not approve of her ways and clothes. She told no-one about her sexual abuse, but to compound her problems, she was pregnant. Eventually, seven months into her pregnancy, she had to reveal her problems. Stressed by the events, she went into early labour and gave birth to a baby that died within two weeks. The baby's death naturally increased her stress but it also brought relief—she wasn't going to be a mother at fourteen.

Her father and stepmother pushed her to improve her grades and she resumed her round of speaking engagements. She won a college scholarship on the basis of her speaking ability.

Winfrey was moved around and accelerated at school, which distanced her from her peers and placed her in groups she had difficulty connecting with. When Winfrey first went to kindergarten, she was found to be too advanced, and was promoted to first grade. Her naturally high intelligence was given a boost by the coaching her grandmother gave her. School was disrupted at the end of first grade when she went to live with her mother, also at the end of second grade when she moved to be with her father, and then again when she was eight in fourth grade and went back to live with her mother. Oprah was moved to an all-white high school, and then moved again when she went back to live with her father.

Not only was she intelligent, but her abilities had been boosted by her grandmother, father and stepmother. Winfrey liked fourth grade because she got on well with her teacher, who especially favoured Winfrey. Winfrey was often asked to speak in front of the class because of her speaking ability. Her intelligence and talent led to some resentment among classmates, and she earned the nickname 'Preacher Woman'.

Following her serial rapes she became even more socially isolated and being younger she was not at the same social development level as her peers. Despite her problems she continued to do well in school and achieved good grades.

By seventh grade, Winfrey was noticed by a teacher as being special because of her grades and the fact that she was quiet and studious. She often had her head in a book. That teacher arranged for her to go to an all-white school; she was the only African American student in the school. Most of the students were pleasant to her and she made friends, but she was different, not just because of her colour but because they were privileged white and she was poor African American. If that wasn't enough, she was carrying the emotional wounds from sexual abuse and a severely dislocated upbringing.

She often had her head in a book.

On returning to Nashville at fourteen, Winfrey had gone through a rebellious period and her grades were poor—almost all Cs. Her father pushed her to perform but failed until she lost her baby. With the loss of her baby she felt that she had been given a second chance in life. Her grades improved and she kept reading and speaking, ultimately winning a four-year college scholarship.

In her senior year at high school, Winfrey became popular. She was elected vice president of the student council and following a conference, was interviewed on radio. Several months later the announcer asked her if she would enter a beauty pageant for the title of Miss Fire Prevention. She won, not only on her looks but for her witty and personality-filled speeches. Her talent led to the radio station offering her a part-time job as a news presenter. She was now getting paid to do what she loved.

She graduated from high school in June 1971, later entering Tennessee State School. She continued with her part-time newsreading job. This was during the volatile times of Vietnam War protests and black power. Winfrey did not join in because she thought that being black and a woman had not caused her to miss out on anything in life. She wasn't liked or supported by classmates and so began to hate college. She continued to win beauty pageants, though she didn't expect to because she didn't see herself as being beautiful.

At nineteen, her radio announcing was heard by a CBS television station in Nashville. She was offered a job, which she declined because she believed she couldn't handle full-time work and college. Winfrey, convinced by both her father and grandmother that a university degree was necessary for a fulfilling career, wanted to complete her degree.

She sought advice from her college professor. It was only after he pointed out that people got degrees to get a job at places like CBS that she took the audition and landed the job, but she took some convincing. The station manager probably was under pressure to comply with the new affirmative-action legislation, but irrespective of that, Winfrey proved her worth. She was in luck—she could work full-time in the evenings and finish her studies for a bachelor of arts/science.

Winfrey's biggest publicly aired personal challenge is with weight. Even while receiving an Emmy Award for Outstanding Talk Show Host, she was humiliated at having to 'waddle my way up to the stage with the nation watching my huge behind' (Krohn 2000). She weighed 237 pounds.

Winfrey has not been married. She had a male companion for many years from whom she split with very publicly several years ago. She has no children.

Interpretation

With an upbringing of serial abandonment from a negligent mother who did not see Winfrey's continual sexual abuse from the age of eight, and tough love from her grandmother and her father, Winfrey was in need of something to bring her love and approval. Fortunately, the tough love from the latter two included a strong commitment to education and, most importantly, public speaking in the form of sermon delivery from the age of three. Winfrey spoke on the church circuit almost the whole time she was growing up, gaining approval from her parents, grandmother and from the congregations.

Winfrey's mother would probably have missed out on love because she couldn't perform what was necessary to please her own mother. Winfrey's grandmother was obviously very stern and was likely to have been even sterner with her own child. This would have been compounded by Winfrey's mother being indifferent academically. Along came Winfrey. Winfrey would have been the beneficiary of the normal grandmother softening and in addition had much for the grandmother to admire. It is possible that Winfrey's mother may have neglected Winfrey because she was jealous of the love Winfrey gained from the grandmother.

It is no wonder Winfrey is an inspirational speaker and has the skills to base her considerable fortune on it. Public speaking and sermonising is at the very centre of the approval she gained as a girl. Winfrey, the outsider, always had this as a constant source of comfort during her physical and emotional upheavals, throughout her childhood and adolescence.

Her speaking skills have given her the edge, and her compulsive need for approval through speaking has driven her to continue year after year, never getting bored despite her obviously high intelligence. She loves what she does and needs the approval that comes from success. In her own words Winfrey said:

> I realize that I was the kind of child who was always
> searching for love and affection and attention, and
> somebody to … look at me and say, 'Yes, you are worthy'
> (Krohn 2000).

The love and approval she received from her grandmother, father and stepmother was tough love, contingent on performance. She gained it by eloquent preaching as an infant and right through growing up. Her skills were highly polished by her late teens, setting the scene for a stellar career in the media.

No doubt, Winfrey has trading intelligence. After all, she has negotiated spectacularly profitable network deals; however, her primary source of income derives from being the 'talent'. She began her other business ventures at a time when she was earning $125 million a year—the businesses were undoubtedly bank-rolled by her entertainment talent rather than the other way around.

But it was not only her skill that has led to success. Right at the core of who she is is the need to speak in order to gain love and approval, and what great approval she has received! She receives it on a daily basis through her guests and her loving audiences. She receives it through the money she is paid, the burgeoning success of her magazine and her book club. She is probably not in any danger of becoming bored or giving up anytime soon because speaking and gaining love through speaking are right at the centre of what she needs.

No doubt, Winfrey has trading intelligence.

References:

Krohn, K 2000, *Oprah Winfrey*, Lerner Publications Company, Minneapolis.

Wooten, SM 1999, *Oprah Winfrey: Talk Show Legend*, Enslow Publishers, New Jersey.

Chapter 19

John Sperling

Forbes information 2007
Rank: 799
Citizenship: United States
Wealth: US$1.2 billion
Industry: education

John Sperling is a true working-class hero. He attacked middle-class educational privilege unflaggingly for more than twenty years before he hit the money jackpot—not that he particularly set out to hit that jackpot; it was merely a by-product of having a profitable educational product.

Achievement

Sperling is the founder of and major shareholder in what is now the world's largest private university system with more than 150 000 students on sixty-seven campuses and in 118 learning centres. He is unusual in that he did not begin on his road to riches until the age of fifty-three, having been a university lecturer with a PhD for most of his working life. He developed market-oriented adult university programs. These programs were both vocational and efficient because they minimised study time and maximised outcomes.

Sperling's university employers would not allow him to deliver the course, despite it being of great benefit to working vocational students. So, he took his program out of the university and developed it into a for-profit program. But despite the market wanting the program, he was obstructed at every turn by the restrictive trade practices of the academic industry.

Academia didn't want to deliver such a program because of its natural aversion to vocations outside the academy. It also didn't want anyone else to deliver it for exactly the same reason. And, because such a course ran outside of its control it would provide alternative pathways for vocational learning, effectively breaking the higher education cartel that universities held. Alternative vocational-based study programs would allow potential students to bypass inefficient study within academia for targeted and efficient study elsewhere, thereby eroding its market share.

Like any cartel, obstruction was the universities' weapon and they used it very effectively. It took twenty years of ferocious effort outside the university before Sperling finally managed to expand his model beyond a few beleaguered campuses.

Sperling was a late-entry billionaire because he never intended to become one. He didn't even plan to be in business—that was an offshoot of his belief in the work he was doing and the need he saw for vocational training for working people. Unlike the other billionaires, he was first and foremost an inventor and product champion forced into what was, for him, the unnatural position of having to take his vision to the market because no-one else would. He passionately believed in what he had to offer and the benefits it had for working people. He says:

> I am an unintentional entrepreneur and an accidental
> CEO. The company I founded in 1972 with $26 000
> in hard-earned savings now has a market value close to
> $3 billion. This stroke of good fortune occurred after
> a largely misspent youth, dutiful but undistinguished
> military service, a graduate education that went on too
> long simply because I had nothing better to do, and a
> lackluster academic career (except for the effectiveness of
> my teaching) (Sperling 2000).

Up until he was fifty-three, Sperling worked with others to develop learning programs for school children, disadvantaged Hispanics, teachers, police and working people. These proved very popular and effective, delivering educational outcomes efficiently while allowing working people to continue working. When he tried to take the courses to the mainstream and make them degree courses, his proposal was rejected. He consulted a Vice President for Development at his university, who he reported as saying something like: 'Educational bureaucracies are dedicated to the status quo, and the only time they innovate is when they have to. The primary spur to innovation is financial necessity' (Sperling 2000). The desire to make his product available to the people who both needed and wanted it turned him into an accidental billionaire.

It was at this point Sperling began his career as an entrepreneur. He recognised that he had a good product and there was a strong market for it, and given his impoverished background and struggle to reach the position he had, he wanted to help similarly disadvantaged people rise above their backgrounds. The product was designed to enable working people to attain reputable degrees as quickly as full-time students.

In the early days, his business was fraught with constant fighting against entrenched educational practices. Regulation was used as a weapon to prevent change and competition. He migrated the program from college to college and state to state, under constant attack as colleges sought to maintain control of higher education.

Starting in California in 1976, Sperling moved operations to Arizona in 1979 where the regulation body was not quite so hostile. Even so, huge amounts of energy and resources were going into the battle to keep the business alive — there were always enough students, but resources were being diverted into defending the program from attacks by academic institutions and regulatory bodies. Sperling routinely worked seventy- to eighty-hour weeks. The resources used up in fighting the battle were huge. But Sperling did not give up. As the years went on, his fighting program became more sophisticated, so that by the time the company listed on the stock exchange it had a strong, national program in place to fight academic industry resistance.

Over twenty years, the company faced bankruptcy several times and had state and federal bodies change rules and generally be obstructive. This included other academic organisations feeding libellous reports to the media and encouraging the FBI to carry out punitive investigations.

Sperling admits having skills in education and politics, not business. Throughout the early growth of his company he has had a varying cast of CEOs and CFOs.

Gradually the company began to claw out a safe position but revenues remained flat. In 1993 it decided, firstly, to be more aggressive with profit targets, and then to float the company on Wall Street. This provided the discipline to grow to the extent that revenues increased from $1.3 million in 1990 to over $3 billion in 2000.

Sperling handed over control of the business but remained in active fight mode and product development. Sperling and his company embraced the discipline of quarterly reports and meeting analysts' expectations within a very narrow range. Growth had to occur and the constant wearing away at the educational cartel began to pay off. The business was gradually able to set up campuses across much of the US, and is now expanding internationally.

Development

Born in 1921, John Sperling was the last of five living children and one dead child, following two boys and two girls. He was born into very poor circumstances in a Missouri Ozark village. There was little food to put on the table and there was seldom any meat. They lived in a tiny two-bedroom house full of conflict. Everybody fought.

Sperling's father was an unemployed, violent drunk. He used to beat Sperling for no apparent reason until he was ten. Sperling threatened to kill his father in his sleep if he was ever beaten again. The beatings stopped. The whole family was relieved when the father died when Sperling was fifteen.

His mother was 'possessively loving' but not encouraging about school work and success. She was intrusive and domineering, demanding to know everything he did. Sperling learned to counter this by lying—a trait that he claims to have worked hard to overcome. His mother was never encouraging about his education—she was educated to third grade and considered it enough. While he claims he loved his mother totally, it was a love-hate relationship—Sperling told her what she wanted to hear while living his life as best he could.

She came from a hard Scottish Protestant background. Her father had been a prosperous farmer and cattle trader. What money came into the family was earned by his mother working menial jobs. Sperling speculates that he got his genes from his mother's side—he is small, and alive and well at eighty-six, whereas the rest of his siblings were large and have died. Given the years of strife that came about from conflicts in academic institutions, he also got her resilience and fight.

Given the Sperlings's poverty and poor diet, it is not surprising that he was sickly. He got most of the childhood diseases going around at the time. At seven he developed pneumonia, and he was chronically sick for a year. Prior to his illness he was a leader of a small pack of boys, full of adventure and bravado and relatively tough. Following his illness, he lost his place in the group, developed sensitivity to pain and lost his bravado. He became an outsider.

As if being away from school wasn't enough, he was moved from school to school, disrupting social groupings. He doesn't recall whether he dropped back a year in class.

While Sperling does not claim to have been dyslexic, he shows all the signs of being so. He found it difficult to learn to read and write, describing reading time as 'painful'. As with many bright dyslexics he compensated for a lack of reading skills by developing an exceptional memory.

Sperling talks about his son, Peter, as being dyslexic, but having a form of dyslexia that people grow out of. Given that Sperling went on to love reading and gain university degrees, it is likely that he had a similar form of dyslexia.

He can barely remember grade school, but unsurprisingly thought of himself as dumb. Undoubtedly others thought so too. He was bullied, and because of his fear of injury did not fight back, hence he developed a reputation for being a coward, which further isolated him. At high school he was the butt of jokes and the subject of taunts. He did poorly in most subjects, and became a loner. While his father was alive, Sperling was ashamed to bring friends home, which tended to isolate him even more.

Once Sperling's father died, he and his mother moved to Oregon. Circumstances improved a little and there was sufficient money for Sperling to have some decent clothes for the first time. The move was positive for Sperling, in that he was able to make some friends and date a few girls. He developed a strong friendship with a bigger boy who physically protected him.

When school ended Sperling was on his own again, working at delivery jobs at the end of the Depression. Sperling was also depressed. He considering himself both ugly and unintelligent and alone in the world without family support. He felt he had no prospect of improving his position.

His real education began when he joined the merchant marine in 1939. Unemployed and depressed in the seaport of Portland, Oregon, Sperling's best friend had gone into the Marine Academy. This route was blocked to Sperling because of his poor education, so he joined a maritime union and took the first job offered after sitting in the hiring hall for three weeks.

Onboard the ship there were well-stocked libraries and many well-educated men who would not have been there if not for the Depression. Sperling's fellow sailors introduced him to a reading culture. He also says that for him this was a time of political awakening and that life at sea was simplified. There were few choices available. By this time Sperling was obviously growing out of his childhood dyslexia and he began to read voraciously. Simplifying his life meant that he could at least in part recover from the mental and emotional trauma of his growing up. He also saw the world, which, along with daily interaction with educated men and his diet of books, expanded his perspective dramatically.

He left the merchant marine in 1941 and went to university to study for a pre-engineering program, achieving such good grades that he was offered a place at Berkeley University. World War II interrupted that path and he joined the Navy and then the Army Air Corps. All during training he continued to go to university, managing to finish a whole year.

On resuming his education at the end of the war, he was suddenly confronted with competition from a flood of tough middle-class men just returned from war. While being intellectually able, Sperling was intimidated and had an emotional crisis.

This proved to be a formative experience for Sperling. It was his first experience of how social class could limit or expand opportunities depending on the class one belongs to, and he resented it. These men took their future careers and professions for granted, whereas the future for Sperling was uncertain. He would have also been socially isolated, a lone working-class boy in a sea of middle-class privilege. This was quite a different situation to his most favourable learning conditions aboard ship where everyone was working class even if they had come from the middle class. Sperling was all at sea.

Despite having had good grades, competing in engineering against the confident sires of the middle class was too tough for him and he changed courses to study history. He got very sick and struggled through to complete his degree in history in 1948. In the meantime, Sperling had found a middle-class wife who nursed him but his sickness continued. The doctor found psychosomatic causes. He entered counselling, during which he realised that he was having problems being a working-class man in a middle-class world.

Like other billionaires in this book, problems at university were essentially social rather than intellectual. Sperling didn't drop out because he had no other options, but he did defect from his first choice.

Having achieved a history degree, he decided to go to Berkeley to study for a post graduate degree in psychology, but faced with a mountain of pre-requisites he reverted to history. In the process he slipped away from his middle-class wife. At Berkeley, Sperling passed his history exams with such distinction that he won a scholarship to study at Cambridge University, UK. He studied and gained a PhD, and along the way had many adventures.

A degree from a world-class foreign university was not enough to boost Sperling into a new socio-economic class. On returning to the US, he began a succession of boring academic jobs at minor universities, eventually ending up at San Jose University for twelve years, where he developed the learning principles upon which he would later base the University of Phoenix on.

He also married his second wife and had a son. Given Sperling's relationship with his mother, relationships with women were never going to be easy. And they weren't. He had two failed marriages, with a child from the second, Peter, later joining him to take up a senior position in Sperling's company.

He joined the teachers' union and soon became the local organiser, growing first his local membership base and later the state's, organising strikes and making demands. These were important times for developing the skills necessary to fight academic authority. Through his battles he became immune to criticism about what he was doing, especially from the university. He learned to battle on, no matter what legal or other attempts were made to shut him down. This toughness became very necessary for the protracted battle he had with academia in order to get his teaching methods recognised.

> He learned to battle on, no matter what legal or other attempts were made to shut him down.

And now that he is rich beyond what he could ever have imagined, he is actively involved in 'giving it back', including a project with George Soros to reverse some of the negative social impacts of drugs and overzealous drug enforcement.

Interpretation

There was never any shortage of adversity in Sperling's life. Right from the beginning he had to struggle. He was guaranteed to be an outsider by the multiple curses of an intrusive mother and an abusive, drunk father, a dysfunctional family, sickness and other schooling dislocations, and early dyslexia.

His success happened much later than it did for the other self-made billionaires because, unlike the other billionaires, he had no early seminal moments of approval to speed him on his way. No bolts of lightning out of the blue. His approval came much later, and in a piece-meal fashion. Approval was firstly for learning and companionship (in the merchant marine), then for teaching (under-privileged children and adults) and for beating the system that gave privilege to the middle classes (seaman's union and teacher's union). He is a working-class hero turned evangelical capitalist.

Sperling was brought up in the lower working classes or, more accurately, the struggling classes. It was a struggle for his mother to put even their modest roof over their heads and meagre food rations on the table. Life was a battle on all fronts for young Sperling. It was only when he joined the merchant marine and later as a university student that he came to believe that his position in life had a political element to it.

His time in the merchant marine also opened his eyes to how education could be used as a vehicle to leave the working classes. He did it, and he passionately believed that others could do it. This is why ultimately he went on to develop courses and teaching methods that were directly aimed at helping the working classes elevate themselves. This has rarely been a goal of universities or academics, so in addition to being an outsider to the academic world by birth and class, he was also an outsider by deeply held emotional commitment to helping working-class people raise their status. He could see what needed to be done but was always going to be at cross purposes with academia.

This is not to say that working-class people don't go to university; many do, and quite a few become academics. Academics may study or take a political position on class differences. They also teach working-class students, but it is rare that they actually get their hands dirty with vocational training—training designed specifically to efficiently impart skills for jobs as opposed to learning a body of knowledge. Some of the older, traditional vocational courses are exceptions; such courses are law, medicine and more recently engineering and architecture, although all of these tend to err on the academic side rather than the practical, relying on job placement to impart the true vocational skills.

As essentially an outsider to academia and never really signing on to the belief of education for education's sake, Sperling eschewed its conventional wisdom. By concentrating on making education useful, rather than the process of academia, he became a revolutionary, and was punished as such.

There were no particular early signs of his future wealth. This may explain why Sperling took so long to become a billionaire. He never set out to become rich or even to be in business. He was a teacher and political activist rather than an academic, who believed in his teaching product. He would have stayed in academia if he had been allowed to expand the market for his product there.

Sperling's fascination was with learning systems and educational outcomes. He developed this expertise over a long period of time and was frustrated in applying this knowledge to aid adults to gain an education. His orientation to adult learning was certainly affected by his own protracted and disjointed education.

The single thing that ensured his success was dogged persistence in struggle. Without his combative upbringing, the expectations of an outsider to go it alone, and wins in the teachers' unions, he wouldn't have had the skills, confidence and toughness to maintain his twenty-year struggle with academic bureaucracy. It is this—along with his intelligence, outsider status, active hostility towards class privilege and an unshakeable belief in the working classes being able to advance through education—that sustained him and made him persist for so long against such formidable opposition.

Sperling is not really a trader and there is no obvious trading history in his immediate family. He is a dogged product champion. Through tenacity and grit he succeeded in keeping his product and company limping along during the years until the company listed. It was the disciplines of the financial market and his professional managers under his influence that did the real money work. Sperling freely admits that his strengths are educational and political—he is a teacher and a (union) organiser, going head to head with authority.

The will to succeed was not only for the sake of success; it was also a class struggle. A David versus Goliath struggle. He says that 'the defenders of academic traditions were protecting undeserved middle-class entitlements' (Sperling 2000). He believes that his upbringing and his lack of awe for academia allowed him to persist.

His initial political position was socialist, but by the time he wrote his book he had become a dedicated capitalist; believing that positive changes mainly come about when there is a market need that people will pay for. In other words, a business opportunity.

He battled for everything he achieved. Along the way he had foes and friends, good fortune and misfortune. Born with a plastic spoon in his mouth, nothing was handed to Sperling, the outsider and working-class hero, on a plate.

References:

Sperling, J 2000, *Rebel With a Cause*, John Wiley & Sons, New York.

Part III

THE BIG PICTURE

Chapter 20

Finding the pattern

The main aim of this book is to attempt to identify patterns that lead people to extreme wealth. Are there experiences that self-made billionaires share? What key factor or factors set them on their paths? What drives them to their great success? In this chapter I am going to look at some of the common threads that emerged from the seventeen billionaires' summaries discussed in the previous chapters. These threads will then be considered in detail in later chapters. I'll also examine some of the factors that, contrary to popular belief, did not play a part in the success of these people.

Are seventeen self-made billionaires representative?

By stacking summaries of these seventeen billionaires end on end, a pattern is beginning to emerge. In revealing the pattern, it is important to see what is common between these billionaires. It is equally important to understand what is not shared.

In survey terms, seventeen self-made billionaires is a small sample. Self-made billionaires make up approximately half of the *Forbes* world's billionaires list, and these billionaires represent only a small proportion of those. I routinely carry out surveys of up to 2000 respondents and would have preferred to have been able to survey all of the billionaires on the *Forbes* world's billionaires list but that was impossible, simply because of the protective layers these people hide behind. To achieve even one interview would have been difficult; any more would be bordering on impossible.

Since a sample of one is not any basis for developing a general understanding, I was forced to fall back on another reputable research method — reviewing other peoples' research. Even so, the number of self-made billionaires covered by biographies and autobiographies is relatively scant compared to the total number of self-made billionaires. It is even more rare to find books that meet the additional criteria of covering the subject's early years in some detail and having some objectivity.

In addition, the subjects must be self-made, which means that they can't start in the family business or with a substantial family shareholding. A large number of billionaires were considered, but only seventeen met the four objective criteria of having a credible biography, having access to information covering their childhood, being self-made and being alive in 2007. The *Forbes* world's billionaires list helped identify the billionaires.

My selection is an eclectic mix to be sure, but that couldn't be helped. The billionaires are generally concentrated in either high-profile industries (media and entertainment) or have chosen to be high profile as part of either their marketing strategies or their personality. Gates, Ellison and Jobs all benefit hugely from being the best of enemies in public, conflict that generates media attention, while Branson has made a lifetime's work out of being a media junkie. Buffett, on the other hand, doesn't need publicity but likes to parade as the gruff sage of finance at his annual love-in. Obviously Lucas, Spielberg, Geffen and particularly Winfrey are rarely out of the news because they belong to the media and entertainment industries — they are the news!

Obviously media stars are written about because the subject's fame and notoriety is what sells books, newspapers and magazines. Fortunately a few of the more private billionaires have gained sufficient public attention to have biographies written about them, including Soros, Ecclestone, Icahn, Schwab, Kamprad, Lowy, Sperling and Lauren.

It would be tempting to believe from media coverage that self-made billionaires mainly come from the constantly evolving industries such as media, computing, software and finance. These industries get the lion's share of media attention. But the top ten industries for the self-made billionaires are retail, finance, technology, service, investments, oil/gas, real estate, diversified, manufacturing, media/entertainment. Anyone would think that media was the most important industry in the world given its huge capacity for self-promotion, yet it comes in at tenth place. Sperling is from such an unsexy industry, education, that he had to write his own book.

Yet even with the obvious media bias towards certain billionaires and industries, all the self-made billionaires in this book fit the pattern. It would be comforting to have one or two self-made billionaires from oil and gas or manufacturing to round out our industry coverage but that is not really necessary. Henry Ford (automotive manufacturing) and John D Rockefeller (oil and gas) don't meet the selection criteria of being alive in 2007, but their biographies indicate similar development patterns to the billionaires covered in this book.

The pattern had not been identified prior to assembling the billionaires' biographies for study, and these billionaires were chosen to meet the objective criteria outlined above, not to conform to the pattern. Yet all the billionaires covered in this book conform to the pattern. While it is not possible to say that all self-made billionaires fit the pattern developed from these seventeen self-made billionaires, a review of others who failed to meet the rigorous selection criteria for inclusion in this book also all fit the pattern. They include Ted Turner, Donald Trump, Sam Goldwyn, Walt Disney, JP Morgan and Sam Walton.

> All the self-made billionaires are different in detail but similar in general.

All the self-made billionaires are different in detail but similar in general. They fit the pattern! Not one deviates from the pattern in any substantive way. Neither their industry nor their media profile make a difference to the pattern. The indications are compelling.

What's out—class, luck, risk-taking and secret moves

Inherited billionaires are born with a silver spoon in their mouths, but these rich-by-birth individuals should not be confused with self-made billionaires. Self-made billionaires come from the full spectrum of classes, ranging in this sample from Gates, the son of privilege from upper-class Seattle, through the professional classes of Buffett, Branson, Schwab, Ellison and Spielberg, to the merchant class of Lucas, to the working-class origins of Jobs, to the migrant classes of Soros and Lowy, to the lower classes, those inner-urban strugglers Geffen, Lauren, Icahn and Ecclestone, and finally the rural dwellers—Kamprad, Sperling and Winfrey.

Lawyers and stockbroking families are well represented with Gates, Buffett, Schwab and Branson belonging to these. Both Soros and Icahn had lapsed lawyers for fathers, and a predilection for philosophy. Other professions are less well represented. Spielberg is the result of the unlikely coupling of an artist and an engineer, while Lucas, Lowy and Geffen come from small business families and Kamprad from both retail and farming in isolated Sweden. There is no discernible occupational pattern except, counter intuitively, business origins are not as well represented as might be expected and lawyers as fathers are over represented.

People often consider that fortunes are made through luck. Luck does play a large part as will be revealed in later chapters, but it is not the kind of luck that people think of as making fortunes. People think of luck as the lottery kind. But to win as much money as Gates has is so utterly improbable it is beyond impossible. He would have to win the lottery something like 11 000 times. The probability of winning the lottery once is huge, something like 20 million to one, twice becomes astronomical, and there probably aren't enough atoms in the earth to represent the probability of winning as much money as Gates has.

The other kind of luck people consider is the 'that person was just in the right place at the right time' kind of luck. It is true that Gates was in the right place at the right time. He and Jobs were right there at the beginning of personal computing—along with many thousands of other people, in an 'industry' made up of professionals, a slew of academics in places like Bell Laboratories and the Xerox Research Centre and a horde of boy wonder electronics enthusiasts all around the world. Tens of thousands of these electronics enthusiasts also subscribed to the very same edition of the magazine that Gates and Jobs bought that inspired him to build his first computer. This computer was little more than a box with flashing lights and switches: no screen, keyboard, mouse, disk drive or anything remotely like present-day computers, yet Gates and Jobs recognised it for what it was—the start of something big.

In fact, both Gates and Jobs benefited considerably from cast-off ideas from all around the emerging industry. While many people jumped on the bandwagon and amassed great wealth, only a few became self-made billionaires through their own enterprise. In Gates's case, Buffett is probably right in saying that Gates would have become a billionaire even if he had started by running a hot dog stand.

Of course there is some luck in all of this. Everyone has luck! Everyone has had the experience of being close to something or someone at the start of something big. The self-made billionaire's luck was that they had the right attributes to convert their circumstances into extreme wealth.

Paradoxically, much of their luck has come from limited opportunity and pain. They had to make the most of what they had because they had little to start with. All created something big from something small and unlikely. Ecclestone is responsible for turning club motor sport into the Formula One racing industry and Winfrey is an industry all by herself. Icahn, Soros and Buffett invented their own ways to trade and Lowy hitched a ride on the shopping mall boom, ultimately becoming a world leader. Even Branson, who hasn't really done anything new, pranked and grinned his way to a fortune, and to his credit started an airline that keeps on going.

People also consider that self-made billionaires are exceptional in their risk-taking ability. That is not true either. A normal person would freeze up if asked to make a decision the size a billionaire routinely takes. This is unsurprising—the quantum shift would be too large. It would have been too large for most of the billionaires too at one time!

None of the billionaires started out making decisions of this size. All started out making very small decisions, much smaller than many adults make on a day-to-day basis. The early Apple business was housed in a garage and only had to find money for a few tens of computers. The early Microsoft had very small overheads—two underpaid geeks in Gates and Allen. Gates originally thought that Microsoft would never get bigger than twenty people. Winfrey made very good wages and even when out in the cold, she had no dependants, family or staff and precious little in the way of financial overheads. The filmmakers Spielberg and Lucas managed large projects funded by other people's money, and they took a share of profits but not losses. Early on, Lowy and Kamprad built their business a shop at a time.

The size of decisions the billionaires made grew with their businesses. Certainly most of their businesses grew rapidly so they had to adapt quickly, but their success is fundamentally not based on risk-taking.

There is a school of thought that seems to indicate that there is a consistent set of secret moves that billionaires employ. Yet there is no discernible pattern of secret moves made by the billionaires. While there may be moves that can be learnt from every billionaire, the secret of secret moves is that there aren't any or, rather, every billionaire has a set of idiosyncratic secret moves that are all related to his or her personality. Doesn't everybody?

What's in—personality, outsiders, difference, direction and drive with a special mention to trading

If there are no secret moves and luck doesn't play a major part, then the only conclusion to be made is that self-made billionaires' extreme wealth comes about through how they think and behave; in other words, their personalities. But what sort of personality?

It is tempting to consider the classic psychology and business personality types, of which there are many. Is there a particular personality type for self-made billionaires?

Most are tough, but Winfrey projects warm, articulate caring, Lucas is nostalgic and does most of his work in isolation, while Lauren and Geffen are neurotic. Soros and Buffett are introverts while Branson and Winfrey are extroverts, and Gates is both an extrovert and introvert in turn. Many are tetchy. Some are gregarious, others are almost total isolates.

All are practical, but not remorselessly so and each of the billionaires have their flashes of inspiration, 'art' even. Even Buffett, whose trips to Paris involve hotel rooms and eating hamburgers rather than trips to the Louvre to visit the Mona Lisa, used his creativity to go against the traditional practices of the stock market. Gates imagined a computer industry and then set about making it. Naturally Lucas, Spielberg and Winfrey are more artistic than their fellows but they could not be considered artists with a capital A.

Despite not being artists in the traditional sense, all are creative in the biggest sense of the word. Most created something huge where there wasn't anything previously and made a fortune doing it. Even those who made money by moving money around did it creatively.

> Most created something huge where there wasn't anything previously and made a fortune doing it.

So how can they be creative but not artistic? How can they be creative and in business? How can they be creative and rich? These questions are redundant. For years there has been systematic bias by the arts industry to classify creativity and art as synonymous and to over emphasise the arts at the expense of business and other endeavours. Every newspaper and TV channel gives more coverage to arts people and arts business compared with businesspeople and business belonging to other industries.

Without denying the importance of artists, business and engineering creativity is more important. While we are culturally much the richer for

Picasso, Dali, Pollock, Hemmingway and Twain, we are even richer for Gates, Jobs and Ellison, not to mention all those faceless business and engineering types who gave us all those industrial products we depend on and take for granted. In addition to Ford, the man who gave us cars, in addition to the Wright brothers, those people who gave us cheap, safe international travel, as well as all the unsung geniuses that gave us countless thousands of day-to-day products. Cheap pantyhose, fabrics, lipstick, bottled water, soft drink, coffee and food on an industrial scale, bricks to build houses and machines to make the bricks. Sanitary products have been extremely liberating for women. Take away engineering, industry and business and you take away civilisation—we all go back to the caves.

Despite a plethora of books on personality and creativity, there is no real agreement on the relationship between the two or even what creativity is. For the purposes of this book, I will take creativity to mean the act of making something with new features. Everyone is creative in some way, but most people are involved in me-too creativity and this seems to be the main difference between artists and artisans.

It is clear when looking at the billionaires—and indeed the great artists, politicians and scientists—that they are different. Of course they are different as extreme achieving adults, but the key to understanding them is that they were different right from the beginning of their lives. They were different during their critical development years and it was being outsiders during those critical phases of their lives that ultimately led to their extreme achievement.

Every billionaire in this book was a misfit and an outsider when they were growing up. There was:

- The flight attendant's son who was expelled from a number of boarding schools, one for having sex with the headmaster's daughter, and who went on to found a successful airline (Branson).

- The dirt-poor rural African-American woman who went on to become the world's most recognised talk-show host (Winfrey).

- The dyslexic Swedish farm boy who went on to found one of the world's greatest furniture chains (Kamprad).

- The two Jewish boys unknown to each other, who, after struggling to survive in Nazi occupied Budapest, went on to huge success in international money trading and shopping centres in new countries (Soros and Lowy).

- The tetchy butt of bullying with no sporting ability who went on to found one of the greatest sporting franchises (Ecclestone).

- The gangly, uncoordinated, mid-western US small town boy who ran away from home and became a great investor (Buffett).

- The runty, unattractive outcast who went on to found a great fashion brand (Lauren).

- The dyslexic son of a lawyer who sustained his self esteem by playing golf and selling golf balls and who went on to found a great discount stockbroking house (Schwab).

- The fractious and unpopular son of a bullying seamstress with no acting ability who became a great entertainment entrepreneur (Geffen).

- The anxious small town Californian boy with the sick mother who developed one of the great entertainment franchises (Lucas).

- The adopted son of working-class parents who, after a period of severe personal hygiene lapses, ended up co-founding a great computer brand and later a revolution in portable music (Jobs).

- The super-bright, fractious, unpopular son of a lawyer who went on to found the world's greatest software house (Gates).

- The bullied son of a difficult and unlikely union between an artist and an itinerant computer engineer who became one of the most bankable film directors of the last forty years (Spielberg).

- The adopted, illegitimate son of a sickly mother and unknown father who spun his way to a fortune in computing software (Ellison).

- The gangly, unpopular child of dominating parents who became one of the world's greatest take-over merchants (Icahn).

- The sickly, impoverished rural boy with poor school learning who, in his 50s, went on to found the biggest private university network in the world (Sperling).

No-one would have picked these children out of their school class to be anything more than mediocre. Most would have been selected for failure yet they all triumphed in an incredibly dramatic manner. That their beginnings were all unlikely cannot be overlooked either.

They were and are all outsiders. A key to understanding their achievements is their difference, and outsiders are different! So extreme are conforming pressures on all children during childhood and adolescence that had they had a choice, they would have chosen to be similar to their peers. They had no choice, they had it forced on them.

Their difference explains the source of their creativity. Indeed it may be that much of what is called creativity is explained by difference. Artists, writers and other high achievers are both different and creative. Maybe difference explains much of creativity rather than the usual explanation of creativity explaining difference, or being unrelated characteristics dwelling in the same person.

However, neither being an outsider nor being different is enough to explain extreme wealth. There are untold millions of outsiders in the world, most of whom don't make the *Forbes* world's billionaires list. It is proposed that being an outsider and different are necessary but not sufficient conditions to achieve extreme wealth.

It is also clear by looking at the billionaires that they have direction; most had set their direction by the time they left school. Even Sperling, who didn't start his business until he was in his fifties, actually was set in his direction fairly much at the point he joined the merchant marine just out of school. He discovered self-improvement of the lower classes by education. His true direction was not business or wealth; that was an accidental direction forced on him when he was blocked by education hierarchies from pursuing his real direction. He didn't set out to be rich; he initially set out to improve his living standards and then those of the working class through education.

A few of the others took time to find their direction. Soros wanted to be a philosopher but couldn't break into the club, so reverted to the skills he learnt during the war—trading. Schwab had an off and on relationship with broking until he established his firm in his early thirties, but he was always going to be a broker. Ellison was a salesman looking for a product until he stumbled on databases. Lowy fairly rapidly moved from shopkeeper to shop owner to shopping-centre magnate on a huge scale, but whatever he did, it was always going to be about shops. Kamprad was always going to be a shopkeeper and mail-order seller.

From three years of age, Winfrey was going to be a preacher. Her church just turned out to be TV and her preaching secular. Gates was always going to play monopoly games on the world whether or not he went into computing, but computing gave him the extra social hook he needed at school. Jobs was drawn to electronics since that was just about the only club he belonged to. Lauren needed fashion to escape the drudgery of his life and Geffen need to be in show business but since he had no acting talent, went into the business part. Lucas and Spielberg both needed to indulge in their own particular brand of escapist movie making. Icahn had to get revenge on the privileged through warrior trading and Ecclestone needed the safety trading gave. Branson needed to trade to please his mother, something he did on a huge scale when he began an airline. Buffett had to trade to please his dad and he needed to pontificate to impress peers.

All the pivotal influences were in place early, even if all the pieces hadn't been assembled.

Maybe it is possible to become extremely rich by jumping from career to career, but these billionaires didn't. Even so, a few moved occupations but they stayed within their occupational theme of trading, selling or creating. Mostly they ploughed a deep, long and profitable furrow believing in the merit of what they were doing long before others did.

Even so, adding direction to difference is still not enough to explain this extreme wealth. What also stands out is that these are eighteen-hours-of-work-a-day folk, seven days a week, 365 days a year, year in year out. Perhaps this is a bit of an exaggeration, but not far from it. Gates had fifteen days off in six years. He didn't 'waste' much time on family or friends. Ecclestone tries to spend half a day a week with his family. Branson is never unavailable for a deal. Buffett never takes a sightseeing break on his international trips, his family was almost exclusively brought up by his wife, and even when he was working from home he hardly had any contact with his family. Lowy spends the whole of international trips immersed in business and never discusses or does anything personal. On their way up, none of the billionaires lay around under coconut trees, except Lucas on one of his fear of failure jaunts to Hawaii.

Obviously another key ingredient is drive. Not your average, common or garden variety drive, but over-drive, shading well into compulsion. This is drive well beyond the sort that comes from being enthusiastic about a new idea and seeing it through. It is a hunger that must be fed. Despite having $3.6 billon and being in his seventies Ecclestone has to keep going; there is no thought of retirement, he will feed his hunger until he drops. Of all of the billionaires, Lowy is the only one to identify his unsatisfiable hunger—derived from real hunger and fear from his life-threatening experiences with the Nazis.

It would be wrong to think that all the hunger is for money, or at least making money for its own sake. Soros is hungry to be a philanthropist. He may well have become the wealthiest man in the world by now if twenty years ago he hadn't started giving his money away to fund his program of philanthropy. Unlike Gates and Buffett, for whom their position on the world's billionaires list is a part of their buzz, Soros is not interested in the score. He is not in the competition to be the world's richest man.

Buffett, on the other hand, is in friendly competition with Gates, and is the second wealthiest man in the world partly because until very recently he never gave away any money, not even to support his local community. Buffett was driven to grow his capital just like his frugal ancestors — frugality is one of the things he received early approval for. Winfrey is driven to gain love through preaching; the money is incidental. Gates is driven to win his game of monopoly with the world and Ecclestone will never be safe enough.

Lauren still needs to hide behind fashion and Icahn needs to exact revenge on the privileged classes, even though he has joined them. And Geffen needs to win his deals, possibly to keep appeasing his dead mother. Lucas and Spielberg still need to film for the remembered emotional warmth it gives them.

The final element is trading. Excellence in any occupation requires skill and the highest level of skill is only achieved if there is an initial aptitude. Great doctors are not usually made from people who wanted to be lawyers nor chefs from motor mechanics or accountants from actors and vice versa. There has to be underlying material to work with. Trading excellence is no different.

Fame is not enough to gain wealth. There are many very famous people who have died poor — Van Gogh for example. His paintings now sell for millions but he died a pauper. He needed a good agent, and if he was operating today may well have been rich due to the trading abilities of his agent. Picasso, on the other hand, died extremely rich because, in addition to being a great artist, Picasso was also a great self-promoter and trader. He always made money. Geffen has become far richer through trading the talent of his stars than his stars ever did.

It is not just art that this applies to. When Amelia Earhart, the great female pre-World War II aviator, was lost in the Pacific Ocean in mysterious circumstances, she had only modest means despite being in the public eye for more than a decade. In fact, she had to complete her flight to stave off hard times and this cash imperative contributed to the fatal decision to fly when she did. Branson, however, is a trader and, while not making money from his adventuring, he uses it much more successfully as a contributor to his cash flows than Earhart did.

All human endeavour that requires mental processing requires intelligence. This book proposes that there is a form of intelligence that leads to trading and that trading excellence requires innate trading intelligence. It doesn't propose that trading can't be learned, just that the greatest traders are naturals. Chapter 25 discusses this in detail.

There is not doubt that the billionaires high up on the world's billionaires list are pre-eminent traders. Gates, Buffett, Ellison, Icahn, Soros and Geffen are all superb traders. But that is not all they are. They have other skills and attributes, but when it comes to trading they just can't help themselves, they have to do it! Soros is the most poignant example. Soros didn't actually want to be a trader, he wanted to be an academic philosopher, but with that door closed to him he fell back on one of his primary innate intelligences—trading. Even so, he was conflicted and suffered an emotional and philosophical crisis until he devised his philanthropy program and began giving money away. Philanthropy and philosophy derived directly from the strong emotional rewards he gained from his father before and during World War II in Budapest. Trading was important during those times too, but Soros was in crisis until he found a way to make all three activities work together.

Not all the billionaires trade as compulsively as others. In fact, it is probable that Winfrey has only slightly more trading intelligence than a reasonably normal, highly intelligent person. She has talent and is the product in an industry that pays outrageous sums of money for talent. The money she earns is related to how much money she makes for others. Spielberg and Lucas are also highly paid talent but it is no doubt that they are better-than-average traders.

The central proposition of this book is that all the billionaires are outsiders, and consequently they are different. This difference contributes to their finding a different direction and their obsessive drive. These factors, along with trading intelligence, are the main reasons leading to their extreme wealth. The following chapter discusses what an outsider is.

Chapter 21

Outsiders and their edge

Everyone has experienced what it is like to be an outsider. It is that uncomfortable feeling you get when you are in a group that you don't fit in with. It feels like being a judge at a Hells Angels barbecue, or a teetotaller at a wine tasting, or a drunk at a teetotallers gathering. Migrants are automatically outsiders, coming from outside as they do, but they can and frequently do adapt. Being an outsider in this sense is generally a temporary state and is fixed by leaving or adapting.

What is an outsider?

By the time most people have reached their thirties, they have begun to work out where they feel like an outsider and progressively edit their experiences so they rarely, if ever, find themselves in such uncomfortable situations. Most people manage their lives so well that they forget that there are other groups that they don't belong to, so they end up thinking that the world is just like their groups.

The term outsider used in this sense means something along the lines of a person who is outside of a group, such as an organisation or club, or from out of town. Used in this way it means nothing more than that the person is not a natural member. This is not the sense in which outsider is used in this book. Being an outsider is not a temporary state for the self-made billionaires!

Outsiders are people whose personality characteristics do not suit the norm and who can't easily find a place where they feel like they fit. It comes with an enduring sense of not belonging, even if everyone actually accepts them. There is always a feeling of discomfort with other people, distrust even. This is why Soros fires people when he thinks they are getting too close, why Lauren has few friends, why Geffen has such vitriolic feuds with erstwhile friends, why Lucas is becoming more and more isolated on his farm, and why Spielberg has become less and less likeable. Buffett was never comfortable with others and neither was Gates. Jobs and Buffett both seek guru status, but are not easily accessible.

Being an outsider has become an enduring personality characteristic for the self-made billionaires. It was hard-wired in while growing up, and while it may be modified with age and experience, it is a continuing personality trait. No matter what they do or how long they live or how much success they achieve, they never overcome the feeling of being outside, being different, not belonging, being a loner, of it being them against the world. Outsiders experience permanently what other people experience only occasionally.

Outsiders are the more interesting characters in fiction, such as the heroic lone rogue cop up against the equally 'heroic' lone serial killer — both are outsiders but operate on different sides of the law. The cop belongs to an organisation but is an outsider nonetheless. He is the rugged individualist standing alone against both the system and crime. Artists and writers are often portrayed as outsiders.

Businesspeople are not often considered outsiders, yet all the self-made billionaires in this book were outsiders at school and have remained outsiders throughout their lives. They are outsiders in the same sense that the heroic lone cop is an outsider — they also operate both within a system but stand outside it as rugged individualists. They make decisions that get the job done but pay only as much attention to making the system work as they have to. Every now and again, there is a novel about businesspeople, and inevitably the super achiever was the bright boy, an outsider in his youth and an outsider right through to the end. This phenomena has been spotted in literature but not generalised to real life billionaires, until now.

An insider is not the opposite of an outsider

I struggled for months to reconcile the terms insider and outsider, attempting vainly to make insider the opposite of outsider, but the terms just don't work together. This is because both terms have recognised meanings operating in different ways.

The term *insider* is not so much a personality characteristic as an indication of how strongly a person belongs to a particular group and how much influence they have in the group. An insider is usually taken to mean someone who is close to or at the nexus of power of the group. It does have as its opposite the meaning of *outsider* that relates to group membership.

But the term *outsider* generally refers to the characteristics of people rather than group membership. In other words, it is most commonly used to loosely describe people's personality characteristics or a set of behaviours. It is usually applied to people who don't quite behave in the way any 'normal' person would behave, normal being in relation to themselves and the groups they belong to rather than having an absolute definition. The term *insider* is not the opposite of this.

> But the term *outsider* generally refers to the characteristics of people rather than group membership.

When insider trading occurs it means someone who belongs to a particular group, say a stockbroking company or an investment bank, trades using information that is only available to someone who is inside the group. In addition, it usually implies that the insider is well inside, right near the centre of power, privy to very privileged information and in a position to know that he or she shouldn't be doing it. This information is not available to the ordinary worker in the organisation and certainly not to people outside the organisation. Paradoxically, it is most likely that it is outsiders (the personality type) operating as insiders (belonging to a group) who are the perpetrators of such trading because they are less bound by the system's rules.

Outsiders are easy to spot at school, but once people leave that artificial social hothouse, their world fractures and everyone goes their own way, which makes outsiders much harder to spot. Instead of there being only one or two or three groups to belong to, there are suddenly a huge number. There are university groups, jobs and careers of various sorts, social groups in the home town or broadly distributed across the nation or the world. A person can become a postman or a brain surgeon or a mother, belong to the local drawing club or car club or mountain climbing club or book club or the Hells Angels. As people get older, the number of groups they can belong to grows.

Every organisation has its own set of rules constructed by its members. Some may be rational and some not, some are written down and some are implicit, but they all have rules. Obviously the rules for joining and staying in the Hells Angels are different from those to join the local life drawing club and are somewhat more onerous. Even the people at the top of the group hierarchy have to obey the rules. If they stray too far they are demoted or ousted. The Hells Angels power struggles are often very violent. The disruptions to a socialite wife's hierarchy may not be as physically dangerous, but they can be very dramatic to the participants.

It is merely belonging to a group that makes a person an insider, and the closer that person gets to the power or the information nexus the more of an insider that person is.

An outsider can also be an insider

Paradoxically, outsiders can also be insiders. The Hells Angels are a particularly clear case of this. The Hells Angels are small groups of outsiders banded together for mutual benefit. It's the Hells Angels against the world, and sometimes even against other motorcycle groups. A senior member of the Hells Angels is an insider to the Hells Angels but would be considered an outsider by most people, even himself.

As people move away from such extreme groups, it becomes less obvious whether a particular group is dominated by outsiders or not. It is a fair bet that outsiders dominate all the extreme sporting groups. Sir Edmund Hillary was an insider to international mountain climbing but was also an outsider by nature. Amelia Earhart was similarly an insider to female adventuring aviation but also an outsider by nature. Elvis Presley and John Lennon were both outsiders, even though they belonged to groups.

This also applies to professional groups. Academic scientists are probably more a mix of outsiders than most professional groups, but may be more socially adapted than extreme sports clubs. Albert Einstein was very much an outsider to the scientific community until his theories were recognised. This recognition process took some fifteen years and only came about because of patronage from a recognised insider. Early on in his career, Einstein was so much an outsider and so poorly accepted within the international fraternity of scientists that without this patronage his groundbreaking theories would still be unknown. His personality never changed. His personality remained that of an outsider despite his colossal success and his later academic acceptance.

The self-made billionaires are all outsiders *and* insiders. Gates, Jobs and Ellison are now insiders to the computer industry but remain temperamentally outsiders. They are rugged individualists and loners. Like Einstein, they were not insiders when starting out. They came up with new ways of doing things—either technical or business innovations—and continue to do so, as Jobs has done recently with the iPod revolution. Winfrey was not a media insider when she started but is very much so now; however, she remains temperamentally an outsider. Geffen, Katzenberg and Spielberg are all entertainment insiders, banded together as a company to magnify their impact, but temperamentally they remain a company of outsiders.

The terms insider and outsider can become a bit mixed up. This can occur when people occasionally talk of people being outsiders to organisations but they never talk of insiders as being a personality trait—it is always a description of status within a group. To make this distinction clear throughout this book, the term outsider will only be used in the personality sense and never in relation to group membership. The term insider will be used only occasionally where it is appropriate and only in relation to group membership.

Outsiders, adapted outsiders and the socialised

Lone heroes may be romantic in fiction or in the newspapers but they are often painful to be close to. However, most forms of success are social in that the success depends on interactions between people. Business is primarily social, club membership is social and recognition in any form is social. Outsiders can and must adapt if they are to have any success.

The seemingly banal saying 'If a tree falls in the forest and there is nobody around does it make a sound?' actually applies more to social situations than physical ones. If someone in the know hadn't heard Einstein, no-one would have recognised the greatness of his work and the world would be all the poorer. While Einstein was an outsider, he was able to adapt just enough to the rules of the scientific fraternity to at least convince one insider to champion his work. As he became more famous and influential, he adapted some more. Equally the nature of the group also adapted to accept him some more, but even in the field of science he was never fully personally accepted, even though eventually his theories were. Actually, he was more loved by the public than by the scientific community. He has come to represent the archetypal scientist in the public's mind, having been voted one of the most popular public figures in the US during the 1940s.

Another example is a New Zealand farmer who was reputed to have flown before the Wright Brothers did. He did it alone and the event went unphotographed. Since he didn't have an insider to support him it might as well not have happened. In fact, as far as most of the world is concerned, it didn't. There must be countless such outsiders with brilliant ideas or who carried out heroic deeds who haven't been recognised. Inventors are in a class all on their own for coming up with brilliant ideas and failing to find a market. They are often simply not socialised enough to cut through.

> Children who are fully socialised generally have an easier time finding a place to fit in than outsiders do.

The job of schools and parents is to impart life skills on their developing charges. The major skills are social—how to behave in normal society. By the time children leave school they are very much hard-wired with their base set of life skills. Children who are fully socialised generally have an easier time finding a place to fit in than outsiders do. They know how the game of life is played and they generally have a good idea of what is expected of them. They have usually been inculcated with what society expects of them and what to expect from society. They still have to adapt to new situations, such as university, a job or marriage, but the adaptation process is generally smoother than the trial-and-error trip an outsider takes.

Fully socialised children have the extended networks and skills to fit in and, since they have strong local networks, they are less likely to move away from the area they were brought up in. They make their transitions so naturally that they don't even know how they did it most of the time. Even when they are reluctantly forced to move from their home towns and become temporary outsiders, they adapt relatively quickly via sports groups, professional associates and work groups. They know exactly what to do and rapidly become insiders. As a rule they don't entirely sever connections with old school friends and relatives.

Outsiders, on the other hand, are much more poorly socialised. They have fewer plug-and-play social skills than others and this causes them problems, especially when they move. Gates experienced this when he moved to Harvard, as did Jobs, Ellison and Geffen when they moved to their universities. All experienced social isolation and fled. In addition, all felt alienated by the learning process and as a result believed it was of little relevance. They couldn't see a future for themselves as academics or easily fitting into someone else's hierarchy after study. Buffett persisted with his studies because he recognised the utility of what he was learning while Schwab recognised it as the barrier to entry he had to cross. Soros and Icahn were both miserable at university but persisted anyway.

Indeed, outsiders are more likely than others to move or be migrants because they have less holding them back, but when they get to their new place they also have less ability to integrate. Engrossing themselves in some personally meaningful activity, such as work, is a tried-and-true solution and all the billionaires did this.

Being in a new situation deeply disconcerted these and the other outsiders and they very rapidly fell back on their salvation path rather than venture into entirely uncharted waters. In every case they were sufficiently socialised to function in their chosen fields at the level at which they started. For example, early computing was made up of a loose collection of enthusiastic outsiders at the time Gates, Ellison and Jobs began work in that area. They looked and acted the part — but today they would probably find it hard to get a job in their own companies!

This is especially so of Jobs, whose landing a job at Atari was something only slightly more probable than being struck by lightning twice. He was a smelly, dishevelled, bare-foot university dropout who needed Wozniak's help to do his job. Not only was he given a job, but he was given the keys to the building so he could work at night and not disgust his fellow workers. The man who employed him was probably an outsider too! Jobs adapted a bit when he was involved in the early Apple company but he was such an arrogant, interfering know-all that he was eventually fired from the company he co-founded. Since this most public of humiliations and years in Apple purgatory, he has returned to Apple as CEO and by all accounts has adapted to that role rather well. But don't be fooled by his cool appearance, wealth and guru status — Jobs is still an outsider and he took a very long, painful time to adapt his persona to become the man he appears to be today.

Gates is also an outsider, but his adaptation process was faster than that of Jobs. Once clear of the social stress of Harvard, he rapidly defaulted to his salvation path with Allen. Gates had a clear objective, which was to beat the world at his particular game, and since he was a game player, he knew that he had to play by just enough of society's rules to enter and stay in the game. He also knew he had to play fast and hard because other geeks were breathing down his neck. While at school he looked sufficiently like a juvenile geek computer/business nerd to convince a company to give his group unlimited computing time. He looked sufficiently like a geek computer nerd and hard-nosed businessman to convince IBM to give Microsoft that key very first contract. Certainly his mother's boardroom standing bolstered his credibility but that is part of the game. Gates has continued to adapt. Over time he has become a computing poster boy, a publicly acclaimed senior businessman of global standing and now a world-scale philanthropist. But don't be fooled—under his veneer of acceptability he is still a moderately adapted outsider.

Unlike fully socialised people, the self-made billionaires have not pulled through any substantial school friendships into their later adulthood. Gates began with Allen, but Allen departed from any hands-on association with Microsoft over twenty years ago, prior to its listing on the stock exchange. Jobs and Wozniak went their own separate ways and Ellison's early partner died. There are no evident enduring early relationships with the others.

The billionaires now socialise as a loose confederation of extremely rich insiders made up of outsiders. Gates and Buffett play bridge against each other. They indulge in a friendly competition to get to the top of the *Forbes* world's billionaires list, and they show and admire each other their works. Like Gates and Buffett, Soros and Sperling have joined forces on philanthropy projects. Lucas and Spielberg have worked together on projects, as have Winfrey and Spielberg. Geffen and Spielberg collaborate, too. Jobs and Ellison have their own rich adoptees' club.

Others are still isolated, even at this level. Ecclestone is so business focused he has no time for people outside his business sphere. But he probably has as many friends as he wants and does just what he wants with them—business. Branson, at the epicentre of his own media frenzy, obviously makes many other rich people very uncomfortable, so he is surrounded publicly by paid models and flight attendants and in private by fellow media stars, also refugees from public attention. Lauren and Icahn are reported to have no close friends. Lowy is completely outside the US billionaire circuit so he is not connected publicly, at least with the US billionaires, but he has many rich associates in Europe. Schwab makes loose match-long connections through golf. Kamprad has only his IKEA family. It is hard to ascertain how many friends Winfrey has from the spray of showbiz disinformation surrounding her.

Many people are naturally inclined to believe that anyone who is rich and powerful is also 'good' until proven otherwise, and even if they have a fall from grace it is usually only temporary. Consequently, there is a natural tendency for the rich to be lionised in the media. They are made to appear more socialised and less as outsiders than they actually are. The latter being easy because they actually have moved the definitions of industry expectations and behaviour in their direction simply by the gravity of their achievements.

Through a process of ageing and experience, they have adapted to become as socialised as they need to be, but not so socialised that it interferes with their ability to do what they do. But it is only by looking at how people behave towards people in their power that makes it possible to get a true sense of their level of socialising. If you look behind the facade of the billionaires' public image, poorly socialised behaviour is frequently evident. Gates is reported to be fractious and bullying to his own staff. Buffett is aloof. Soros fires staff out of hand, simply because he has seen too much of them. Branson and Ecclestone nuke staff through others. Ecclestone and Geffen bear venomous grudges and Geffen disables people with his voice. Lauren plays staff off against each other. Lowy and Kamprad demand superhuman efforts. Spielberg has become cold and Lucas almost a hermit on his isolated ranch in California.

Little is known about Winfrey. Apparently blessed with much more in the way of social skills than the men, she may actually be what she appears to be, a personable outsider.

Of course, one should be slightly sympathetic to the plight of the super rich. With wealth they have become super attractive. They are often surrounded by sycophants and targeted by gold diggers. Geffen has suffered this particularly. He knew when he was young that he was feared and loathed. Now he is older, nothing really has changed except for his wealth. Yet now people want to be his friend. He is deeply suspicious that people only want him for his money and he is probably right. The other billionaires all have similar problems.

The biographical information suggests very strongly that these billionaires left school as outsiders and that they have remained outsiders the whole of their adult lives. It's reasonable to assume that being an outsider persists through life because brain development, and hence personality formation, is largely complete by the time a person reaches adulthood. But since brain development does not entirely stop at adulthood, adult humans can adapt to their environments as they age and this is exactly what seems to have happened. These billionaires have become adapted outsiders—they have become semi-socialised. Some are possibly less adapted than others but all have adapted; however, all remain essentially outsiders.

I had the opportunity to discuss the topic of this book with a very rich New Zealand businessman who I met with to discuss an entirely different business matter. New Zealand is a tiny nation at the far end of the earth and is curious for punching well above its weight in the number of super rich it produces per capita. I was expecting some comment about the term 'outsider' but upon seeing a draft copy of the book cover he made no comment. When he was asked about the appropriateness of the term he merely shrugged and said, 'Of course they are. I play golf with three of them'. Perhaps this is not rigorous scientific proof but it is nevertheless compellingly indicative.

Difficulties in spotting outsiders

Almost everyone belongs to a group, some to many. Most can quickly spot people who are not of their group. A rich socialite wife can spot a professional woman at a gala function and vice versa, and they can both spot a working-class woman. It is easy to differentiate a military man from a businessman even if they are both in casual clothes. Railway enthusiasts can see hot rodders are not like them, despite having the same amount of ingrained grease on their hands.

We believe that we can tell the difference between an artist and an engineer. Flight attendants can apparently tell a rich man from an expense account flunky in first class by the shoes and watch. But these visual cues can lead to incorrect conclusions. The air hostess would mistake Icahn for a flunky because of his shabby clothes and shambling manner. Icahn wouldn't care—his wealth is predicated on being seen to not be an insider and being consistently underestimated. Billionaires, given their wealth and power, can sometimes get away with not looking like what we think they should, but most other people cannot.

Many social rules are set up to identify who belongs to a group and who does not. Many religions and ethnic groups have practices that easily identify people. Such things may include where they buy food, what they eat and how it is prepared. WASP high society has an arcane set of rules associated with using cutlery that differentiates those who belong from those who don't. This is all about group identity, and the adherence or otherwise to these rules can make it apparent who is part of a group.

Many outsiders, having experienced the pain associated with being noticed through their critical development years, tend to keep to themselves and take up isolated occupations. Many others need to make their way in organisations or groups, so are forced to adopt the manners of the groups they belong to. Like Lauren, they will adopt camouflage for protection and benefit until they get to the top and, like Lauren, will often revert to their true type. It may be a long, slow process full of mistakes and pain, but even outsiders can adapt, and as they adapt they become harder to spot. Socialite mothers, professional women, Hells Angels and sportspeople will easily spot who doesn't belong to their group but they often won't spot the outsiders in their own groups.

People expect others to look and behave according to group norms and will punish them with social isolation if they don't. Being recognised as an outsider is almost a guarantee of isolation and humiliation unless the personality edges can be smoothed and an effective disguise adopted.

Artists need to wear their flamboyance on the outside. Indeed they need to be seen to be outsiders even if they aren't. Dentists need to be much more conservative. Salvador Dali, the extremely flamboyant Spanish artist, sported an outrageous moustache with waxed tips that curled up, wore bow ties, used a silver-topped cane, pronounced gobbledygook in public and scandalously had nude models prancing around his exhibit at the 1939 World's Fair in New York. A local dentist may get away with a bow tie, but is unlikely to get any closer to adopting Salvador Dali's manners without risking going out of business. The dentist certainly wouldn't get away with nude models in the surgery nor having too much of Dali's unsettling art on the walls. Dali's image required him to be outrageous—he would have failed in the market if he behaved as a dentist does. The dentist may be an outsider with Dali inclinations but would lose customers if too much of his inner Dali crept into view.

Businesspeople also need to conform, or rather need to be seen to conform. An expensive suit, shirt with cufflinks and a watch can be an effective disguise. I have met many adapted outsiders in senior positions in business who are testament to this. Indeed, there seems to be a concentration of them at the top. They adopt the expected mannerisms at least when things are running smoothly, although their difference often peeks through. But the disguise can get a bit frayed when the chips are down and big decisions need to be made in a hurry.

School is probably the only time in our lives when we are forced to rub shoulders with everybody, but it can still be difficult to spot the outsiders at school. Some can look like they fit, especially if they are among the sporting elite. Many of the remaining outsiders become invisible; people tend not to notice them and, even if noticed, people tend to discount them as irrelevant, as indeed they are to the social pecking order at school. This natural process means that outsiders often disappear from view. Lauren did it, eventually resurfacing like a fashionable phoenix rising from the ashes. Like Geffen and Ellison, outsiders tend not to be in the school yearbook. They are also the ones whose faces and names won't be remembered at school reunions. Or, if they are remembered, they can be the ones like Lucas and Buffett who hung around the fringe of a number of groups but never quite belonged to any.

This doesn't mean that the outsiders have really disappeared; some might, but others, like these billionaires, go on to do really unusual things. Outsiders John Lennon and Elvis Presley became internationally loved pop singers, very much in the public's eye. Some make huge amounts of money, though many don't.

Most self-made billionaires remain secret and functionally invisible to society at large, even if they run high profile operations. Take, for example, Chaleo Yoovidhya (Thai) and Dietrich Mateschitz (Austrian). These two men own Red Bull, the international caffeinated soft drink franchise, along with Red Bull racing and the Red Bull air race sporting franchise. They keep their names out of the limelight and it is almost impossible to find out anything insightful about them.

There are countless experiments in psychology in which attractive people are rated better than unattractive people, deemed to have higher intelligence, better morals and be better companions. Tall men are attributed as being authoritative. This is the reason why news anchors tend to be apparently tall, attractive males, irrespective of their other qualities. Elite sportspeople will be seen as highly moral even if they really have the morals of an alley cat.

Being rich makes a person appear much more attractive, intelligent, moral and likeable than they actually are, hence self-made billionaires are not usually considered to be outsiders. This is one of the reasons it has taken so long for the outsider phenomenon to be discovered.

> The billionaires' success is predicated on them being outsiders and making their own way, irrespective of prevailing opinion.

The billionaires' success is predicated on them being outsiders and making their own way, irrespective of prevailing opinion. Buffet is a stark example of this. He went against all his frugal instincts to buy a plane just so he wouldn't be given tips by financial insiders and others at airports. He may seek information but never investment advice. All the others are rugged individuals in their own industries. Gates and Microsoft may not be the first to develop software but he very much set his own agenda about how Microsoft will proceed.

The self-made billionaires aren't alone. Outsiders are everywhere. In order to survive, most have adapted and become invisible. Next I'm going to look at the particular ways outsiders vary from everyone else.

Outsiders are different

As discussed earlier, success is personality driven and the main personality characteristic common to all the billionaires is that they are all outsiders. The billionaires are variously prickly, isolated, gregarious, introverted, extroverted, party animals, compassionate, ruthless, moral, amoral, emotional, rational, friendly, confiding, secretive, and pugnacious.

Outsiders are different from others. As will be discussed in greater detail in chapter 22, the process started with their biology, being too bright or small or tall or dyslexic or sickly or ugly or just plain fractious or any number of other things. It was enhanced by difficult home lives and by systematic ostracism or bullying at school, sometimes compounded by geographic and other dislocations. They started school a bit different from their peers and as time went on, particularly during those critical teenage years, the differences were exacerbated.

Denied a place in the mainstream, the billionaires were pushed to the outside. Without being given a life, they had to invent their own life. They couldn't adapt sufficiently to find an acceptable place in the pecking order, and since they had to be somewhere doing something they had to invent a life to fill in the time. They did what they had to in terms of officially sanctioned activities—some they liked (such as Winfrey and Icahn enjoying school work), some they didn't like (Ellison, Lauren, Lucas, Branson, Spielberg and Sperling doing school work). None enjoyed the officially sanctioned sporting activities; most, like Gates and Jobs loathed it. The official activities were character building but in most cases for these billionaires the character it was building was anti-authority. This in itself would begin to create a schism between the developing billionaires and others.

Outsiders behave differently

Outside of official school activities, the young billionaires became increasingly isolated. Other students were bouncing balls, skipping ropes, talking about boyfriends and girlfriends, discussing the latest pop phenomenon, going to the local cinema in groups or the local teenage hangout and generally doing what children and teenagers do. Irrespective of the specific activity, what they were really doing was socialising themselves and their peers. They were adopting the dominant culture and developing implicit and explicit rules of belonging.

The billionaires didn't belong to the mainstream. If they belonged anywhere it was to a loose affiliation of similarly afflicted outsiders who were also inventing their own lives. They had time on their hands and they had to fill it with something, and in the absence of conventional social forces they filled it with whatever was available that took their fancy.

If outsiders are lucky and don't make too many mistakes, they make it safely into adulthood. But they frequently operate without a compass in uncharted waters, so the possibility of mistakes is high.

Luckily for them, our seventeen billionaires did not become delinquent. Although they had their scrapes, these billionaires avoided being so antisocial that they would be later disabled in public life. Buffett ran away from home; Winfrey also ran away from home, became pregnant and had a premature baby. Geffen and Jobs truanted and Gates biased the school computer to put him in a class with more girls than boys

—and still failed to get a girlfriend. Branson had sex with his headmaster's daughter and was expelled from school and then had his problems with Her Majesty's Customs. A criminal record would have severely damaged his airline business, making it almost impossible for Virgin Atlantic to fly into the US. On a more trivial level, it would have destroyed his chances of becoming Sir Richard Branson. Countless others who may have made it into this book slipped and disqualified themselves early.

Simply by doing different things to the mainstream, the outsiders began to see the world differently, began to do different things and this process built on itself.

Outsiders see the world differently

Excluded from mainstream society and thus from group think, the outsiders did what they could within the boundaries of what was available. They became seekers, looking for things to do that suited their personalities.

Buffett was always fascinated with numbers, counting and stock prices. Intermittently rewarded by his father, this developed into a fully-fledged obsession with the numbers of business. Winfrey was fascinated with reading and preaching, Gates with games and computing, Jobs with electronics and the supply of electronic components, Lauren with fashion, Icahn and Soros with philosophy. Lucas, Spielberg, Gates and Jobs were fascinated with science fiction, the former two extending the fantasy via film, while the latter two made some of it real through personal computing. Ellison and Jobs spun stories to their outsider buddies. Branson, Buffett, Schwab, Kamprad, Geffen, Gates and Ecclestone all started businesses or traded well before they left school. These activities were not mainstream!

They all did what they could do to fill in the time, to keep themselves interested and to give themselves a tiny place to belong. It wasn't what most of their peers were doing. The young billionaires understood the basic social rules, but the more subtle rules were not ingrained or hard-wired into their brains as they are with highly socialised people. They had been forced to stand aside for that part of the normal development cycle of children. But these are bright people. They could see they didn't fit and ultimately worked out in which ways they needed to appear to fit and which ways they didn't. Unlike highly socialised people, at some point they had to think about the rules and then decide which ones to adopt and which ones not to.

For example, it is certain that Buffett does not observe the complex dining rules required in upper class society. He will certainly know they exist, but will have dismissed them in a nanosecond as being trivial and of no advantage to him. To him, there is no material consequence in appearing uncultured. Money keeps coming in and he can fill stadiums for his annual talk fest. He would be quite happy to sip his raspberry cola from a glass while others drink expensive champagne from crystal flutes. But the rules are not trivial to the society matrons. They put a great deal of store in such rules because they clearly show who belongs to their group and who doesn't. So ingrained or hard-wired are these rules that they are seen as almost god-given rather than just social conventions. Buffett couldn't care less—he is his own group of one and that is enough.

This example of manners may seem trivial, but examples like this and myriad others are core differences between outsiders and the rest of society, and the self-made billionaires in particular. Many of the ways billionaires behave had to be adapted to suit society where it was necessary and not where it isn't. Since they had fewer and different interactions when growing up, their social skills are often lacking. This is bad if you place a lot of importance on manners and convention, but good if you value originality and irrelevant if you are super rich.

As they grew up separated from and generally reviled by their peers they developed hard-wired ways of behaving that were idiosyncratic. They also developed different ways of thinking because they often had some completely different intellectual inputs from the norm. They became different. By the time they left school they thought and behaved differently to people in the mainstream.

People who are fully socialised, like the society matron, can become entirely rule bound. Good manners are conventions, pointing or not pointing is a convention. Helping your adult children or siblings is a convention. Declaring your intentions in a negotiation is a convention, as is keeping your word. Being a nice person on a company board is a convention, one that Icahn fully exploited—unsettling his opposing negotiators by being both unpleasant and upredictable.

A key difference is that outsiders in general and these billionaires in particular became rugged individualists. They learned over time that most of what goes on in society is because of made up rules and many of the rules are completely arbitrary. They observe the rules if they must but may choose to operate outside them if they are inconvenient. This has worked well for all of the billionaires. Gates and Ellison easily blindside opponents and Buffett simply doesn't take any notice of insider knowledge. Kamprad and Lowy simply keep going with sheer doggedness as if their lives depend on it, never allowing opposition to stand in their way. Neither Geffen nor Ecclestone are bothered by what others would call gentlemen's agreements. Soros understands that money and the whole international monetary system is just a convention, so he is willing to distort the rules and invent new products. Different behaviour has been beneficial to the billionaires because it often gives an edge. Blindsiding the opposition or surprising allies can be very advantageous.

It would be a mistake to imagine that all of their differences are rational and a process of choice. Much of their different behaviour has been hard-wired through development. They are lucky that their hard-wired behaviour wasn't so bizarre and intractable that they couldn't function in society.

As children and adolescents, they had filled their time doing different things compared with others, so the billionaires also know different things. Their influences are different and consequently they have a strangely eclectic view of the world. They accept as normal what other more socialised people would think was strange, obscure or irrelevant. They eschew group think because they can clearly see that is what it is—they became strong individualists. Even if they came from the same town, the billionaires would seem to have come from somewhere entirely different, almost from another planet.

Speaking of other planets, sci-fi and fantasy certainly played a part in the early lives of the male science buffs. These two forms of fiction have the ingredients that an outsider needs. They have the rugged individualist (outsider) who possesses secret powers or knowledge up against some hidden threat that only he or she can solve. Usually the hero comes up against a misguided authority that is either the problem or obstructs the solution. The hero triumphs over all danger through almost superhuman effort and intellectual cleverness, while at the same time having the satisfaction of both saving the establishment and showing it up as inadequate. The outsider conquers all. The hero may have a small group of outsider followers or may be entirely alone.

The relatively recent hit franchise of Harry Potter follows this model exactly, and has made the author JK Rowling a billionaire. Her story very cleverly appeals to outsider children in particular, but also draws in other more conventional children who suffer the arbitrarily applied authority of school. They love Harry sticking it up the school teachers and the bad teachers getting their comeuppance—something they can't do but at least Harry does as their proxy.

Back when the billionaires were growing up, fantasy fiction such as Harry Potter was a less dominant genre than it is now. Science-based fiction was much more popular. It had rockets going all over space with faster-than-light drives. Dr Spock, Captain Kirk and the rest of the Enterprise crew said, 'Beam me up Scotty' in every episode of *Star Trek*. The impossible was done routinely. All around were bits and pieces of equipment that did amazing things; the equipment had flashing lights, tape drives, buttons, switches and screens. They were control systems, and even if they weren't called computers, that's what they were.

These TV shows were in mass circulation, as were movies and serials such as *Flash Gordon*. The real buffs devoured comics and countless sci-fi books. The tradition began with Jules Verne and HG Wells in the late nineteenth century but exploded in influence and circulation from the 1920s. It was technology-based with the rugged outsider saving the day. The hero may even have been a science geek. Adventure appealed to a fairly broad base, but that combined with technology and some big, strange ideas appealed to science and technology buffs.

While there are no figures on who the sci-fi audience is, it is generally accepted that they are usually young males with a science or technology bent, and it is a fair bet that there are a large proportion of outsiders in that following.

Perhaps the seminal moment in personal computing happened when *Popular Electronics* published an edition in 1975 with a picture of a crude, build-your-own computer on the front cover. Millions of people passed that edition as it sat on newsstands, but it was a call to action for the tens of thousands of boys who were both sci-fi and electronic buffs. They recognised it for what it was. Rather than being a crude box of bits, the future had arrived! Here was a way to build what they had always coveted, a computer. Gates and Allen, Jobs and Wozniak and undoubtedly Ellison's partner, Miner, were strongly influenced by this event. While it is not recorded, undoubtedly thousands of boys and a few men built a copy of this early computer, and a few may even have taken it a bit further. From sci-fi they had already seen that the future was full of computers—the race was on to make the future happen!

We all know who won that race. It is interesting to note that it was won by outsiders to the main outsider group. Technical geeks don't usually have much business sense but, strictly speaking, Gates and Jobs weren't technical geeks. They were refugees from mainstream society who had gained serendipitous membership of the tech-geek world. Unlike the other geeks, these two were mainly game players and traders who sought refuge with the geeks. They had a double dose of outsider's edge. An unusual combination of skills and ideas won the day. Ellison, by joining with Miner, achieved the same as a team.

Science fiction was brimful of other ideas too. Another key element was different life forms (aliens) and transformation of humans—obviously the process of Scotty beaming people up involved a complex matter transformation. It is a fair bet that the scientists involved in bio-engineering and genetics have a strong grounding in sci-fi.

Enough of the technology of sci-fi of old has come to fruition, which makes technology-based sci-fi less appealing. It has been overrun by fantasy—maybe the outsiders of the future will put metaphysics on the map. Outsiders now haunt curious corners of the internet and play computer games. Outsiders will ensure that strange things will continue to be created. This is where many new billionaires will see the future and then make it real.

It is now a brave new world for outsiders. The world has become much more complex than it was even when Gates and Jobs were growing up in the 1950s, 1960s and 1970s. The revolution brought about by personal computing and communications means the information world has become much more diverse than at any time in history. There are incredible opportunities for new products, such as YouTube. These opportunities exist not only in cyberspace but in conventional products and brands as well. Red Bull, for example, is really an older product re-branded and hyper marketed. It is the outsiders who will spot these new opportunities.

There has been a long history of people analysing how rich people made their money, with the hope of emulating their 'secret moves' to become wealthy. The bad news is that there are no secret moves that can be copied slavishly. Each billionaire is different from the other and from everyone else. It was their being different that made the difference. The good news about this is that opportunity is part of the inherent capability and creativity of the individual.

Knowing different things is good because it often gives an edge. It may not be obvious to people in school when the emphasis is on fitting in and knowing the same stuff as everybody else, but life isn't modelled on school. Life outside school is a free-for-all and there is no telling when and where non-curriculum knowledge will be handy if not critical. As outsiders, all of the billionaires had substantial bodies of knowledge their peers didn't when they left school. They also had different skills.

This is one of the reasons migrants can do well in business. In addition to the necessity of finding something to do and being closed out of conventional occupations by the incumbent society, migrants see things differently to the surrounding socialised society and see opportunities where most people don't. In a sense, the billionaires are almost migrants of the mind.

There needs to be a special mention of creativity. Creativity exists in every field. Dentists, long held to be the most boring of the medical fraternity, are constantly creating new processes. Architects are considered creative but engineers rarely, despite some of the loveliest structures in the world being created by engineers. Few of the architectural flights of fancy would even stand up without engineering innovations.

Businesspeople often eschew being called creative, as creativity is used as a pejorative term in business, like 'creative accounting' being a euphemism for borderline fraud. Everyone is creative to some degree, and the billionaires are creative in the extreme.

The billionaires were all wildcards when it came to career choices. While their peers marched off to do more or less conventional things, there was no conventional place for them. They had to create their own place and, being rugged individualists, that is exactly what they did. But before they did that they had to have direction.

> Everyone is creative to some degree, and the billionaires are creative in the extreme.

Direction is critical

Difference is all very well, but it may be merely entertaining or painful unless it actually leads somewhere. We all know people that have changed course when studying at university, hopped around in their careers, been a social worker one year, a poet another and a shrimp boat captain the next. It may be very romantic but it is hard to get ahead that way and difficult to become a billionaire. Sperling makes a lie of that proposition with his seminal foray in the merchant marine and near lifetime career in academia, finally setting out on his business in his fifties. There is hope for all you career butterflies out there; not much, but a little.

All the rest of the billionaires concentrated on one thing almost right from the moment they left school. It was a different path to everybody else's and luckily it went through very fertile soil. Did the billionaires know that it was going to be so fertile? They probably had little more than the hope that it might and a deeply ingrained compulsion to do it. Having nothing much in their young lives to lose and everything to gain, that is the direction they were compelled to head in. Even Sperling, who came late to the final turn in his journey, had little to lose having already watched his family disintegrate. He had little holding him back except his dubious academic tenure. Already branded an outsider, his future in academia was doubtful and he had little in the way of career prospects, so why not start his own university?

The other billionaires were all young at the beginning of their odyssey, so they had plenty of time and generally no responsibilities. There was little at stake if it failed and everything to gain if it succeeded.

Besides which, as outsiders the billionaires had little choice. Ordinary jobs were out of reach for most of them. They were either unqualified or temperamentally unsuited for most positions. They couldn't or wouldn't fit into other people's hierarchies. Lucas was never going to take over his father's office supply business nor Gates join his father's law firm. Branson wasn't going to be a fourth generation lawyer because he was not able to read well enough. Winfrey wasn't going to be a cleaner or a beautician nor Ecclestone a bank clerk. Icahn had the intellectual capacity to be a doctor but was sickened by actual sickness. Soros tried to be a philosopher but didn't make the cut. Spielberg had no recognisable job skills when he left school—it was filmmaking or nothing.

Again, it would be a mistake to think that their final direction was chosen rationally. Their saving grace was their 'salvation' direction. There was a fair chance that this direction was so emotionally satisfying that they would have embarked on that course irrespective of success, bearing in mind that their success only appears certain in hindsight. They were lucky that their salvation direction was sufficiently in alignment with the times to be turned into billions of dollars. Gates and Jobs were lucky to have become fascinated with computing rather than valve radios or steam trains. There must be millions of people in the world who have embarked on their salvation direction to find less success or, worse, a dead end!

Drive or hunger?

The billionaires didn't get rich by lying around on a sofa listening to music and smoking dope as many young people do. Fun in the normal sense of the word just does not feature in the billionaires' lives, and parties were conspicuously absent from their program. Even Branson set about partying as a way of getting ahead. Outsiders tend to have few real friends, and since they had little social contact when growing up they are used to spending long periods of time alone. They are loners, and parties make them uncomfortable. Gates, Buffett, Soros and Ecclestone are all eighteen-hour-a-day, seven-day-a-week, fifty-weeks-a-year guys. Don't expect to find them at parties. Even on the rare occasion that they do attend a party they will probably be found off to one side. Every now and again, an outsider can be sociable in short bursts but it doesn't last. Fame, of course, changes the demands on their time, and as they get older they are seen more and more at parties and functions.

With the exception of Branson, none of the others are the life of the party. Branson is the life and soul of his own parties but by all accounts there is little real connection with his guests. He uses parties as a means to motivate staff, treat journalists and save him from falling into an existentialist hole. They are frantic diversions that don't appear to be much fun.

As already discussed, billionaires are obsessive workaholics. They had to do what they do because it gave them what they needed in the past, and since everything they have done since reinforces this activity, they have to keep doing it. They become workaholics. It is lucky that their hunger made them rich.

By now the hunger of all the billionaires should be obvious. There is the real hunger of Lowy and Soros, borne out of actual wartime hunger and terror. Sperling and Icahn had a hunger to right the injustices of the world. All had an early desire for safety, love, approval and belonging. Without this hunger, the billionaires would not have been able to sustain the extreme effort required year in, year out to become extremely wealthy.

Trailblazing to success

Microsoft, Oracle, Apple, IKEA, Charles Schwab & Co, Virgin and the University of Phoenix are huge corporations. Icahn, Buffett and Soros are small businessmen who own large corporations. Ecclestone, Geffen, Lucas, Spielberg and Winfrey have huge media businesses. Lowy's Westfield Corporation has shopping malls around the world. Looking at them now it is easy to feel that where they ended up was always certain, and that all they needed to do to succeed was get on their own super highways to success.

But it wasn't like that for any of them. They have all nearly failed innumerable times and perhaps would have failed if it were not for true grit and lack of alternatives.

When they started, the vocational super highways they created did not exist. They couldn't or wouldn't pay the toll on someone else's super highway, so they had to go their own way. Blessed with limited choice, they struck out across country and blazed their own trail. A trail they turned into a superhighway all of their own. This was their key decision — had they not started out, they would not be the billionaires they are today. They all avoided the greatest failure of all — the failure to start!

Most of these people started off as small business start-ups and some — like those run by Icahn, Buffett, Soros, Ecclestone, Geffen, Lucas, Spielberg and Winfrey — remain as small businesses.

One thing the billionaires didn't do was to feel sorry for themselves. They were all discriminated against but they didn't sit around licking their wounds. They didn't blame others. All had a lot to be angry about. Some got even; all got on. They used their disadvantage to advantage. Since the best revenge is success, they used their outsider's edge to make their extreme wealth.

Having started, our self-made billionaires kept going. Luckily they had their difference, direction and drive—their outsider's edge. But was that enough? Chapter 25 looks at trading intelligence—that essential ingredient that separates the doers from the owners. But first, I am going to look at how they became outsiders.

Part IV

BEGINNINGS MATTER

Chapter 22

Development pain

Chapter 20 established that the personality factor linking the self-made billionaires is being an outsider, in particular having difference, direction and drive. I will now examine how this came about.

The key common development factor for all these self-made billionaires is that while their personalities were forming they had significant problems in *all* three of the great life domains: family, school and friends. The details and intensity vary from billionaire to billionaire, but the pattern is the same for all of them.

In order to understand what happened to the billionaires when they were growing up, this chapter will describe how children's personalities are hard-wired as they develop. First, and most importantly, children's personalities begin to develop through early interactions with their primary caregivers, usually their mothers. Fathers usually have a minor role, but their influence can be important. School is naturally important but much less so for the education it gives than the sense of belonging it does or doesn't engender in children. In particular, there is a lengthy discussion about the critical role school sport plays in establishing boys' social standing.

Social standing is affected by other related things as well, such as real or apparent disabilities, being dislocated by moving, being accelerated or held back in school, or bullying. War had a dramatic impact on two of the billionaires.

It is also obvious that there are fewer female self-made billionaires than males. The reasons for this will be discussed later in this chapter.

It mainly happens before eighteen

> Surely no wider circle is really interested in what Ingvar Kamprad got up to as a small boy — things going badly for him in school, being shy with girls, or when young, making a political blunder that he would bitterly regret (Torekull 1998).

This came from Ingvar Kamprad — and how wrong he is! What happened to Kamprad from birth right through to the end of his schooling is much more important than what happened later. This may seem a surprising statement, since most of his wealth was made later, but the wealth was a consequence of his personality and his personality was dramatically shaped as he was growing up. This is true of all the self-made billionaires featured in this book. It is true for other extreme achievers in all walks of life. In fact, it is true of everyone — people are a product of both their genes and their environment, and early environment is particularly important for personality development.

The Catholics said, 'Give me a child until he is seven and I will give you the man'. Perhaps they were exaggerating, but only a bit. They should have made the age eighteen.

Biographies tend to downplay childhood and the biographical subjects themselves tend to downplay this time even more. There is a kind of tacit agreement that this time of a person's life is unimportant — babies are babies and we were all like that once. We all cried, soiled, cooed and were totally dependent on our parents for everything. And who likes to think of themselves in this state? Babies, infants, small children and even older children are not very interesting to adults unless the adult is a close relative.

In addition, few high-achieving male adults want to talk about their childhood because the image of dependence and weakness undermines their hero status. Admitting to being vulnerable, at any age, runs counter to the appearance of super achievement. Childhood images of famous people are usually only used in the media if they are to gain sympathy. For instance, in the case of convicted murderers subject to a public campaign to prevent execution, or the slightly different tack of the media showing a picture of a baby adjacent to the picture of the criminal and asking how such a sweet, innocent-looking child could turn into such a fiend.

We were all babies once, and the question that goes mainly unanswered in biographies of super achievers is how do babies end up becoming who they finally are as adults? How a baby turns into someone exceptionally 'heroic' like Gates or Buffett is a question that is rarely asked and needs to be answered.

When male adults talk about their childhood, it will generally be couched in suitably heroic terms, dwelling largely on tales of derring-do, when they won rather than lost, and if they lost it will still be couched in heroic terms. Branson's example of being forced out of the car at four years of age and made to find his way home is told as a heroic adventure. The infant Branson made his way calmly across country into the approving embrace of his mother. The reality was probably quite different! Chances are he was terrified and howled his eyes out all the way home. He may have been helped to get back home by a kindly adult; who knows? But it is certain the event did not happen as told. Branson should feel no shame if the alternate scenario described here is what actually happened, because this is what most children would do.

In addition, it is well known that specific memories of childhood trauma are often repressed. Since the hypothesis of this book is that it is childhood events and particularly trauma that lead to the personality required for extreme wealth, then it follows that self-made billionaires will also tend to have repressed many, if not most, of their early problems. Indeed, people with problem upbringings tend not only to forget their upbringings but to idealise them, hence Branson's recall of his cross-country adventure.

People with more normal upbringings tend to have realistic memories of both their upbringing and their parents, with fairly clear understanding of their parents' strengths and weaknesses.

But never mind, it is not necessary to have a blow-by-blow account of the billionaires' childhoods to understand the environmental forces that shaped their personalities. We only need to know the big things. How the billionaires were generally treated by their mothers, fathers, friends and at school. How frequently they were uprooted and in what circumstances and, when they were uprooted, did they fit into their new place? Were they sick for extended periods of time? Did they have any disabilities that prevented them learning or made them the object of scorn or bullying? The finer details of most of these events are not necessary to know, just knowing that they happened is enough.

Sperling is a rare male for the candidness of his disclosure. He was small, sickly, vulnerable and terrified for most of his childhood, and he tells it that way. Winfrey has the advantage of being more used to disclosure; even so the level of her disclosure is unusual, evangelical almost.

The literature on personality shows that it is between 60 per cent and 80 per cent genetically based. In other words, most of our personality comes from the genes of our parents and other ancestors. These numbers have been established over a long period by the now famous twin studies. In these studies, groups of identical twins, non-identical twins and ordinary siblings separated at birth by normal processes, such as adoption, have been compared. It has been found that the personality of identical twins match each other most closely, and the conclusion is that since these twins share identical genes, the genes are the major contributor. Non-identical twins are less similar, and other siblings can be quite different since the genes contributed from a long line of ancestors on both sides can combine in many different ways.

Given the apparently minor contribution of environment in personality formation figures, it would be tempting to write early childhood development off as a factor in forming billionaires' personalities. But even if the environment contributes only 20 per cent to personality, that is a lot if it is focused in key areas. There may also be a wild card combination going on. Genes come as combinations from ancestors. Personality then depends on how a person's genetically directed development interacts with his or her developing environment. A person's final personality may be much more different than the sum of the genes plus environment.

It is also probable that the impact due to early environment is greater because the twin studies are silent on the effects of trauma on the estimates of the environmental contribution to personality development. Luckily, other literature is not. There have been many studies carried out on children brought up in institutions deprived of appropriate attention, especially love and positive feedback. These children are usually distressingly maladjusted, in some cases almost emotionally catatonic. Since most of the twin studies are carried out on children in relatively normal situations, the studies almost certainly underestimate the impact of negative environmental factors on personality development.

In addition, identical twins have identical physiques, so will tend to be treated similarly by different people. They will be identical in such categories as height, attractiveness and sporting ability, so if one is admired or reviled, the other will be too. How people look affects how they are treated, which affects their personality!

Whatever the relative contribution of genes and environment and the possibility of wild card combinations of both, it can be taken as a given that early environments can have a dramatic effect on personality development.

The latest work on brain development shows that babies are born with only a fifth of the brain cells of later life, but only two years later, they have three quarters. As the infant's brain grows, it wires up. The newborn infant not only has fewer brain cells but also relatively few connections between brain cells. But as the brain grows and develops from birth, the brain cells are wired together into circuits with synapses. Early on, the synapses are connected at a rapid rate.

As the brain matures during middle to late adolescence, most of the synapses that aren't used are destroyed. The brain removes its redundancy and leaves the circuits that have been used while the child develops to adulthood. The late adolescent brain takes on something close to its final form. Personality and learning, while not totally fixed, is quite difficult to change from that time on.

It is not only the psychologists and physiologists that find this declining effect of learning with age. Studies by economists also confirm the declining learning pattern with age. They find that money spent on early childhood development is a huge benefit to a country's GDP. The benefit of early schooling is also high, but declines as the child gets older. By the time a child gets to late secondary school and university, the contribution to GDP of education has almost plateaued. Unfortunately, investment in education is the reverse of this curve. The biggest investments are made at the times of least impact.

Early brains are full of potential to learn; in fact, learning is the primary job of infants. I am not talking about school learning; while important, school learning is relatively trivial compared to the scope of learning that goes on prior to school. Infants have to learn the really big things in life, like listening and talking, moving about without hurting themselves, and how to relate to other people. The last of these is an incredibly important skill to learn as we are social animals and, even as adults, almost totally interdependent on others for everything—even the self-made billionaires are dependent on others. After all, they wouldn't be rich if there wasn't a market and their wealth would be irrelevant if they were the only people on earth.

Whatever the mechanism of learning, it is accepted that there is a physical wiring-up process that goes on; in other words learning, or indeed living, changes the brain.

Children learn what to do when mother smiles, father growls, the dog barks, the wind howls, the sun heats them and the snow cools them. They learn what to do near a cliff and there are some amusing psychological experiments that show this. They learn to speak the particular languages they are exposed to, they learn to walk, to run, to control their bodily functions and so on. Since they are so utterly dependent on others for everything they learn how to interact (or not) with other people, and this is the key to personality development.

The job of children is to grow up and become the best adults they can be given their biology and their environment. That is what they are programmed to do. Bodies grow, brains grow and learn, personalities develop. The job of those adults around them is to help them grow into the best adults they can be according to the environment they are going to grow into.

What is best for any particular child is not able to be determined nor prescribed. While parents have a critical and legitimate role in helping their children move into adulthood, their aspirations for their child are often misaligned with what the child is willing or able to do—for example, Lauren's mother insisted he be a rabbi while Icahn's mother wanted him to be a doctor, Gates's parents thought computing was a good hobby but not a career, Soros's father favoured philosophy, and Sperling's mother thought any education above third grade was a waste—and he went on to achieve a doctorate and found a university. Few of the self-made billionaires' parents insisted their child go into business.

So if parents, as the major custodians of their child's development, shouldn't be prescriptive, what should they be? Again, the literature is very clear. Parents provide the environment for children to develop in. There is an ideal way for children to be brought up, but not a perfect way. There is no perfection because life isn't like that, neither for a child growing up nor as an adult. Life is full of unpredictable joy, adversity, tough times and good times, poverty and wealth, arguments and fun, sickness and health. Children need to grow with some chance of dealing with what life throws at them.

An ideal development environment for a child includes (after food, water, shelter and clothing) love and expressions of love through sound, sight and particularly touch, predictability and a growing sense of being able to influence their environments. Also, since life won't be predictable all the time, a bit of uncertainty should be thrown in. An ideal upbringing is mostly loving, predictable and responsive, but sometimes not any of these things; whereas a perfect upbringing has a sense of rigid order about it that paradoxically can't be ideal.

I'm now going to discuss the ideal development in terms of mothers, fathers and school.

Mothers make the world go round

Mothers are usually the most important people in an infant's life. Infants can do without their birth mothers as did Jobs and Ellison, but it is never the same as if they had them. Both felt abandoned and different. Fathers and other relatives can sometimes substitute, but for most babies, mothers make the world go round.

Generally, mothers have a strong influence on the environment that babies grow up in. It is important to note that there is no one model that is more 'ideal' than another, provided it has the essential elements of physical care, expressions of love, predictability and safety, with a growing sense of the child being able to influence its environment.

In an ideal environment the following sorts of interactions happen. Pre-mobile infants make noises and after a time mothers understand what the noises mean. There is obviously the distressed cry, but there is also the moderately hungry cry or the lying in bed contentedly gurgling sound. As the baby develops, the noises become more meaningful and mothers can become very closely attuned to them—the baby and its mother have developed a pre-verbal way of communicating. The baby understands that if it uses a gurgle it will mostly be left alone to do what is obviously giving it pleasure, and if it screams then there will usually be more urgent attention. It is important that the mother makes appropriate eye contact, touches and communicates with her baby.

If mother behaves in a manner that is mainly independent of what the baby is communicating, then the interactions between mother and baby become disturbed and problematic. This may come about if a mother completely ignores her baby when it is screaming in hunger, or disturbs it to feed when it is contentedly gurgling. Of course the baby's needs will sometimes be out of synchronisation with what the mother needs to do, so occasional mismatches are inevitable and probably desirable. But if mother and baby synchronise only randomly, then baby can't develop a sense of having any influence on what happens to it and its development is impaired. Of course, if the interaction is mainly negative then development is even more impaired.

As the child grows, communication generally becomes more sophisticated. The baby may, for example, be playing. It expects to be left alone to play, but when bored or hungry or just needing love and assurance, it may complain or scuttle back to its mother and cling to her leg. The mother will usually be appropriately responsive—a cuddle, soothing words, food or another activity. The child learns what to expect. This pattern goes on right up to the point the child leaves home as an adult. Over that time interactions should become more sophisticated and dependent on the development of the child. This ideal, warm, bump along, learn from each other as we go type of child development happens about two-thirds of the time. Or, rather, two-thirds of mothers are capable of doing this.

Naturally there are times of misalignment between mothers and their children and these can be particularly strong during adolescence. While this may be unpleasant for all parties living through the misaligned times, it is normal and necessary. But too much misalignment may point to problems with either or both parent and child.

If a child is brought up substantially deficient in one or all of physical care, expressions of love, influence, predictability and safety then their development is impaired. The physical care issues are obvious but the others perhaps need a little elaboration.

For example, children brought up in extreme institutional environments may be deficient in all the elements, but even if the physical care is assured, the deficiencies in the emotional care and physical affection area can lead to near catatonic emotional states.

In many cases the love that the self-made billionaires received from their mothers was intrusive. In other words, it frequently did not take into account the immediate needs of the child. We don't know exactly how the billionaires' mothers were with them, but we do know how intrusive mothers usually behave. Intrusive mothers constantly interfere with their child to suit their own needs. An example of this would be if a child is playing happily and its mother comes along, picks it up and gives it a big cuddle, puts it down and walks on. Cuddles are generally good, but out of context it can be intrusive. In exactly the same situation at another time, mother walks by and scolds the child. Yet another time she ignores the child. Or if the child is distressed, she does any one of these things—picks it up and cuddles it, or scolds it or simply ignores it. A mother's random responses make it very hard for children to learn to interact with their environment.

Every mother gets interaction with her child wrong some of the time—this is normal and even desirable. But if it happens too frequently and the response consistently appears random to the child then the child begins to fear interaction with its mother. This is doubly so if that interaction is intrusive in that it forces the mother's response on the child irrespective of the state of the child. As adults we would hate that.

As adults we have all been in situations in which we are doing something we want and someone comes up and demands that we do something else, or we feel like a cuddle and we get rejected or we don't feel like a cuddle and we are made to. Imagine now how you would feel if you were forced to remain, for ten years, close to a person ten times your size who came along and consistently acted out of sync with your moods and needs. Many of us have been in this situation for extended periods without the obvious difference in physical power. It is distressing!

The art of relationships at any age is getting the type, intensity and timing of interaction right. It is important between adults, and even more so between adults and children because children are unable to defend themselves against the inappropriate behaviour of others.

Mothers generally take on another role within the family. They act as social secretary, connecting families with one another. If that works well, there is an interplay of diverse social connections between families and friends. They also tend to be more involved with mothers' clubs. These clubs, among other things, act as a sort of information clearing house. Mothers get early warnings about what is going on at school or in the community. Working mothers are often excluded from these clubs and it is this, as well as lack of time, that can make mothering stressful and difficult for working mothers.

Luckily for Gates his mother was connected to the mothers' club; so connected that she ran it. She was also a socialite, so there would have been many occasions for young Gates to interact with others. Many of the other billionaires' mothers weren't in the mothers' clubs and didn't have people around socially. Gates's mother was intrusive in other ways, so she almost certainly helped young Bill develop a fractious personality by the time he got to school.

David Geffen is reported as having probably the most fractious personality of all the billionaires. His mother was intrusive with everyone and the family was socially isolated. She gave hard, gratuitous advice to anyone in her orbit. Geffen, as the apple of his mother's eye, would have been given special attention, which would have been as much a curse as a blessing. While there is no doubt she loved her young god, there is also no doubt that would have made her doubly intrusive. She would have demanded he love her in the way she wanted on her schedule of needs, not Geffen's. Her emotional breakdown and hospitalisation when Geffen was six is an indication of the quality of her relationship with Geffen and a source of both anxiety and shame for him. When she was hospitalised, young Geffen would have been anxious, because as difficult as she was to live with, she was his mother and her total withdrawal would have felt like abandonment, making his world even less predictable. He would also have felt shame because of the stigma attached to mental illness.

Geffen probably had few good times with his mother. His good times included going to movies together. These would have been special times for young Geffen because he had the affection of his mother, and she was constrained from intruding on him because she was paying attention to the screen. It is no wonder he was drawn to show business. When he scalped tickets, when he skipped school and when he entered show business would have been among the few times in his life he felt safely loved.

Buffett's mother was also emotionally unstable. As he grew older, Buffett increasingly withdrew from the tempestuous unpredictability of her behaviour, but he would have been unable to do this as a baby or infant. Understandably, Buffett did not like bringing friends home. Fortunately for him he had his relatives close for much of his growing up—these relatives gave him much needed approval and reinforced his central small business and frugal inclinations.

Icahn and Lauren had intrusive, demanding mothers, and both had rigid ideas about what jobs their boys should have. Lauren's mother moved him from school to school in an attempt to achieve her ambitions for him to become a rabbi, even forcing him to travel through hostile territory. Both families were socially isolated.

Kamprad's mother is surprisingly absent from any discussion of his upbringing; the focus, instead, centres mainly on a dominating and intrusive grandmother. It is likely that the mother had her abilities to mother usurped by the grandmother, which would have left little Ingvar exposed to the vagaries of his grandmother. Both his grandmother's husband and son committed suicide, so as dedicated as she may have been to Kamprad, her love was probably fierce and intrusive.

Lucas's mother was loving but she was forced by medical reasons to be unpredictably absent. Lucas would have suffered multiple separation anxiety along with the uncertainty of her return. That, coupled with the 'loving' harshness of his father and emotional austerity of their housekeeper, made life hard at home when his mother was hospitalised. It is no wonder his predictable, doting, movie camera toting grandfather provided such a compelling role model.

Lowy's mother became his dependant during the war and part of his 'hunger' involved feeding and protecting her. Soros's mother was overshadowed by Soros's father.

Spielberg reports that his mother was close to ideal, a playmate who compensated somewhat for his problems at school. That may indeed be true. It is also true that she provided a completely unstable environment for the young Spielberg to develop in. There was a constant, high-volume threat of his parents separating, probably reinforced with arguments about which child would go with which parent and whether they would ever see the other parent again. This would have provided ongoing fear of separation right through the critical formative years. It probably would have been better to have actually completed the separation and put the poor kid out of his misery. That, coupled with the constant uprooting of the family, would have been enough to induce extreme anxiety in Spielberg.

Branson similarly praises his mother, but her strange behaviour in forcing young Branson to find his way home overland indicates more than a single lapse in mothering. This is confirmed by sending an obviously learning-disabled boy to boarding school then continuing to send him to more boarding schools after he failed at the previous. Young Branson paid a price for his mother's undue emphasis on going to the right school. This experience would have been the equivalent of sending him to a series of concentration camps, and indicates a serious failure in her duty of care. She did, however, praise him for trading and being adventurous.

Winfrey's mother abandoned her and then, when reunited, rejected her. Luckily, Winfrey had the tough early love of her grandmother for a period and her father and stepmother later. Her grandmother's love was almost entirely contingent upon Winfrey's preaching and reading, hence Winfrey's later predilections, which were reinforced by the stern love of her father. Even when Winfrey was living with her mother, she was rejected in favour of her younger half-siblings. Her mother also set up a situation in which Winfrey could be serially raped by relatives. It is no wonder Winfrey struggles with self-esteem despite being one of the most publicly loved women in the world.

Mothers have mothers and Winfrey's situation is one of the few in which both her mother and maternal grandmother are mentioned. Winfrey's mother is a product of her own interaction with her mother, a mother who only dished out love contingently. If, as would appear to be the case, Winfrey's mother did not preach or read much, so she would have missed out on her mother's love. In addition to taking feelings of rejection into adult life, these feelings would have been made even more unbearable by seeing her own daughter getting the love that she missed out on. Winfrey's mother probably moved away in part for this reason, and rejected Winfrey when eventually she came to live with her.

Sperling makes no secret of the fact that his mother was intrusive and demanding. So intrusive was she that he had to become a compulsive liar to escape her attention. She was also socially isolating and he never wanted to bring any of the few friends he had home. That was not all his mother's fault as his father was a violent drunk and they lived in a shanty.

Ecclestone is silent about both his parents, but given that he never went home after leaving and that he didn't go to his mother's funeral, it is almost certain that he had a severe problem with both his mother and churches.

Both Ellison and Jobs were adopted and certainly suffered from feelings of abandonment. Ellison's adoptive mother was not able to protect Ellison from the constant attacks by his adoptive father, while Jobs's adoptive mother appears fine but probably out of her depth with her super-bright son.

Little is known of Schwab's mother.

Mothers are important to the development of their children. For most of these billionaires there appears to have been serious issues with their mothers and that, coupled with other things, led to a great deal of pain for their children. The final result was their children entered school with unusual and often unpleasant personalities. They were set up to be social outcasts at school.

Dads—bit players in the family drama

By and large, fathers don't play a major role in raising children. Certainly there are exceptions, but even in these times of equal opportunity this is one area in which men usually don't step up to the plate and take over. If that is so now, it was even more so when the billionaires were growing up. Nevertheless, fathers have a role that becomes particularly important in the absence of a strong mother or, conversely, almost invisible in the presence of an overly strong mother.

Whatever Gates's father's role in the family, his mother was dominant. Gates senior was also busy and reported to be a remote presence. He was a bit player and probably had little effect on Gates junior, except for encouraging games and inculcating him into the games that lawyers play. This is also true for Branson.

Geffen's father was so dominated by his wife that he chose invisibility and eventually death to escape the constant emotional battering from Geffen's mother. Lauren's father was equally invisible.

Kamprad's father was slightly more present but still suffered the emotional battering of Kamprad's grandmother, so his sphere of influence was curtailed. He did not commit suicide like his father and his brother.

Icahn had a strong, dominant mother and an unconventional, cold and over-intellectual father. While stripped of some traditional male power, his father, a lapsed lawyer and amateur philosopher, still had a significant role in Icahn's life. Rather than playing knock-around games with his son as fathers often do, he played cold, intellectual games. He provided contingent approval for participating in and winning philosophical word games, games that Icahn would use on his enemies in business.

Soros's father could have been cast out of the same mould as Icahn's father. Also a lapsed lawyer, he was short on simple fun and uncontingent approval and long on approval for philosophical debate, later coupled with philanthropy.

Lowy idolised his father but lost him during the war. His mother became his dependant and hence he developed his hunger.

Lowy idolised his father but lost him during the war.

Spielberg's father was a constant source of both physical and emotional instability for young Steven. The computer engineer was at war with his artist wife and the threat of divorce and family fragmentation was always imminent. If that wasn't bad enough, he was also given to uprooting the family at short notice, disturbing Spielberg's fragile social networks and compounding his almost intolerable anxieties. But he did provide the all important movie camera that Spielberg made his first movies with and plenty of quirky material to be used in Spielberg's movies.

Lucas's father was not able to provide any compensating emotional warmth for the random separation of Lucas from his mother. In fact, he seemed to have no idea that this was required and installed a hard-hearted housekeeper to take over from his wife. In addition to this, he set up humiliations for the young Lucas by shaving his head for lice or taping his ears back. As a small businessman, he did provide contingent approval for Lucas's forays into business when Lucas ran a newspaper, mowed lawns and especially when he charged admission to his dioramas and movies. By being around his father, young Lucas had learned to mobilise money to solve problems, which gave him an edge over his young film school colleagues and later enabled him to take on large expensive projects.

Ellison's adoptive father was abusive and intolerant, constantly berating Ellison for failure. There was nothing Ellison could do to win praise. His abuse more than negated any positive effect the mild adoptive mother may have had.

Both of Jobs's adoptive parents have the appearance of being good folks but way out of their depth in dealing with their headstrong and obviously highly intelligent son. Once he hit puberty, Jobs would have felt like an alien both at home and at school. Jobs senior did take Jobs around weekend markets, which awakened in Steve trading skills, skills he used very effectively in sourcing components for the fledgling Apple Computer Company.

Sperling's father was an ignorant, bullying alcoholic whose abuse of Sperling was only curtailed when Sperling threatened him with retaliatory violence. His death was a welcome relief to the family

Winfrey's father was by all accounts a good man, but not a dominant force in Winfrey's early formative life because he was not found until Winfrey was at school. By then he was married. Winfrey was gladly accepted into his family but her loyalties were conflicted and she yo-yoed between her mother and her father. When with her father, he reinforced the preaching and school work orientation set in train by Winfrey's grandmother.

Buffett's gruff, aloof stockbroking father provided a safe haven for young Buffett, and an escape from the difficulties of home and his emotionally unstable mother. Approval would have been sparingly given and the only way Buffett could consistently achieve approval was by chalking up stock prices. Like Buffett, Schwab also participated with his lawyer father in stock trading. Little else is known about him and his relationship with his son but it was probably very similar.

Almost nothing is known about the relationship Ecclestone had with either his mother or father, but the indications are that relations were never good.

Those golden school years revisited

There are many people who claim that their school years were the best years of their life. It was not so for the seventeen self-made billionaires in question. For most, school was a misery that had to be endured, for the rest it was a matter of indifference.

Academic achievement is not a pre-requisite for extreme wealth

It is relatively easy to deal with the academic side of school, at least as far as the self-made billionaires are concerned. Academically, the self-made billionaires varied from extremely successful in Icahn, Winfrey and Gates; to very successful in Buffett and Jobs; to modestly successful in Schwab and Soros; and barely successful to near failures in Geffen, Ellison, Lauren, Kamprad, Sperling, Lucas, Spielberg, Ecclestone and Branson. Lowy's prowess remains untested as his education was interrupted by war and never really resumed. He only had a few years of primary education.

Clearly academic excellence or failure was irrelevant to achieving extreme wealth, except perhaps as the pre-requisite to enter a university course leading to a chosen occupation. This will be covered later. Success in the classroom may have provided the achieving billionaires some relief from teachers, maybe even praise, but it was not enough to compensate for the humiliation at the hands of other students, both in the class (for being nerds or other varieties of misfit) and on the sports fields (for being incompetent).

Winfrey was good at school and achieved well. She continued from school to gain a degree despite her employer strongly suggesting that it wasn't necessary — education had achieved all that was required, she had the job. Despite this, the conditioning from grandmother and father was so strong, she persisted.

All the rest of the self-made billionaires are male. As men, their experience is different from that of women. Most of this chapter will deal only with males at school. However, women at school will be discussed in a later part of this chapter.

The apparent irrelevance of school education for the extremely wealthy is not an argument that school-based education is irrelevant to individuals or the economy overall. These billionaires became wealthy at a time when the background level of literacy and numeracy in the population was high and benefited from that. The billionaires that were low on literacy could find someone to do the work that required literacy.

While academic performance varies markedly across the billionaires, there is one area of school life in which the male billionaires are absolutely consistent. Some flirted with team sports, but none really played!

Sport defines boys' pecking order

Boys' status tends to be based on direct physical power. Put in extremely simplistic terms, if you are a boy and you can't physically beat another boy then you are subordinate to him. This is one reason why sport is so incredibly important to boys and in most school situations establishes the power hierarchy and boys' status.

Teams have similar importance, with the added bonus of enhancing group identity or status. It is very tribal and very primitive. If the home team beats the away team then the home team is better — this is very simple. The group's status rises, therefore one school's identity is enhanced over that of the other. This is great for the school because in the wider world, winning schools attract better students and better parents, even though in reality there is no proven relationship between sporting prowess and success in later life, which is, after all, what school should be about.

Elite schools recruit elite sportspeople to enhance their market position. Charles Schwab freely admits to being 'assisted' in his enrolment at Stanford University and given academic latitude while there because of his golfing prowess. His academic abilities were not good enough to gain entry without elite sport, nor were they good enough to remain there if he had managed to gain entry. Buffett, on the other hand, did not get into Harvard because he wasn't quite Harvard material, which is undoubtedly code for not being good at sport. He wasn't given any free kicks!

There is status in being a good team player without actually being the best player. Belonging to the winning team is nearly as good as being the best player on the field.

On the other hand, being a high academic achiever or artistic is usually a source of scorn unless it is tempered with sporting prowess. The bright, unsporting boy is labelled a swot, geek or nerd, the artist any other term that throws his masculinity into doubt.

Adolescence is a particularly important time for forging identity, and pressures to conform are extreme. If a person is forced at that time to become an outsider, then the brain will wire itself that way and this person will always be an outsider. Conversely, if a person derives a great deal of personal benefit from conforming and playing by the rules, then they will be wired that way. Sport and academic endeavours promote the paradoxical need for high levels of personal achievement within highly prescribed activities. It is compelling for those who can play that particular game and humiliating for those who can't.

As in any human endeavour, there is a large range of sporting abilities. There are the highly competent and aggressive with abilities across a whole range of sports and who are consistent winners. There are the mildly successful who sometimes win, and then there are the absolutely dreadful, the ones who always lose.

Whatever the physical benefits of sports may be and social benefits to the winners, to always lose is humiliating as both Gates and Jobs demonstrated. Neither would play games they couldn't win, so team sports were out.

People who always lose at anything will fairly soon withdraw from the competition if they can. This gives schools a problem. Since sports excellence is relative — in other words, it has to be against someone else — for every winner there has to be a loser or the whole thing becomes pointless. If the very worst boys withdraw, then the next most incompetent sportsmen become the consistent losers and are a withdrawal threat, and so on. The rot of non-participation moves up from the bottom. The winners have fewer people to win against. Schools try to stop this rot with the time-honoured method of making sport compulsory. But as the saying goes, you can lead a horse to water but you can't make it drink. When forced to participate in sport, boys at the bottom of the sporting hierarchy tend to adopt all sorts of pain avoidance strategies, such as fooling around, getting sidelined for forgetting their sports uniforms or failing to appear.

It is hard for a boy without sporting prowess to break into male power structures and find his place. It is a safe bet that most male comedians were poor at sports so developed very useful verbal skills to bolster their standing in the pecking order. Boys love a laugh and will adopt a comic as a kind of mascot if the joke is not at their expense. Branson was just such a school joker. This is doubly useful as girls prefer boys with a sense of humour and this also seems to have worked for Branson, both while at school and outside. He appears to be the most loved male billionaire.

While some comics may be blessed with a warm humour that pleases all and offends none, most comedy is based on making fun of one person while keeping the others on side, and usually it is the other outsiders that are the butt of jokes. It is often a case of outsiders turning on other outsiders to gain status with the in groups.

In addition, there is systematic bias by teachers towards their sportspeople and away from the others. An elite sportsman who, for example, is drunk at the school dance, fights the other boys and gropes the girls will often be treated as a naughty boy—after all, boys will be boys. Their papers will be graded much more generously. In the adult world, this bias exists also. Elite sportsmen are shown much more tolerance than ordinary citizens.

Non-sportsmen are treated much more harshly. Branson suffered a large fall from privilege at school when he permanently retired injured from sport. While he was a sportsman his slow learning was indulged. As soon as he stopped being a sportsman he was permanently in trouble and labelled a dunce. Nothing had changed academically for Branson; he was always dyslexic, he had just tumbled down the school's status league. Branson probably would have escaped expulsion for having sex with the headmaster's daughter if he had still been in the top football team and the girl would have taken more of the blame for leading him astray. But then if he had been in the top football team, he wouldn't have been seen as an academic or a behavioural problem. Also, he wouldn't have been expelled from his first school, so he would not have been in a position to have sex with that headmaster's daughter anyway.

'Delinquents' are thought to come from the non-sporting groups. It is often thought that they are delinquent because they are not involved in sport so, logically, making them participate in sport will stop them being delinquent. It may be that boys who are not part of the sporting scene are more delinquent, but it won't be because of the intrinsic physical value of sport. It will be because they have no other way of getting attention, that their other pursuits have little status, that they have more time on their hands, have burned off less energy and that they suffer systematic bias against them by other boys, teachers, girls and possibly even their own parents. They may be just plain angry at the injustice of it all!

It is by no means proven that non-sportspeople are more delinquent. The only thing that can be said is that people think they are more delinquent because they apply different judgements to one group and not the other.

Outsiders can be good sportspeople. Jack Kerouac, the famous beat generation writer of the 1950s, was a brilliant footballer but as part Indian was never quite in the school hierarchy. Boys who have moved around schools will also not have long-established bonds and be only loosely bound in the hierarchy.

There is no doubt, however, that outsider sportspeople are better off at school than they would have been if they didn't play sport. Whether they are better off outside school has yet to be determined. It may be that sport blunts their outsider's edge and they don't achieve as much as they could have.

None of the male billionaires played traditional team sports to any great extent, although several claimed to. Ellison and Lauren flirted with basketball, and undoubtedly most were forced to play the odd game or two of something.

None of the male billionaires played traditional team sports to any great extent, although several claimed to. Charles Schwab was very good at golf while at school. It certainly helped his standing at school, and more particularly at college where they play more adult games. It is interesting that Schwab chose golf. As a sport, golf is nearly perfect for an outsider. It is not a team sport and at school it is very much second tier, which means few people pay attention to it. If the boy loses, so what, it is only golf. In addition, the boy can play alone without declaring bad scores, only declaring scores and handicaps when they are good enough. This can be kept up for years without anyone knowing or caring.

A boy with no sporting ability and no comic abilities must fall back on other tactics to establish himself. Some will choose to become 'invisible', but that is not always possible or what they want. Lauren claimed to be on a school basketball team but rarely, if ever, got a game. He was more like a mascot than a participating sportsman.

Branson, once retired hurt, adopted his semi-comic prankster persona as a way of fitting in and deflecting abuse. Ellison was briefly on a basketball team but was humiliated by scoring a goal for the opposition and being reported in the paper for doing so—hardly an elite sportsman! There are no school photos of him, so whatever sporting career he had it was short and ignominious. But it was for this reason Ellison developed his storytelling abilities and some pranking. He could belong to a small group of boys this way through charm and storytelling—great talents for making billions of dollars. Soros played some soccer in junior school but was mainly interested in tennis and boxing. The war interrupted his sporting involvement.

The ultimate irony of school emphasis on boys' sport is that unless the boy is going to be a professional sportsman, bodyguard or do work involving heavy lifting, sport does not necessarily lead to post-school success. It may or it may not. In this world where money is made from brain work, muscle work is very much the province of low-paid workers. Certainly, billionaires can and do hire legions of disposable muscle men to do their muscle work.

Sport may be most useful in establishing social connections and providing males with a common language. This post-school socialising made possible by sport is of considerable benefit to some individuals, along the lines of Dale Carnegie's 'make friends and influence people'. Equally it may be of little or no benefit to others; we don't know the real post-school impact of sport.

There is no doubt that some people appear to benefit greatly from involvement in elite school sports. There seem to be plenty of examples of people who have used their connections via sport to achieve success. Sport doesn't appear to stop people being outsiders in the broad development sense, but it does seem to give some outsiders the ability to enter and rise to the top of hierarchies.

The argument some people make that sport helped them get where they are is untested. It may have helped them, but conversely there may have been better choices to make. Individuals' lives are a great uncontrolled experiment and they don't know what the results would have been if they took different routes to the ones they did. Taking the easy route of relying on sporting connections may actually prevent people from reaching their full potential.

Gates, sensibly, wouldn't play anything he couldn't win and still doesn't, but even after all this time both Gates and Jobs are sneered at because of their extreme distress at not being able to win at school sport. But not playing anything he can't win has set Gates up very well in business. He never wastes time on things he can't win, and precious little time on sport either. He doesn't carry an outmoded sporting code into his business and look where that oversight got him.

Buffett probably doesn't know that sport is going on unless he sees it as a good investment.

Ecclestone didn't play school sport but went into motor racing after school, a very non-school type of sport. Nevertheless he undoubtedly felt that he had missed out at school by not being in a team and entered a sport where he could use money rather than muscle to qualify. He wasn't particularly talented at that but he went on to make a fortune in motor racing as one of the greatest sports entrepreneurs.

Lowy has worked assiduously as sports administrator for Australian soccer. He never played, but his enduring fond memories of watching soccer with his father prior to the war and just before his father was killed by the Nazis meant that he has a lifetime attachment to the sport.

Luckily for some, they were compensated by being able to attract a small band of followers, usually only one or two people. Intellectually, Gates could beat the kids two years his senior in his accelerated grade and was hated for it, but it was this ability coupled with his very early deals that won him power and admiration in his computer club. Buffett had his small band of semi-outsiders that he went into business with. Ellison spun his stories and gained admirers. Branson didn't seem to manage any real friendships at secondary school, probably because of his constant expulsions, but his charm would have deflected some of the pain. Lauren adopted style and became a mascot. Geffen had a single very brief period in the social sun when his manic organising style contributed to an acting team win, but that didn't actually translate to acceptance. Lucas probably had a position in the school hierarchy somewhere near the bottom. He knew his place and so did everyone else. His position was probably more invisible than painful. It was only when he began flamboyant model making and then filming that his status improved. Late in his schooling, Spielberg found his strategy for saving himself from the bullies and fitted into a group with filming. Jobs, like Gates, refused to play games he couldn't win, but he was briefly in a school band. He could win at electronics and gained his standing in a small group of wireheads doing that.

Others seem to have never been attached to even small groups at school. Ecclestone saved himself from the bullies but, unlike Spielberg, he never managed to fit into a group that he didn't buy. He bought safety without gaining social status. Icahn seems to have been completely isolated. Kamprad, in his desperation to stop his isolation, had an unfortunate interlude with the Nazi party. Soros and Lowy's time surviving the occupation of Budapest by the Nazis meant survival was the issue, not their standing in the boys' pecking order. Sperling played sport, but once he was invalided at a young age for an extensive period he completely lost his standing in the hierarchy, never to recover.

School sport has obvious social benefits for the boys that are good at it. They gain status at school that is reinforced by the teachers and their peers alike. Sometimes that standing carries over into adult achievement and sometimes not. And, even if it does, it does not seem to carry over into extreme success such as that shown by the billionaires. It almost certainly doesn't carry over into other forms of extreme achievement either, possibly with the notable exception of being a sportsperson.

Counter-intuitively, Sir Edmund Hillary, the first man to climb Mt Everest (with his climbing partner Tenzing Norgay) was a failure at school sport and, like Gates, was accelerated two years at school. Neither John Lennon nor Elvis Presley played school sport. Neither did Einstein nor Freud nor Picasso nor Walt Disney. It is handy for a male politician to be a sportsman, since politicians need status and the veneer of conformity to gain popular support. President John F Kennedy was a school footballer and this helped overcome other disadvantages he had. On the other hand, President Franklin D Roosevelt, who was reportedly 'delicate' at school, did not need such help with his status.

Boys with no sporting prowess are very much on their own. They become outsiders during their critical development years and remain so for the rest of their lives. They are forced to find a way to manage in the power hierarchy at school, and since they can't compete in a conventional way, they have to invent non-conventional ways or merely suffer extended periods of pain and humiliation. They have to make up their own lives.

It is interesting that there are not systematic studies about the relationship between schoolboy sporting prowess and success in later life. Sport is taken as 'a good thing' and certainly may be for those lucky boys that are good at it. It certainly guarantees higher social standing at school than would otherwise have been the case. But this study points to a negative relationship between high achievement at school sport and extreme achievement in adulthood—involvement in school sports works against extreme achievement.

Since this study is only dealing with self-made billionaires, it is not possible to draw any inference about sport and the success of the rest of the male population. There are moderately successful adults that have been among the elite school sports players as well as those that haven't. Sports reporting is so extremely biased in our media in general and society at large that it is not possible to make any inference about the real association between school sport and later success.

At school a boy is usually low on the social pecking order if he isn't an elite sportsman or in a team. He is fair game for bullying and other abuse by anyone higher up, including the comics that act as court jesters to the kings. Boys low on the pecking order will be considered more negatively by boys, teachers and girls than if they were the same person but good at sport.

Growing up as they did in the long shadow of World War I (Buffett, Ecclestone, Sperling) and World War II, strange as it may seem now, the schools the billionaires went to had as part of their ethos to build suitable character for military service. Military character is intended not to help the boys but the nation. The elite schools tended to act as feeder schools to the elite military academies such as Westpoint in the US and Sandhurst in the UK, and may still have pretensions to do this.

After all, 'The Battle of Waterloo was won on the playing fields of Eton'—except it wasn't. The Duke of Wellington, the general who led the British forces to beat Napoleon, went to Eton. He has been reported as a dreamy boy who didn't play much organised sport and, in any event, there actually wasn't much organised sport at Eton at the time, just disorganised games put on by the boys for their own entertainment.

By the time Winston Churchill, the UK's wartime prime minister, went to a private elite boarding school, sports had been institutionalised and Churchill was a failure at them. Ironically, he now has a specialist sports school named after him. Churchill left school mentally disturbed. To be fair, he also had profound failures in relationships with parents, school and peers, and probably wasn't in good mental shape when he entered school. His character was appropriate to guide Britain through the war but not for peace time and he died a lonely, disturbed old man.

Many of the sports teachers at the time the billionaires were growing up probably modelled their teaching methods on army drill sergeants. In this model of motivation, poor performers are deemed to be lazy and unmanly irrespective of aptitude and are constantly humiliated. Even if the humiliation could not affect the performance of the student, it acted as a spur to motivate the others. But accumulated humiliation damages people. By and large, school administrations, other teachers and parents often gave tacit approval to these methods as sporting prowess is deemed to be good and failures are indeed lazy and unmanly.

There are encouraging reports that some present-day boys school sports programs are beginning to uncouple from the military model these sixty years after World War II. Some are reported as being able to accommodate the consistent losers without humiliation.

If the reports about the link between obesity and lack of sporting participation are true, then it would appear that sport is suffering a market failure among significant parts of the population. Some minorities of the population don't find participation in sport appealing and appear to be using their consumer right to opt out of sport from an early age. Since the authoritarian road to participation sport is becoming increasingly unavailable to ensure participation, and if sport is indeed found to be beneficial, then it is time to rethink its nature to increase its market share again.

Indeed, there is increasing evidence that as the coercion model of education is breaking down, education will suffer real problems until it can move to a market model — the market being the consumers; children in other words. Unless children want to consume the education on offer, there will be increasing participation and disciplinary problems.

There will be some readers that will be angry at what they consider to be an unwarranted attack on school sport. These will mainly be the consistent winners at sport, and as with anybody who has had a positive experience of something, they will passionately believe that what was good for them is good for everyone else. There will be a smaller but equally passionate group of people who will be cheering what they see as a justified attack on school sports. They will come from the consistent losers, those regularly humiliated on the sports fields.

But this is not an attack on school sports per se. What is important is the vigour and extent to which any sport is used to establish and reinforce pecking orders, to define winners and losers and to provide positive rewards or humiliation. Boys' sport was certainly used this way at the time the billionaires were growing up.

There is only so much time and head space

Everybody has to be somewhere doing something. The convenient thing for schools about many academic subjects and sport is that they are great time fillers.

Even without the historical obsession and untested perceptions of 'good', it is easy to see why some schooling practices keep going. Sport in particular can absorb huge amounts of time and resources and the great thing is, like the weather, while it keeps changing it always remains the same. It is content free and requires no curriculum. The score is clear at the end of the game, so the teachers aren't involved in marking. Boys run around and burn off all that testosterone. There is much joy if one likes that sort of thing.

But while they are thinking about sport, travelling to and from venues, training, gathering equipment and playing sport, sportspeople have their time and head space taken up. They can't think about other things and they don't have time to do other things. Outsiders, on the other hand, have their time and head space taken up with other things. Sportspeople probably suffer from having too much structured time and become too dependent on group or team activities. Outsiders may suffer from having too much unstructured time, but there are obviously some unexpected benefits from this.

In addition to the time and head space taken up with sport, there is another factor at work—group think. If a person spends large amounts of time with others, sooner or later, what they think about, the way they act and what they do begins to line up. There is a group norm. They begin to agree about what sort of beer they like, who they like, which cars they like, what is good to watch on TV, whether books are good to read and, if so, which books. Which people are cool and which are nerds and who is in and who is out. Each thing on its own may not be very significant, but over a long time there is a very large accumulation of attitudes, values and behaviours that become wired in.

With their time and heads free of sport, outsiders can concentrate on other things. With their attitudes free of group norms they are free to choose other attitudes. In fact, they may even perversely eschew group norms. The self-made billionaires certainly did. Forced onto their own devices, they cobbled together a life and invented their own activities. They became obsessed by different things. By the time they left school they had radically different attitudes, interests, skills and views of the world than those of their peers.

Any obsession drives out the capacity to concentrate on other things and since creativity seems to come mainly from the outsiders, it is just possible that sport as promoted by schools is an engine of conformity simply because it drives out the capacity to think about other things.

But it wasn't all bad for these outsiders. While the sports nuts had their eyes on the ball, the outsiders won the prize!

Difference matters

Adolescence is a time of key identity formation and the pressure is on to conform to the very rigid standards imposed by fellow students. Non-conformity leads to social isolation at best and humiliation and pain at worst. Being an outsider is a punishable offence!

Imagine what happened to Gates when he was accelerated two years at school. Undoubtedly Gates was already fractious. He certainly didn't have the temperament or looks to be taken on as a class mascot. He was always his own boy. In addition, this difficult, gawky upstart was bright. Even though he had been accelerated two years, Gates was operating both below his intellectual level and well above his social and physical level. Even if he had been inclined to play sport, he was too small and uncoordinated compared with his classmates to compete on their terms. He would inevitably be hurt and beaten if he played with them. The classroom was the only place he could compete and win. In class he humiliated the jocks. Outside of the class and in the playing fields the jocks would have had their revenge. Gates found refuge in computing with the computer nerds. He did different things to those who played sport.

Jobs was also accelerated at school. He was a boy with high natural intellect, growing up in a family who were not his intellectual equals, mixing with peers who were not his intellectual equals either. Like Gates, he was small for his class and like Gates he behaved peculiarly in his own way. He also hated losing at sport and, given that some sporting participation was compulsory, had suffered the distress and humiliation of loss often enough. Being forced just once to undertake an activity in which loss is inevitable has a tendency to upset.

> Being forced to lose time and again will inevitably lead to some sort of crisis.

Being forced to lose time and again will inevitably lead to some sort of crisis. Jobs became strange, an unsurprising outcome for a bright boy who had to invent his own way because he couldn't adopt an appropriate conventional persona.

Even Buffett and Icahn, who both had the benefit of being demonstrably bright and tall, struggled socially at school. After moving schools Buffett became sick, so he was sent to stay with relatives who cared for him. He also ran away from home. Hardly the reaction of a happy, well-adjusted boy. Icahn became invisible outside class, except when picked on by neighbourhood bullies. Both boys were tall, normally an asset in the male power hierarchy but in their cases not so. Just by existing, tall boys present a physical challenge to smaller boys trying to establish their own position in the power hierarchy. Both Buffett and Icahn stooped and shambled in a vain attempt to become less visible. Icahn still affects that shambling, dishevelled manner as he extracts revenge on the power hierarchies for past hurts at both school and university. Now, as then, his adversaries underestimate him, to their detriment.

The billionaires that weren't demonstrably bright suffered even more. The term demonstrably bright is used advisedly here because many of the other billionaires had learning disabilities, notably dyslexia. They were physically, not mentally impaired, but were treated as mentally deficient—dumb in other words. There are no objective reports of their intellectual capabilities, but it would be safe to assume that at worst the billionaires vary in intelligence from slightly above average to extremely bright. Becoming as rich as 10 000 college professors requires high-level processing capabilities.

If being a tall outsider is a problem — these individuals are fair game for some physical challenges — then a short outsider has this problem magnified. Short outsiders are alone, unprotected and frequently the butt of jokes. They are often bullied by those just a little bit further up the power hierarchy. It is no wonder Spielberg was chronically anxious and Ecclestone's bullying protection solution became the compulsive behaviour that it has.

Lauren made himself cute enough to be a kind of mascot while Lucas quietly hung around. Spielberg wasn't in any school long enough to be anything other than scared until he was protected by his bully. Geffen skipped class and disappeared from school as soon as he could. Sperling was mildly bullied and Ecclestone was severely bullied. Kamprad was bullied and lonely.

There needs to be a special note on what is pejoratively called 'the small man's syndrome'. This is the generally accepted but not proven folk wisdom that small men are more aggressive than men of normal height. There may, however, not be such a syndrome, because typically folk wisdom is based on every example proving the point and every contrary example going unnoticed or being discounted as an exception. But if this folk wisdom is true then small men have just cause for aggression. Right through their key personality formation years they were treated at best as mascots and at worst as easy targets for bullying. At no time do they get treated with respect unless they become super aggressive. If they want to equal others in sport they have to try that much harder, and even then face the simple physical disadvantages of height and weight. If they are poor at sport they run the risk of being treated even more poorly. By the time they leave school their personality and social style is largely fixed; any extra pugnaciousness will be locked in, as it was for Winston Churchill. If there is a small man's syndrome, it is made by other people and it is grossly unfair to blame the men in question.

It is a tragedy that schools and parents often fail in their duty of care with outsider kids. On the other hand, outsider kids are not always easy to help.

Going it alone — the boy against the system

It is not all bad for outsider kids. While they are subject to various traumas at school they are also freed from social mores and conventional thinking. While education in the major academic skills, such as literacy and numeracy, is ostensively school's major purpose, schools have a far greater purpose in keeping children off the streets until they are old enough, and socialising children to help them fit into society. A big part of schooling is to adjust children's expectations; in other words to socialise them.

Most people are acclimatised to expect to go into some sort of social hierarchy and that they need to work diligently to achieve increased social standing. This is based on them first accepting that social standing is a worthwhile thing to achieve. They are taught to play within the rules of the hierarchy to make their way up it, and school in general and sport in particular is a start of the acculturation process. There are rewards for doing what the hierarchy approves of and punishments for just being neutral, let alone opposed.

Of course, social learning isn't over once school is out. The acculturation process proceeds. Like schools, all hierarchies have their own sets of rules and behaviours. For example, the social welfare system is different from the manufacturing sector, which is different from the military, which is different from the mothers' club at school, which is different from the Hells Angels. Hierarchies punish or reject people who stray too far from their largely unwritten rules. Outsiders either adapt rapidly or go. Gender is just one of the many ways a person can be an outsider; males entering female organisational structures suffer as much as females in male structures.

Having suffered through school, outsider kids don't expect anything of hierarchies. In fact, they are almost certainly deeply suspicious of them. This is most likely one of the reasons Gates left Harvard, because even with a Harvard degree, he was going to struggle if he started on the bottom rung of an organisation and tried working himself into a position of power. No doubt he could have done it, but he had neither the temperament nor the belief that any organisation would reward him sufficiently soon. He was right!

With the exception of Winfrey, Sperling, Spielberg and Geffen, it is significant that none of the billionaires spent any extended periods of time in someone else's hierarchy. Buffett went straight from university to his own investment company. Icahn, Soros and Schwab were briefly in broking companies, then established their own businesses. Lowy was briefly a factory worker but almost immediately became a commissioned food salesman—not really a waged position—then shopkeeper and shopping-centre developer. Spielberg was a wandering resource at a film studio and Lucas went straight into making his own films after a bit of tutoring. Ellison spent a little time as an employed computer 'programmer' and Lauren as a fashion salesman. Kamprad started IKEA when he was five and has never worked anywhere else. Ecclestone started almost right from school with his own motorcycle trading company. Winfrey did spend a few years employed in radio and TV networks, a substantial portion of that in a kind of professional purgatory for being different — ultimately developing the style she made famous and that made her rich.

Geffen did belong to hierarchies but he played by his own rules, which completely unsettled the hierarchies. He behaved almost like a virus, attacking them from within to his colossal advantage.

Despite working in the educational sector for many years, Sperling was an uncomfortable fit. While he was in the hierarchy, he was never really part of it. It tolerated him just as long as he toed the line, but he never thrived since his ultimate objective of providing efficient education for working people did not line up with the objectives of the employing institution or the sector. When he developed his teaching program he had to either leave or desist.

On the other hand, people who look conventionally accomplished have the advantage of being offered places on the first rungs of the career ladder much easier than those who don't. Having a good qualification from a good institution is one such mark of conventional accomplishment. Sporting accomplishment is another. Getting on the first rungs of the career ladder early looks like an advantage, certainly in the jittery years around the end of education when everyone is scrambling for a start in life. But an easy start is not necessarily a good start or if good, not necessarily the best.

Many of the self-made billionaires could have done something easier and more conventional. Most would have if they weren't such outsiders. But they wouldn't have become so rich. If Lucas, for instance, had played sport or even done a bit better at school, he probably wouldn't have left Modesto. His fate would have been like one of the main characters in *American Graffiti*. If he didn't have quite enough angst to power his exit, he would have been stuck in small town America running his family's office supply company. That was the easy, conventional route he could have taken. But he did have enough angst, so he left and made a film about it and became one of the great filmmakers of the twentieth century.

In addition to expectations about the disadvantages of being in hierarchies, outsider kids don't learn the rules of 'good' social conduct or, if they do, they either ignore them at will or use them against the insiders. They are not polite. Why should they be? They were always the butt. And why would they be? There was never any reward for being so. Manners are a social convention and outsiders haven't experienced many benefits from social conventions, even if they have used them. Besides which, social behaviour becomes ingrained through repeated use and ongoing cycles of rewards and punishments, some subtle, some not. If the result for the outsider is always punishment irrespective of good manners, then good manners have no utility and won't be hard-wired as a way of behaving. Many actually learn that bad manners get them further.

It was probably more effective for Gates to get his mother's attention through bad manners than through good. He then later used bad manners at school. Now Gates doesn't worry too much about whether his behaviour is seen as bad. Neither do Jobs or Ellison worry if their behaviour is seen as duplicitous spin. Ecclestone certainly doesn't care to keep gentlemen's agreements and doesn't mind the world's press reporting it. Buffett and Soros completely sidestep the problem by having little to do with people. Soros's 'attack' on the Bank of England has always been construed as bad manners and unchivalrous, but for Soros he was just playing by the rules. He had offered to help the authorities change the rules, so people like him couldn't do that, but he was refused, as if the expectation of chivalrous behaviour is deemed to be protection enough.

Outsiders don't slavishly believe what they are told. They know that the rules they are meant to obey are just conventions. They begin questioning everything that is told to them by everyone—teachers, parents, peers and media. They first question the cornerstones of the education system. They query the value of sport, the usefulness of English as it is taught in senior school and whether an intimate knowledge of Shakespeare is really worth the drudge. Gates and other billionaires are routinely derisive of the curriculum taught in business schools.

We all chuckle at the historical belief that the world was thought to be flat or that blood poisoning could be fixed by leeches. While these have been proven wrong scientifically, there are still many things that we don't know about. Most importantly, we have our knowledge and behaviour ruts, long acculturated and rarely challenged. Not surprisingly, many adults find the world is frequently different from what they are told it is. It is this knowledge gap that outsiders use to their considerable advantage!

While at school Gates and Jobs were almost certainly influenced by that most outsider of literary genres—science fiction. Both imagined that computers could be something other than one-tonne machines taking up whole rooms, drawing enough energy to power a small town and costing millions of dollars. They imagined that a computer could be small enough to fit on a desk or a wrist, be cheap enough for the normal person to afford and that there would be countless millions of them. They believed that there would be a consumer market for computers. They had seen it in science fiction and they had the nerve to imagine that personal computing could be more than a kid's fantasy and that they could make it happen. And guess what? The early market for computers was drawn from exactly the same interest pool. This is why early computer clients did not worry too much if the thing worked exactly as specified; they wanted to be part of the development process and gave considerable latitude to the fledgling companies of Microsoft, Apple and Oracle.

Lucas, also influenced by science fiction, made his billions bringing the unfashionable medium back as escapist entertainment.

It is probably a good test of whether a boy or girl was an outsider at school by whether or not he or she was in any of the year books. Most of the billionaires tried to stay out of the firing line and, with the exception of Schwab, none were involved with sport. Geffen slipped out of school without picking up his diploma.

Certainly the male billionaires were outsiders when they got to school but school undoubtedly exacerbated this tendency. They suffered constant isolation, humiliation, fear and rejection at school—fifteen years of that kind of treatment on an evolving personality is bound to have a permanent, hard-wired impact.

On the upside, however, they escaped from being over-influenced by conventional wisdom. They had little handed to them on a plate, so they were free—no, compelled—to invent their own worlds. This gave them what others didn't have—a different world view with a different sense of what was possible. Certain that no-one was going to give them a free ride, they invented their lives.

University or richer than 10000 college professors

As with schooling, it is relatively easy to deal with university. Of the self-made billionaires Icahn, Buffett, Winfrey, Schwab, Soros, Sperling and Lucas achieved degrees by their own efforts. Others claim degrees but that seems unfounded, and several have honorary degrees.

Gates, Jobs, Ellison, Lauren, Geffen and Spielberg dropped out. The first two could have easily achieved a degree and Ellison, Lauren, Geffen and Spielberg probably could have too, despite their school performance being less than impressive. They reportedly dropped out because they couldn't see the relevance. This is probably true, but unlikely to be the major cause as lack of relevance in course work is the rule rather than the exception both at school and university, and is a frequent cause of student complaints.

More likely they suffered a social failure at university. They got to university and had to start all over again trying to fit into a social hierarchy without the personality or sporting prowess needed to achieve any kind of social integration. They were probably even more lonely at university than at school. Jobs wandered off to reconnect with electronics and Wozniak. Geffen, alone as usual, went straight into showbiz, and Ellison, expelled for lack of performance, drifted into programming and business. Spielberg, really only marking time at university, received a better offer from a movie studio and left.

But lack of credentials does not mean lack of smarts nor does the presence of credentials guarantee smarts. Having qualifications only proves a person's ability to attain credentials and does not necessarily indicate any ability to do anything else.

Gates is super smart and he didn't need a degree for what he wanted to do, so he left to recreate his computer club in the business world. It is interesting to note that one of the few friends Gates made during this time, the one person who tried to integrate him into the social life at Harvard, Steve Ballmer, is now Microsoft CEO and a billionaire in his own right. Kamprad, Ecclestone, Branson and Lowy did not go to university at all.

So, what does this say about university and the creation of extreme wealth? Probably that like the latter years of schooling the academic side of university is not very effective. The economics studies of education's contribution to GDP confirm this. Later years of schooling and university contribute much less to GDP compared to pre-school and early school years.

With the exception of Winfrey, those that gained degrees used them as entry tickets to occupations with academic barriers to entry. Buffett seems to be the only one to have directly benefited from university teaching. Having failed to get into Harvard University he met his mentor, Benjamin Graham, at Columbia University.

Moving about

Modern electronics are wonderful; they plug and play. One can plug a new amplifier into the home entertainment unit and generally expect it to work. The computer plugs right in there too. Leads can be run to all parts of the house and music and images are sent to every room. In the near future, home security systems, zone temperatures and even the toaster may be included in one mass of interconnections. Look at the back of any electronics system and one can see masses of plugs and wires running all over the place. When electronic systems are running well, they are a thing of beauty and joy. The system is simply switched on, with never a thought of how it all connects.

Despite the fact that most of the elements are supposedly plug and play, setting up a new system with new elements is often challenging. Even if you move or replace an element, you can be in such trouble that it may take days to sort out or may even require the help of an expert. There are often unintended effects. Some things that should work don't. The audio for the video player comes out distorted and only from one speaker, or not at all.

Human society is a bit like a modern home entertainment system writ larger and more complex. In well-established groups, more interpersonal connections run between people than in less established groups. The connections build up over time and may become very complex. They include friendships, hostilities, transactions, tradition, habit, trust and distrust, and everyone fits into a highly evolved pecking order. Connections are built up around activities such as sport, a local band, theatre, business or gardening. If a person has lived in a place for a long time, especially if they were born there, the connections will be numerous, ingrained and taken for granted. People usually don't realise just how interconnected they are until they move away.

Like the home entertainment system, if a group is working people rarely look at the connections to see how complex they are or why the system is working, and even fewer are inclined to change any of the units or connections. Anyone who dares to do this is usually branded a troublemaker. This can be so even if some of the connections are bad and some of the units are malfunctioning. Some people remain in toxic communities for the whole of their lives, held in place by their connections.

When people move from one place to another, it inevitably means moving from one community to another, or unplugging from one community and re-plugging into another. Unplugging is relatively easy, you just tear out the connections, but re-plugging is usually much harder. Re-plugging a home entertainment system is complex enough. Doing this with interpersonal connections in a new community can be extremely difficult and time consuming. Obviously, levels of re-plugging skill are important, and so are the units that people have to plug into, not to mention the compatibility of the leads and plugs.

Move an elite sportsperson from one school to another, and sooner or later—but probably sooner—that sportsperson will plug into the power structure. There would be a bit of jostling, a number of the locals may be bruised in the process, but fairly soon the hierarchy will fit the new person in and vice versa. A moderately good but enthusiastic sportsperson will take longer but will usually find a place.

A boy who is not involved in sport will struggle since he has little with which to break into the power hierarchy. His plugs don't fit, his leads are too few and too short and his bits of equipment are incompatible. Maybe he was already an outsider from the place he came, and he will become even more so in his new place. Move him again and he will become even more of an outsider. If he is going to make friends, the only friends he will make are fellow outsiders, and because he is outside, or at the bottom, of the power structure with no power and no protectors, he is a candidate for bullying, teasing and other humiliations.

No wonder Spielberg had anxiety attacks, cried at children's cartoons and retreated to fantasy. Having struggled to establish connections in one place, such an anxious, strange little guy with no interest in sport was in trouble every time he moved. With every move he became more of an outsider, which made it more difficult for him to connect. Ecclestone still carries the trauma of being bullied when he changed schools—it is what powers his hunger. Buffett ran away from school, made friends with other outsiders and concentrated on what gave him approval from his family—making money. Sperling became invisible, Branson pranked and Schwab found golf and associated business.

Even if they didn't move towns, almost all the billionaires changed schools. Gates not only switched schools but was accelerated. If he had any hope of plugging into his new school, that chance was destroyed by the acceleration. He could not jockey for power by physical means with classmates two years his senior and he wasn't going to be anybody's mascot. Similarly with Jobs. Lauren yo-yoed between schools and finally adopted his fashion strategy as a way of gaining status. Geffen just became more and more fractious. Kamprad joined the Nazis, Branson had sex with the headmaster's daughter and Ellison learned how to spin ever more elaborate stories.

Women's social systems are almost always much more complex than men's. They are plugged into many more people and activities far and wide. They also can much more easily plug a new person into their network than a man can. When they move they often don't unplug everything from where they came and they rarely, if ever, completely unplug from their origins. Suspect extreme trauma if a woman disconnects herself completely from her birth family, as is the case with the feminist Germaine Greer.

Women may run awfully long leads and not use the connections much, but they rarely completely abandon all historical connections, whereas men often do. This explains why couples often end up living close to the woman's parents and female siblings at the expense of the male partner's birth family.

Only Winfrey didn't appear particularly troubled by moving schools and peer groups. Winfrey was offered the opportunity to be involved with peers when she changed school but she declined. This was for another reason than her ability to make connections. She learned to make connections quickly and uses this skill daily on her shows.

Communities do many things that have symbolic meaning, are demonstrations of tribal loyalty or are emotional hooks with no real content. Sport is a particularly good example of this. If a person hasn't played any football and has no tribal loyalties to any team, then football is just a bunch of men moving a ball around on a field. Nothing much is achieved, and what's more they will go on and achieve nothing much every week until the season is over, and then start all over again next season.

Stripped of its symbolic significance, tribal loyalties and other emotional hooks, all sport is equally banal. Motor racing involves cars circling a track for a seemingly endless time. Golf involves hitting a little white ball around kilometres of countryside and ending up in the same place it started from. Yet billions of dollars change hands every week and many grown men and women are rendered almost senseless for hours, days and sometimes years watching the sports of their choice.

Sport is an easy target for this kind of analysis but it isn't alone. Women have their own rallying points, which are essentially senseless if stripped of symbolic meaning, tribal loyalty or emotional hooks. Fashion is a prime example. Overhear a conversation between two women in a coffee shop and it is likely to move to fashion at some time. It will also range over the relationships of those near, not so near or famous. Princess Diana was a real loss to the magazine industry because of her near universal appeal to women due to the heady combination of, among other things, glamour, an ever-changing parade of frocks combined with a dysfunctional relationship—all of which are followed by many women much like some men follow sport. These things have value to women and, therefore, are the basis of huge industries. This is why women are much more likely to know Pierre Cardin than Tiger Woods.

The girls Winfrey was invited to connect with had their own local emphasis of female topics. Any set of topics is equally valid as any other set, but may be equally meaningless to an outsider. Topics such as which boy is seeing which girl, who is wearing what to the prom or which is the right lipstick to go with the clutch purse and will it go with the shoes. Winfrey was already well past those girls and couldn't connect with the banality of it all. She had been molested, so the girls' concerns about losing their virginity or other normal sexual or relationship issues may well have distressed her. She wasn't of them. She had an unloving and unreliable mother, suffered molestation at the hands of male relatives and didn't have a regular boyfriend, so she couldn't share their valid little middle-class concerns. All her issues were much bigger than theirs. Not that she felt superior, just unable to connect. It's likely that she was unable to disclose her own experiences and, since that is one of the keys to female intimacy, felt unfulfilled. Undoubtedly she has deliberately set about righting this problem in her later career, being more than frank about both her past and her day-to-day issues with millions of women daily.

While moving about is stressful for everyone and especially stressful for outsiders and others with little ability to plug into the new society, it is not all bad. On the upside, since outsiders can't or are disinclined to plug into the prevailing culture they do other things. They are freed from being conventional because they can't be conventional. The more unconventional they became the less they connected with others, which leads them to become even more unconventional. There is obviously danger in this if it is taken to extremes. Jobs gave up washing for a time and could only work at his computer job at night because he was an unacceptable co-worker.

While the billionaires' unconventionality accelerated their outsider standing, it also meant they had thoughts that were less influenced by conventional wisdom and social expectations. Both Gates and Jobs were drawn to science fiction, science, electronics and computers—the ultimate in nerdy interests—and could imagine themselves doing great things. Unrestrained by the shackles of their peers and their families even, they did it. Lucas, excluded from any meaningful participation in boys' society, made toys, dolls' houses, castles and stop-motion films, and started a whole new direction in movie making and franchising. Buffett built his confidence by doing so much business at school that he earned more than his teachers. He proved to himself that conventional ideas about jobs and making money were just that, conventional. He knew he was unlikely to profit from them.

This final 'benefit' comes with a health warning. It is likely those taken to be delinquents also come from the outsider groups since outsiders are unattached to and often unconstrained by convention. They are also unprotected by good will, so will tend not to be given the benefit of the doubt. They might also be more than a bit angry! So expect 'senseless' violence, vandalism, fast cars and excessive drugs and drinking from young male outsiders. Mind you they are not the only ones to do this—football teams do their share but are more likely to get away with it.

The billionaires were lucky that they didn't go to the *dark side*, as Lucas's characters in *Star Wars* would say. Even if they don't go this way, being an outsider can be very painful. It is almost certain that if given the choice when growing up of being an outsider or having a normal, stable, loving set of relationships, they would have chosen the latter. However, they wouldn't be the people they turned into and almost certainly would not have been billionaires.

While at school, almost all the billionaires suffered some form of social dislocation due to moving schools or being accelerated. This disrupted their social networks and made it increasingly difficult for them to fit in, which increased the pressures on them to be outsiders.

War

Most readers will not have lived through a war, and despite the help of Hollywood can't imagine the sheer emotion-wrenching terror of it. There is the uncertainty of the outcome as the enemy advances and overruns positions, along with the noise, danger, death, rape, separation, maiming and general mayhem. This is followed by the despair of seeing much of what was familiar damaged or destroyed, people moaning or even screaming, services broken down, starvation and a lack of clean drinking water. Then there is the period of adjustment while the new set of rules for living are understood and finally adjusting to the occupation.

The Nazi occupation endured by Soros and Lowy in World War II Budapest was barbaric and their young minds were certainly traumatised. Every day was a challenge to stay alive. These two were relatively lucky compared with the ones that were sent to the death camps, even the ones that survived. Unlike the children in the camps, Soros and Lowy had something to do. They weren't forced into passivity. Forced passivity in the face of danger is bad because it engenders a sense of powerlessness. While these boys didn't have much power, they had things they could and did do to survive.

Soros assisted his philosophically inclined father to help fellow Jewish people escape Budapest. Soros's main role was to trade gold, other items and cash so those fleeing had assets to take with them. Hence the unbreakable link in Soros's personality between trading, philanthropy and philosophy. Soros became driver, whereas his father, a veteran of

Russian concentration camps, was not. In the absence of his father, Lowy protected and fed his family, hence his enduring hunger.

War undoubtedly had a profound affect on these two. Their hunger has become deeply programmed into their brains. They can't stop, they have to keep going.

Disability at school

Every one of the self-made billionaires was disabled in some way, and since disability causes stigma it also causes social problems. The disabilities the billionaires suffered were all the more a problem because some were not considered to be disabilities and some are still not.

The first one has been dealt with at some length — the inability to effectively compete at sport. Others have been touched on: being too short or tall, unattractive or having a fractious personality. These are all physical or social disabilities that contribute to a negative spiral when it comes to social and personality development. Being different is a disability and it often has unpleasant consequences. Different children have to work harder than others to establish and hold their place in the pecking order at school.

> Being different is a disability and it often has unpleasant consequences.

Two other key disabilities are obvious. The first is extended illness. Sperling and to a lesser extent Lucas both had lengthy periods off school and both suffered irreparable disruption to their social standing.

The other is physical disability leading to learning problems. Most prevalent in the billionaires is dyslexia. There is the possibility that Ecclestone, Schwab, Soros, Lucas, Spielberg, Kamprad, Sperling and Branson were all mildly to profoundly dyslexic. Dyslexia has not been confirmed in a number of cases, but their early difficulty in reading is certainly indicative.

Dyslexia is a physical problem that generally arises from some inability of the eye to scan written words properly. Reading is difficult to impossible depending on the severity and, in a written-word driven system such as school, even mild dyslexia can be a severe problem. Sometimes people grow out of it, sometimes they don't. Sometimes the problem is mild, sometimes it is severe.

Reading is critical to school learning, so a person who can't read will be unable to keep up. When these billionaires were growing up, dyslexia was not understood so they were uniformly treated as being dumb. Dyslexia coupled with a lack of sporting ability put these boys right at the very bottom of both the peer and teacher pecking order. Yet as boys these billionaires weren't dumb, as their later extreme performance demonstrates. School was torture, a daily ordeal of pain and humiliation.

Dyslexia can be worked around if it is treated properly. Some researchers claim that dyslexia can be beneficial overall, in that dyslexics develop compensating abilities, much like blind people develop extremely acute hearing to compensate. Some of the billionaires appear to have done just this. Both Branson and Ecclestone are reported as having prodigious memories, but then so do non-dyslexics Buffett and Soros. Lucas and Spielberg think pictorially and hence became model-makers and filmmakers respectively.

Developing compensatory abilities is probably not the greatest benefit of dyslexia. Like all other disabilities, dyslexia contributes to social stigma and guarantees the affected person the 'benefit' of a lower position on the pecking order.

Overbrightness is the flipside of being 'dumb'. Like the 'dumb' the overbright are singled out for special treatment and as a consequence stand out in ways that are not approved of by fellow students. Gates and Jobs were accelerated two years and Winfrey and Buffett one. Icahn and Buffett were very bright and odd. All of these billionaires did not fit, and they could not make themselves invisible. They had to resign themselves to special, favourable attention from teachers and special, unfavourable attention from their peers.

If being an outsider can be considered a 'benefit' then dyslexia and other disabilities should be greeted with enthusiasm.

Why boys and not girls

So far, most of the attention in this book has been directed at men. This is because men far outweigh women as self-made billionaires. The reason for this stark difference needs to be explained.

There is only one female self-made billionaire in this book, Winfrey, and she is qualitatively different from the males. Without casting any doubts on her business and trading abilities, she is more like actors or rock stars whose wealth comes from their appeal to the public. While Winfrey is more than this in that she owns her own production and publishing companies, her star quality is still the cornerstone of her wealth.

JK Rowling, the author of the Harry Potter books and owner of the franchise associated with the brand, has recently become a billionaire. Clearly this is self made, but again it is qualitatively different from wealth generated from direct business involvement. Her achievement is more akin to that of Agatha Christie and Ernest Hemmingway than Bill Gates.

There are other female billionaires, such as eBay CEO Meg Whitman, undoubtedly a tough, competent woman but she is not self-made. Like Microsoft's billionaire CEO Steve Ballmer, she was recruited after the company was started. While it is also true that women are poorly represented in the ranks of high-flying CEOs and there are many theories as to why this is so, it is not the topic of this book, which is about self-made billionaires.

Coco Chanel is a rare example of a self-made female billionaire whose wealth has been made in her own business. She had all the hallmark characteristics of an outsider—she was abandoned by her father then orphaned from her mother as a child. She started her working life in a convent sewing room and had amassed the equivalent of $4.5 billion when she died in 1971. However, she doesn't qualify for this book as she was dead in 2007.

Big surprise, men and women are different!

To state the blindingly obvious, there are differences between men and women and between boys and girls. Aside from the obvious biological differences, there are a whole set of hidden personality features that become clear through behavioural observation.

First, it is important to note in which ways boys and girls are similar. The most important way being that there is absolutely no evidence that boys are brighter than girls. The different genders tend to excel or fail in different things, but objective testing indicates no overall quantitative difference. In any event, even if there were differences across the mass of boys and girls, there is always a huge spread of abilities within genders. While historically on average girls have achieved poorer grades in maths and science than boys, there have always been girls that beat most, if not all the boys, in these subjects.

Fewer women outsiders

Fundamentally, male and female power structures are different. As discussed earlier, sport is the predominant method for establishing the male pecking order at school. While it is not all sweetness and light for girls at school, their power structures are more diverse. Sporting excellence is celebrated, but much more emphasis is placed on participation than excellence, and when the school sports team wins, its achievements don't always drown out everyone else's achievements. Girls' schools and the girls themselves also tend to celebrate artistic endeavours—it is perfectly acceptable to be involved in the orchestra, with drama or debating and not in a sports team. Even those girls who just want to talk about boys, fashion or the latest TV show can usually find a group to belong to.

Certainly there is plenty of bullying, bitchiness and general unpleasantness among girls, but there is also more individual choice as to how a girl can fit in and make her mark. The female power structures are more diverse than the boys'. If a girl is ejected from one group she may be able to find another of suitable status.

Girls move from school to school just as much as boys, but it is probable that girls also will find moving from place to place slightly less traumatic than boys because their heightened communication abilities makes it easier for them to plug and play, as discussed earlier.

Winfrey was an outsider even before she got to school. She was able to read in preschool and was accelerated a year into first grade. Already she had set herself apart. As an older outsider she was one of the few African-Americans in school and not surprisingly felt out of place. She decided she didn't want to spend time with the other girls and opted out of their groups. She would rather study in the library than discuss frivolous things with the other girls. Certainly she felt disconnected, but she had a choice. Most of the boys didn't. Like Winfrey, the boys generally started off in school as outsiders and were kept outside right through school. Winfrey suffered too, but her suffering was more to do with her family situation and being constantly uprooted. School itself was rarely, if ever, a source of additional pain.

Undoubtedly there are girls who are forced to be isolated but it is probably much rarer than for boys. Therefore, there are most likely far fewer outsiders among girls than boys, and since this would seem to be the key prerequisite to be a self-made billionaire, there will be fewer female than male self-made billionaires.

Transactional versus social thinking

To further thin the ranks of potential female self-made billionaires, it is obvious that men and women think differently. Earlier I discussed how women are much more socially connected than men. The sample of women in this book is too small to generalise, so I will draw on my copious professional experience in business management consulting.

When two men get together, they are often uncomfortable discussing personal issues. They are usually more comfortable talking about tangible things and events. And here is another great reason for males to bond over sport—there is something going on out on the field that isn't personal that they can both relate to. Sport being largely transactional fits the male 'social' model, the men are doing something together. The rules are clear and everyone knows what is expected. Even if the men are spectators, they came to watch an event in which the players are just out there to get a job done. The spectators don't have to talk except to cheer or boo, and when they do talk it is about the game. If there is a woman present, she is often frustrated because she wants to talk about other things and the men become irritated because of this.

Women are much more likely to ask how another woman is and expect to get a personal answer. The people who have been to both male and female dominated events will notice the difference in the noise at the beginning. Men's events start much quieter until the alcohol kicks in, women's start noisy and it is much harder to get the official program moving because women network—most of that networking being about personal stuff.

Poker is an interesting analogy for male business because it has all the elements men require. It is a much more popular game for men to play than for women. If games are mentioned about the male billionaires, inevitably poker plays a part.

A male poker game typically starts with little conversation. You don't need to know your partner, so casino gaming is popular. Rich men will travel around the world to play against strangers in casinos where there are high-roller rooms for visiting whales, as they are called. If the players are close friends it may take five minutes for the game to start rather than nano-seconds, but once the game starts there is really not much difference. The point of poker is to beat everybody else, and to do that you must take calculated risks and have a poker face. Even a slight slip in body language can mean annihilation. Everyone is your opponent. A man can beat his best friend, totally humiliate him, bankrupt him even, and that is acceptable, indeed expected. The defeated player is expected to take his losses like a man and not complain.

This sounds very much the sort of game Branson plays with his business partners or Gates with the computer industry. They are not alone. Icahn turned onto his business method while playing poker in the army.

Women sometimes play poker and some are extremely good at it but it is not a game of choice. They generally prefer games with more social interaction and with less transactional outcomes, and sometimes they even forget to play very hard. Even if they choose the same game as a man, say golf, the nature of the way they play is different. A team of women will make much more noise, make many more concessions to each other and be slower players than an all-male team. Women simply don't transact in such a concentrated way, as frequently and as ruthlessly as men!

Even professional women rarely get together just to transact, and when they do they explore issues together. Women socialise decisions much more. They talk the issues through and take a more collective view. This means that when women do deals they are much more likely than men to have consulted a greater range of people. They have socialised their decisions and taken some of the risk out of it. But by doing this, they reduce both the risk of failure and the risk of extreme success.

But in minimising the risk, they remove the chance of wild-card success. Any decision based on a socialised decision-making process is more likely to succeed but less likely to break new ground, hence the consistent successes of women in small business and equally consistent failures of men. But in minimising the risk, they remove the chance of wild-card success. All the billionaires have succeeded through what appeared, at the time, to be wild-card activities, even Winfrey. They did something wildly different. All could have and some nearly did fail spectacularly along the way. Had they sought advice from peers, parents and business advisers they undoubtedly would not have started at all. This is not generally a woman's way of doing business.

It is impossible to be a rugged individualist if you consult your best friend about your next decision.

In the family way

Women make up nearly half the labour force. There are certainly many more women in the labour market than there ever used to be and many more operating at much higher levels than they used to. There are women in serious corporate positions and it is now acceptable for young women to enter professions, corporations and government with the realistic expectation of rising to a senior position.

But there are fewer women than men unequivocally in the labour market. Leaving aside any barriers placed in their way by men, corporations and just plain inertia of large systems, women are often conflicted in their ambitions. Women often want families; well not just families, they often want children. Having children and families deflects attention from work. Sure high-flying women could hire full-time support or, if lucky enough, find a partner who is both willing and able to step into the breach, but that would miss the point.

It is not only the having of the children that is important, it is the ongoing experience of them. It is almost impossible to be involved with a family while working seven days a week, eighteen hours a day, year in year out like Gates, Buffett, Ecclestone and Kamprad. The male billionaires have wives to look after the family. In any event, the decision to have children or not probably wasn't theirs, so they are unlikely to feel that the constant care and responsibility for the children is theirs anyway.

The male billionaires may experience their families from time to time if it suits. Buffett was a virtual stranger to his children. Ecclestone tries to spend half a day a week with his family, which may or may not include his children. Ellison has children from an estranged wife. Gates now has children and is reported to be very happy with them, but it is his wife who has the main family role. Geffen is gay and without children. Lowy is a family man of the old autocratic style and his children were mainly brought up by his wife. Branson is constantly moving around the globe while his wife is at home rearing their children.

In the male self-made billionaires' households, family care is mainly women's work. The male dips in and out of family life as it suits but has no real direct role aside from bringing in a river of cash. The men are more or less absentee landlords.

Generally such a reversal of roles is unsatisfactory for women. High-flying women with children try to be involved with their children. When at work they are often wracked with guilt about not being able to spend more time with their children, or when with their children they are wracked with guilt about not spending more time on the job. Women can be driven close to madness because the demands of high-flying jobs, or any job requiring long hours, are completely in conflict to those necessary to raise children. The conflicting demands may be worked around but they can't be fully reconciled.

Many women are forced to choose between their careers and children. Some choose not to have children; others, like Winfrey, can't have children so are not placed in a position that requires that choice. Women who work in demanding jobs and choose to have children have to make time concessions. They may be able to do all that is required of the job but may be unable to spend time on something else, say office politics — after all there are only so many hours in the day and something has to go. This could mean that their career suffers accordingly.

Running your own business does provide more flexibility and there is an increasing trend for women to start up small businesses. Women's start-up companies tend to fail less than men's, and women are becoming so good at it that in some countries banks are beginning to view women's applications more favourably than men's. Be that as it may, the point of these companies is usually to allow women to make a decent living without sacrificing involvement with their children too much. Few of the companies are set up to make the woman outrageously rich and few of the women wish to compromise their families to do so. Of course there are exceptions to this but they are in the absolute minority.

The reason that there are fewer self-made billionaire women than men is largely a numbers game. There are almost certainly far fewer female outsiders than there are males. Women are naturally more interested in social interaction with people than merely transacting and, in addition, since women's lives are usually less single-focused than men's, such a split focus means they can't dedicate the hours nor the concentration necessary to become super rich.

Combinations

It will be obvious by now that every one of the self-made billionaires features in most, if not all, of the above categories of woe. While there is some lack of clarity about the family life of some or the schooling of others, there is sufficient detail about each of their lives to readily infer that they conform to exactly the same general pattern.

When these categories are collapsed to the three great domains of life for the developing child (family, school and friends) it is clear they had substantial to near catastrophic problems in *all* of the three great domains. All became outsiders, developed unconventional coping strategies, and made billions of dollars as a result.

It is also clear that becoming a billionaire had more to do with what went wrong in their lives rather than what went right.

In each of their miserable young lives there was one beacon of hope. Unencumbered by conventional expectations and armed with unconventional personalities they were headed frantically towards the light. The next chapter will discuss how that came about.

Chapter 23

Salvation

Every one of the billionaires was in pain while growing up. As anyone who has suffered unrelenting pain even for a little while knows, pain can be debilitating. Luckily, and this is the luck the billionaires had, there was some relief available. It was only a small amount of relief but it was enough to work with and work with it they did, with such obsession that they turned their relief activity into fortunes.

Saving themselves from the shipwreck of their lives

Shipwrecked and drowning in the seas of their own misery and unable to board any of the life boats that should be and usually are provided by mother, father, school and friends, our young self-made billionaires try to head to the light of a far-away beacon. It may not be much, but as they scan the horizon it is the only light they can see. Unable to swim fast or far enough, they spot a piece of flotsam floating in the sea. They grab it and hold on for dear life. There may be someone else on the flotsam or they may be alone.

As they bob up and down on the wreckage, they look at it and find that they can make something of it. Soon they start accumulating bits and pieces of other floating wreckage and begin building a boat, with the original piece of flotsam as the keel. They build furiously, as if their life depends on it — as indeed it probably does. They don't really have a plan, and in any event how it ends up depends to a certain extent on what floats by and what they recognise as useful and what the sea is like.

Boats full of other people pass by. Mostly those people don't even notice them because they are busy on their own course, but some do and throw them a few bits and pieces of useful material or food. But many just hurl abuse.

The boat grows in size and begins to get some form of power, maybe some oars or perhaps a sail. Eventually the boat takes its final shape, size and power, which will depend largely on the skill of the person building it, but also on the original piece of flotsam and what floats by. As the boat grows, it can begin to move and pick up bits and pieces of flotsam. It can also absorb other boats through direct assault or by buying them. The captain becomes more skilled and aggressive. All through this process the boat inches and eventually speeds towards the beacon.

Eventually the boat grows very large. Some boats are built as submarines with very little showing above the water, others are highly visible above the water but the captain remains out of sight, and some grow huge and the captain wants — demands — to be noticed, wanting credit for building the boat and maybe wanting to take on passengers. Other captains don't want any attention at all because the only times they have had attention in the past have brought pain.

This may sound a bit flamboyant but the image is broadly accurate. The young billionaire's life is a misery until he or she begins to accumulate bits of floating flotsam and begins building a metaphorical boat. Everything that young people should be able to rely on has either failed them or turned on them. They are psychologically and emotionally hurt and are looking for a safe place. Once they find that safe place they work ferociously to make it impregnable.

In this metaphor, the beacon provides direction, and the original flotsam is a starter set of skills or activities. They may have someone on this original piece of starter flotsam with them, as did Gates and Jobs, or they may be entirely alone, such as Icahn. In the early stages what they will achieve is not clearly defined.

In Gates's case, for example, while he stated that he was already moving towards the light when he saw the seminal *Popular Electronics* cover, he had already seen his salvation in having a computing club; the cover merely gave him a sharper focus and the realisation that there were going to be a lot of people like him who were going to start building personal computers. He got going and motivated Allen to join him. He, Jobs and most of the sci-fi buffs in the world thought personal computers were coming but all of a sudden Gates and Jobs could see how computers could be put on everyone's desk. It made Gates put on speed rather than substantially change direction, but in Jobs's case, he saw the light and found his direction.

One of the keys to extreme wealth is that in all cases the young self-made billionaires suffered constant pain and misery, and were rescued from that pain by some small thing or things that they latched on to. These small things have given them what they haven't had before. Safety was given to the terrified and admiration to the despised. The billionaires worked with passion and obsessive drive. They furiously built what looked to others like an unpromising beginning but they turned it into something of value. They had little choice. It was the only thing they found to do that gave them what they needed. What they needed wasn't billions of dollars, it was a place to fit in and some admiration to go with it. Having billions of dollars may have been the result, but it was never the original objective.

> The billionaires worked with passion and obsessive drive.

In every case, the self-made billionaires went through a pattern of pain and salvation, or as the metaphor above indicates, they were shipwrecked in the sea of their own misery and they found a way to build a boat so they could float to a light they eventually spotted. Almost by accident, they made a boat that was so successful they became the richest people in the world.

Paradoxically, if asked if they would change anything in their early lives, they would have changed much of it, and having made the changes they would certainly have failed to become billionaires.

Cobbling together a life out of found experiences

When young, these billionaires were profoundly unhappy in all the three great domains of family, school and friends. They were shut out of many normal development experiences that the children around them were going through or, if forced to be included, were frequently humiliated. They had to find a way through, a way to ease the pain, to give themselves some of what they were missing out on. They had to find somewhere to belong and something to be admired for. This they did.

Being shut out of orthodox activities, they invented their own activities, and these had four key ingredients.

First, the elements had to be available and recognisable; second, the elements had to align with an interest or talent they had or could develop; third, the associated activities had to give them some sort of reward, even if it was intermittent and unreliable; and fourth, whatever they did had to be repeatable. It is the alignment of these elements in an unorthodox package that gave the billionaires an edge.

The first two points work together. The elements have to be available, recognisable and align with an interest and talent. Two people in the same environment with a different starter set of innate intelligences and interests will head in different directions. This is a common enough occurrence with siblings. If Buffett had been born into Spielberg's family he probably would not have been a filmmaker or an artist. He probably would not have taken an artistic course after his mother because he had no talent in that direction, but he might have taken an interest in computing from the father's side and by now might be beating Gates, Jobs or Ellison at their own games. The father's camera would just have been a bit of equipment hanging around. It would not have inspired him to become a filmmaker. If he used it at all, it would have been the starter equipment for a media business, say a television network with someone else behind the camera.

In the Spielberg family there were at least three obvious directions that Steven could go. He could have gone to the purely artistic side, the technical artistic side (filmmaking) or the technical side (computing). He chose the middle path. Buffett would almost certainly have chosen the technical path and Winfrey would have chosen the artistic path.

Because the selection of activities is undirected by some external authority such as family and school, the child puts together a mix of activities that is all its own. But the mix has to do something for the child, and the something it has to do is provide the child with some reward, generally some satisfaction, recognition or love even. The child keeps doing the activity and refining it to increase the rewards. It was not about the money!

The child starts out and gets some reward, such as Gates did playing games. That worked in the family but not quite as well outside, until he discovered computing. He had already read sci-fi and knew that personal computing was the future. He joined the school nerds in a computing club and that worked for a while but that was not enough — he was ejected. His place could only be secured by controlling the club's computing business. To stay in the club, he began to make work for his friends by finding and closing deals, dealing progressively into bigger and better deals. Gates received major early rewards from making computing deals, which led to the birth of Microsoft.

Buffett was similar, he felt he needed to do business to keep his friends bound to him. Kamprad started a business to save his family. Unlike Gates, as the natural boss, he didn't take his friends into business with him. Lauren gained approval with fashion, and as with fashion, he had to keep renewing it, staying ahead of his peers and in the limelight of approval. Winfrey's preaching became better, her skills increased faster than those of her peers so she remained the centre of the congregation's attention. Lucas grew better at making models and filming. He had to, otherwise the audience would get bored.

These children were still outsiders, but had gained some acceptance for their unorthodox pursuits. Even in their chosen area they didn't receive unreserved approval. Their activities would have created admiration in some people and not others, or some days were better than others. As they grew older they needed to work harder to get the same approval.

Approval was intermittent! This is the stuff that addictions are made of and there is every indication that the billionaires are addicted to what they do.

Chapter 24 explains how people learn and become addicted. Intermittent rewards given to people with few other rewards is one of the recognised ways in which people become addicted to anything. This applies to gambling, especially addictions to poker machines. It also applies to things that are considered beneficial, such as sport. If Branson had continued to play sport he probably would have been addicted to that and not become a billionaire. Food can be addictive as Winfrey and millions of other men and women know.

These are very big statements, claiming that billionaires have become addicted to what they do because of intermittent rewards from doing unorthodox things. Well, by now the fact that they are unorthodox should be clear, but becoming addicted from having intermittent rewards in very few areas of activity, isn't that a bit far-fetched? It is far from being far-fetched as you will see in chapter 24.

Chapter 24

Learning about learning

Children are programmed to learn—that is their job until at least early adulthood and, for many of us in this ever-changing world, right into old age. It is clear that while growing up the billionaires learned things that were substantially different from what others learned and pursued those activities with much more vigour than is normally the case. We need to look at how learning happens to get a better understanding of what happened to the billionaires.

Pavlov's dog and other animals

One of the greatest contributions to the understanding of the psychology of learning didn't start out with a psychologist at all but with a physiologist, Ivan Petrovich Pavlov. He discovered that a dog would salivate at the sound of a bell if it had become used to hearing a bell just before it was fed. He also found that the dog would salivate at the sound of the bell even if it wasn't fed. This is called a conditioned response.

This became the starting point for a large body of work by the behaviourist school of psychology, which was carried out during the early and mid twentieth century. This work showed that animals could be conditioned to behave in certain ways through cycles of reward and punishment. This is not surprising, as animal trainers have been doing this for millennia, but it was important work because they gave such learning a scientific basis and generalised it to that most adaptable of animals, humans.

Because the behaviourists overemphasised the similarity between animal studies and human behaviour, and since people generally don't like to think of themselves as animals, the behaviourist school of thought fell into general disrepute They compounded their error by claiming everything in human behaviour could be reduced to simple action and reaction, and that interaction could be modelled on animals in the lab. They also fell foul of the general mood against using animals in laboratory testing, and lost the support of future generations of psychologists who dubbed the discipline the study of 'rats and stats'.

Despite their unpopular claims and lack of political correctness, there is a lot to be learned from their work. So let's try a thought experiment using a situation that most people will be familiar with—pet dog behaviour. Anyone with a dog will know that there are certain sounds that a dog will respond to in very particular ways. There are sounds that it associates with rewards or pleasure, such as opening the refrigerator or the sound of the cupboard opening that contains its lead, or its owner putting on a hat and coat, or the word 'walk' or simply the front door opening. These are all sounds that it has learned will precede pleasant experiences—food, walking and attention.

At the other end of the spectrum are the not-so-pleasant sounds, such as its owner calling it with an angry voice—this could lead to a smack. Such unpleasant sounds could also include the dog groomer's voice on a home visit or the clanging of a cage that will carry the dog to the vet.

Dogs can become remarkably sensitive to very particular sounds. In any dog's life there is a spectrum of sounds that can mean pleasure (go there) or pain (get away), and sounds that are irrelevant. But there is an additional class of sound that is very confusing, such as hearing its name called lovingly (pleasure) just after hearing water running in the tub (pain). The water heralds a bath, which is generally hated, and the loving voice is associated with good things, so the dog becomes confused and generally behaves that way. It may come but whine, or slink away with its tail between its legs. These sounds are mixed.

For dogs there are pleasure sounds, pain sounds, irrelevant sounds and mixed sounds. If the sounds are repeated with the same consequences and only those consequences then the dog will rapidly learn that the sound and consequence go together. Once that link has been made, the consequence need only be associated with the sound every now and again to reinforce the link. If the proximity of sound and consequence stops, never to be repeated, then eventually the link will be extinguished.

This explanation crudely represents a particular type of animal learning. There are many books available if you want to pursue this further, but the above should suffice for this discussion. In essence there is the stimulation (in the case of the dog example, sound) closely followed by a consequence (pleasure or pain). For the animal the stimulation becomes inextricably linked with the consequence, and after a time the animal will respond to the stimulation even if the consequence rarely follows.

A very important finding that the behaviourists made was about intermittent rewards. Animals responded much more vigorously to stimulation if they did not receive that stimulation all the time. People are the same—eat steak all the time and people will get bored. Eat steak as a treat once a month and it becomes very important. If that happens when we are growing up, we will probably love steak for the rest of our lives. Food habits learned while young are very hard to break—it contributed to Elvis's death. Perhaps this explains Buffett's love of hamburgers and raspberry cola.

Equally, animals and people have to receive the stimulation some of the time to reinforce the activity. If it only happens once, it is unlikely to have a lasting effect.

Primitive learning in people

People aren't dogs. Our lives are much more complex and not so easily determined. In a day, we have to differentiate between literally thousands of sounds—people, events—and decide what to pay attention to and what to ignore.

By the time we are adults we have to attend to and process a river of information to get through a normal day. Most situations have been learned about and once learned we respond in a relatively automatic, conditioned way. Having learned about how things work and using similar but more complex inputs than a dog might, we largely travel on autopilot. Our emotions are very finely tuned to the possibility of pleasure, pain and relevance, they operate extremely rapidly, much faster than rational thought, and protect us from anticipated danger or lead us to anticipated reward. If a new situation passes the basic emotional tests then it can safely be processed in a number of other ways, such as more conditioning or by rational thought.

> By the time we are adults we have to attend to and process a river of information to get through a normal day.

Young humans are really just cute little animals. Babies don't have any rational thought because they don't have enough experience in their cute little heads to make any rational decisions. Babies recognise the signals from their bodies telling them whether they are comfortable or not. As they get older they associate sounds and activities with things that happen and they learn or are conditioned. Mothers are usually associated with many of the pleasant things, and generally babies learn that their mothers are good and can be trusted, so they begin to relax around their mother and trust what she does. Mothers are then responsible for introducing new experiences at a controlled rate.

This is what happens to about two-thirds of infants. Unfortunately for the other third, mother provides painful or mixed signals—both are bad and, like the example of the dog, these signals could produce lasting behavioural problems. This appears to be what happened in the early lives of many of the billionaires. Intrusive mothers provide both pleasure and pain simultaneously or unpredictably, and infants want to go to them and want to get away from them. This may be one of Gates's problems and almost certainly is an issue for Buffett, Icahn, Geffen and Lauren.

Learning about life

As people get older, they grow apart from their mothers and have a far richer range of experiences, but their primary way of understanding the world is still very similar. They rapidly become conditioned by stimulation and its consequence. School is one of the next great learning experiences, and what a child learns in the classroom and schoolyard is critical to how it progresses through school and what lessons it takes into later life.

I'd like to return to the male billionaires and school sport. Many boys, perhaps most, enjoy school sport. There is the pleasure of emerging skill, beating the odds, rushing hormones, camaraderie, perhaps rewards for being a hero, establishing oneself in the pecking order, beating someone else, and admiration from peers, teachers and girls.

Sure there is a bit of pain and effort but that is outweighed by the pleasure. Sport and pleasure become inextricably linked or conditioned together. Some boys want to play more sport, which leads to more pleasure. Over time these associations become incredibly strong, so much so that sport and pleasure become inextricably linked in sportspeople's minds. Their mind wires up in this way.

For people who strongly associate sport with pleasure, the love of sport will endure long after active or even regular participation has ceased. While still actively playing sport, they may do as much as they can humanly fit in. Even after their active sporting life is over, there is frequently ongoing reinforcement — usually discussing the football at Monday morning's business meeting reinforces the feeling of belonging to a 'tribe' and restimulates the love of sport. With this level of involvement, the love of sport often endures for the rest of their lives. This also explains the silly debates that can be heard about one type of sport or one type of football being better than another. There is little objective difference between sporting codes. The differences are really all in which code the person gained pleasure from when they were growing up. They are really arguing about who had the best childhood!

But sport and pleasure aren't inextricably linked — this is not a god-given association. There is perhaps a minority of children who lose much more than they gain when they play sport. They suffer humiliations and they may get hurt because they are small, uncoordinated or simply unable to perform well enough. Not playing sport adds to their loss of standing in the pecking order, causing even more humiliation. Gates, Jobs and most of the other billionaires belong to this group. For these people sport and pain are inextricably linked, and quite naturally they avoided sport as much as they could to avoid the pain. If they were forced to participate even by well-intentioned people, people who associate sport with pleasure, the hostile reaction in these boys would become even greater. Boys will associate pain with the people who forced them to endure pain and hate them too.

Often it is the occasional sports hero who becomes the most addicted to the sport because the intermittent rewards were all the sweeter than those received by the constant hero, and both receive better rewards than the constant failure.

In the development of boys, sport is merely the stimulation and not all that important in itself. It is the pleasure or pain associated with sport that endures.

Finding the inner workaholic

Even if a child had a miserable time playing sport, there are often many other things in life that can give pleasure. Many people get by on being associated with the family or being in another social group such as Scouts or joining a hiking club. Most people can point to a number of things that give them pleasure. They often have a surfeit of choice. On Saturday they may make a choice between sport, either as a participant or spectator, going to the theatre, having dinner with friends or relaxing with loved ones. All of these things have given pleasure in the past and can be expected to do so in the future.

But people who have had significant failure in the three great domains of family, school and friends usually don't have such rich choices. They have a limited choice when it comes to doing what gives them pleasure or avoids pain.

This is what happened to the billionaires. School made them miserable, as did home. But they all found something that gave them pleasure, and because this was unique in their lives they worked hard at it. Every small, intermittent reward fed their appetite. The more they did of this activity, the more they narrowed their focus and the more they were dependent upon it for pleasure. This led to them repeating this activity until it became a self-reinforcing cycle and they became obsessed. They became addicts. This is exactly the type of behavior seen in chronic gambling, shopping and other addictions. People can become pretty much addicted to anything if the pleasure derived from it is so great that it overwhelms everything else. These billionaires became addicted to business and work. This is why Branson is both a deal and attention junkie. It's why Gates built Microsoft in the image of his school computer club and it's why Ellison spins his stories. It also explains why Kamprad has to keep expanding IKEA and it's why Winfrey keeps going.

Mostly things that are socially desirable are not seen as addictions, but the mechanisms for becoming addicted to them are very much the same. It doesn't matter if the activity in question is socially acceptable or not. People can be addicted to sport either as a participant, spectator or club member. This is rarely seen as a problem in our sports-oriented culture. In recent years the terms shopaholic and chocoholic have been coined to cover very specific female addictions. Many males have equivalent technical addictions, needing to be up with the latest phone, gadget or computer and many people are addicted to their mobile phones and text messaging. Addiction to BlackBerry use seems to be very common among some businesspeople who check every few minutes to make sure they are still thought of.

The term workaholic is usually only applied to people who are addicted to work and not so effective at it. Being a workaholic does not make a person wealthy — it merely makes that person work hard and long. After all, the world is full of people who work very, very hard and make very little money.

Billionaires are workaholics; they *are* addicted. They are addicted to their work for the simple reason that it provides not only the intermittent pleasure they need in their lives, but also allows them to avoid engaging in the things that cause them pain. They gained both direction and drive, and they all developed physically punishing work schedules with a mono-focus. They keep going because it still provides them with the social rewards they need and the connection with the original circumstances that started it in the first place.

This is the reason all the billionaires worked so slavishly once they had found their salvation. When they were young it was one of the few things they had in their lives that gave them moderately reliable pleasure. They invested everything they had in it, to the exclusion of just about everything else. Intermittent rewards focused on a very small range of activities will do this.

Balanced personalities don't become addicts. And, like any addicts, workaholics aren't balanced, therefore it follows that self-made billionaires don't have balanced personalities! While each followed a different route to a similar state of work addiction, the result was the same. It must be stated that being a workaholic is not generally about the money, although that does come into it. After all, Gates keeps score by it and gains a lot of approval for it. But in the early days, at least, it was about getting that hard-to-find emotional reward.

Many people are obsessed, but few become billionaires from their obsession. In addition to having some commercial value, there has to be an ability to convert that obsessive effort into wealth. Trading is required. Chapter 25 explores trading intelligence.

Chapter 25

Trading intelligence

Almost everyone has some experience of IQ tests. Despite having been extensively developed and carried out on millions of people there is a sense of unease about these tests in the general public. This is because almost everyone has had experiences in which their own assessment of a person's intelligence is different from that shown by these tests. Putting aside the normal bias that you may have about your own results or those of your children, it is often difficult to reconcile personal experience with test results.

A short critique on intelligence

There are people who are thought to be 'dumb' but score brilliantly on tests and there are others who score poorly on tests but are considered bright.

Now I'd like to return to the great Professor Albert Einstein. There is no doubt that he was a genius. He was a near failure at school, extraordinarily adept at a few subjects and an almost complete failure in others. He failed his entry exam to the Zurich Polytechnic, and did so poorly in his doctoral class he found it nearly impossible to get even a lowly tutoring position. If there were IQ tests at the time, he may or may not have scored well. His score would have depended in part on whether or not he was feeling cooperative. Even if he had cooperated, he may not have achieved a high score because his genius was very strongly focused in a few areas and he was relatively weak in others. In addition, his genius was not based on the convergent thinking required for normal academic performance. Convergent thinking is that which recreates what is already known. His thinking was divergent—he was a creator in the greatest sense of the word, and that isn't recognised by tests because by its very nature creativity cannot be given a standard score.

Despite his undoubted genius at theoretical physics, Einstein's intelligence was unbalanced. He was very much a social and organisational cretin. He couldn't function properly without one of his string of women and assistants looking after his day-to-day life. The man could barely look after himself. Isaac Newton, another genius physicist who discovered many of the laws of motion, was a sociopath. He spent most of his adult life cloistered at Cambridge University and died a virgin. Although Einstein had considerable charm to offset his social and practical shortcomings, neither Einstein nor Newton were poster boys for balanced intelligence.

Then there are plenty of other people who are considered to be very intelligent but who also score badly on tests. There is the nearly illiterate motor mechanic who can get a broken-down car going in the middle of a storm apparently by just jiggling a few wires or the 'unsophisticated' bulldozer driver who can carve a near perfect thirty-kilometre track out of the bush without using a survey map. The midwife who can deliver a baby better than any gynaecologist, and the working mother who can close that critical deal in the afternoon and still get her child fed and to tennis by 6 pm. These are real tasks that require real intelligence to perform, intelligence that is not covered in any real way by intelligence theory or tests.

It is now clichéd to consider that IQ is what intelligence tests measure. IQ is taken to be intelligence when in actual fact it is only what is measured by the tests. IQ tests are constructed to serve particular purposes, which are mainly related to succeeding in education. This is a key failing of IQ tests because very few are designed to predict success in life after school. Indeed, having seen the irrelevance of the self-made billionaires' academic performance it is tempting to also conclude that school performance is no indicator of post-school performance, at least as far as becoming a billionaire is concerned.

Unfortunately intelligence tests are used as barriers to entry for many children. Mrs Branson knew her little boy was smarter than the tests told her but couldn't prove it. Intelligence tests have changed a bit since Branson was a boy — these new tests may have gone some distance to helping Richard had they been used then.

Intelligence tests, or IQ tests as they are now known, are quite good at predicting academic performance, or rather they are good at predicting performance if the person tested has the same level of motivation to perform on the test as they have during schooling.

But as Sperling found, academia is much more interested in serving its own industry rather than the working world in general. This is only natural since academic standing depends on the opinion of peers.

Radical change in education, as with most industries, can usually only come from outsiders with nothing to lose and everything to gain. There are many examples of this, such as when Charles Darwin introduced his theories or Einstein tried to introduce his.

Not only is the general public becoming increasingly frustrated with academia but so are decision makers. The general level of education has risen in the population, particularly since the surge of degrees earned during the 1960s and 1970s. There has been a jump in the proportion of senior managers with degrees and an increasingly credentialed workforce. Senior managers aren't as impressed by degrees and doctorates as previous generations were. They want the people that they employ to be able to produce results.

The general level of education has risen in the population, particularly since the surge of degrees earned during the 1960s and 1970s.

Underneath the general angst between decision makers and the public on the one hand and academia on the other, is the fundamental difference of opinion about what an education should achieve. People outside academia almost universally want it to lead to productive activity. They may want a good general grounding in liberal arts as cultural garnish, but fundamentally they want economic results. By and large, academics aren't interested in economic results, they are interested in perpetuating academia and their place in it. Hence, definitions of intelligence are self-serving and are designed almost exclusively for predicting academic performance, so there is a fundamental conflict between the meaning of intelligence as used by academics and as used by the public in general and decision makers in particular.

When an academic speaks of intelligence it usually means the demonstration of abilities needed to achieve academic results. When a layperson talks about intelligence it is usually in relation to a person being able to achieve something useful. Accomplishment of academic results is only of relevance to non-academics when they or their children are studying, but it is always relevant to academics. Unfortunately there is a whole world of human achievement out there that is not explained by academic formulations of intelligence.

Laypeople expect a spread of abilities that goes way beyond achieving good results in school. They expect people to function in the world across a broad spectrum of activities. For them, intelligence is about doing things. School work, puzzles and little tests are all very interesting but if it doesn't lead to useful outcomes in the real world, the public gets frustrated.

The general model of intelligence understood by the public and employers is actually about demonstrations of useful abilities — it is all tied up with function.

It would be selling the intelligence theories short if it was maintained that IQ tests represented the sum of knowledge about intelligence, but they do tend to dominate. Perhaps IQ tests would be less confusing if they were renamed Schooling Aptitude Tests.

There is no generally applicable model of intelligence that relates to everyday life; consequently there is a need for a radical re-think of intelligence. A tentative start is proposed in the following section, based on first principles, which looks to explain intelligence in everyday activities and trading in particular.

Power and multiple intelligences theories

The work on intelligence points to intelligence having two important dimensions.

The first is intellectual power, which is what IQ scores are supposed to represent when they are produced as a single score. This is roughly comparable to intellectual horsepower or processing power. This is such a well-understood concept that there is no need to discuss further.

The second concept is where all the confusion comes in. The concept in question is multiple intelligences. When people talk about intelligence they actually choose one or two attributes to describe a person. Laypeople's model of intelligence could easily include Einstein and Newton, but they would become perplexed on contact with these professors because they wouldn't understand how a person can be a genius in one area but so manifestly unintelligent in others. Both Newton and Einstein could have been variously called genius or simpleton depending on which intellectual attributes were being described. Both are correct!

Multiple intelligences theories have existed for a long time. They were first formalised by Louis Leon Thurstone in the 1930s. There have been various new formulations up until the present time, one of the latest theoreticians being Dr Howard Gardner. At first glance all of the multiple intelligences theories seem to have validity; that is until they are tested against real situations. Developed by academics using students as their lab rats for consumption by the education industry, multiple intelligences theories as they are currently formulated are unsatisfactory for use on people in the real world.

Gardner proposed seven intelligences, namely: linguistic, logical-mathematical, musical, bodily-kinaesthetic, spatial, interpersonal and intrapersonal. Initially, these intelligences have a certain face validity—they look like they could explain different abilities and to a certain limited extent they do. It's easy to see that a university research scientist would be strong in logical-mathematical intelligence and to also see that Soros and Buffett would be similar; however, on a multiple-intelligences test there would probably be little to differentiate between Soros and Buffett and such a scientist, but clearly life and economic outcomes tell us differently.

The tests probably couldn't differentiate between, say, Jobs or Winfrey and an English lecturer; or Gates and a law lecturer; or Icahn and a philosophy lecturer; or Schwab and a business school professor. There would be little to differentiate between the academics and the billionaires on these multiple intelligences, yet plainly there is a great deal unexplained and it can't all be just a matter of learning.

In reality, Gardner's multiple intelligences are merely schooling aptitudes dressed up as intelligences. They are what are needed for school performance in language, maths and science, sport, music and socialising. They are not enough to explain the intelligences that are required to live out of school.

Since Gardner, there have been two important extensions of multiple intelligences, or perhaps elaborations, proposed by Daniel Goleman—these are emotional and social intelligence, which overlap with Gardner's interpersonal and intrapersonal intelligences. How could these have been overlooked for so long? It is impossible to live in society without them! Emotional and social intelligence merge into the ways of making money proposed by Dale Carnegie—make friends and influence people.

These two intelligences when combined with the other multiple intelligences still fall very far short of explaining human behaviour. Perhaps they explain some of the social and family side of life and some other basic skills such as navigating around without bumping into things and talking to each other, but they don't explain much about vocational choice or functional strengths and weaknesses. The term functional is used in its broadest possible sense to mean what people do to live their day-to-day lives—it may be mothering or fathering, farming, fishing, soldiering, law making or enforcing, teaching, health care, music, storytelling, or the subject of this section of the book, trading.

It is proposed that there are multiple functional intelligences. These intelligences are there to put food on the table, shelter over our heads and clothes on our backs, as well as to find a mate and maintain a family—humans have to do things. The better people are at all of those things the more likely their offspring are to grow up to do the same, and so on in perpetuity.

Having said that, the two concepts of intellectual power and multiple intelligences are still useful—the latter needs to be extended rather than abandoned.

Intelligence is for doing things

Intelligence is of no use if it is not used to do things. That is its point! Academics are right from their point of view—intelligence tests are good at predicting academic performance, so they are valid if that is all you want to predict.

But most people want to do more than just pass tests. Even while still at school and university, most people have other things they need to do. People need to work, to travel, to do jobs for their parents. They also need to make and maintain relationships.

As human society became more complex, individuals were forced to specialise. It is possible that we have to learn every skill from a standing start, but unlikely. This would be dreadfully inefficient, and since adaptation is one of our greatest assets it is most likely that there is some genetic adaptation over a relatively short span of time to give our progeny a head start in life.

Genetic theory is still undecided on the length of time it takes for human genes to adapt. At one end there is the theory that we haven't changed much for 100 000 years or so, and at the other end that we have adapted to the hamburger we had this morning. As with all these things, when the experts finally get it measured, it is likely that some genes may be found to change over relatively short spans of time depending on the conditions and what they are about. Such spans may be in the order of ten to 500 years—not so fast as to cause chaos, but not so slow that the species gets wiped out before useful adaptation takes place.

There is undoubtedly genetic change in humans over time in response to their environment and it's equally likely that these changes have helped us function in our ever more complex society.

Trading as a natural or innate intelligence

It is proposed here that in adapting to their environment, humans develop innate tendencies to perform particular functions. These tendencies take the form of specific functional intelligence. It is further proposed that trading is one of these intelligences and that trading has some biological basis and is affected by genes. These propositions can't be tested in any formal sense but there is some compelling evidence.

It is also not likely that there are specific genes—for instance, a trading gene. Trading, like any of the other multiple (functional) intelligences, may be encoded in the gene structure in a diffuse way, merely providing a weak aptitude and interest to be built on if the environment is right.

Nor is it proposed that it operates as a fully-formed intelligence from birth. People tend to gravitate to what they are both good at and rewarded for—the verbally inclined are rewarded for speaking, the logical for analysis. These skills don't start out fully formed, and without reward may remain largely unformed. But Icahn's almost instant uptake of poker in the army and then extending into playing poker with corporate boards suggests he had a very strong innate trading intelligence just sitting there waiting for the opportunity to be developed and used. It also suggests such an innate intelligence may be stronger in some people and weaker in others. But we all have to trade to get through the day.

First, there is strong evidence of there being biological variations between people on the type of intelligence they possess. You only have to look at school performance to see that there are major irreconcilable differences between the science and maths geeks on the one hand and the literature and arts clique on the other.

Despite having very much the same education up until the end of primary school, specialisation is almost inevitable by the time a child enters secondary school. No matter how hard the English teacher tries to bludgeon the science and maths geeks to understand, let alone take an interest in, *Wuthering Heights* or *Macbeth,* mediocrity is the best anyone can expect. On the other side, the budding literati can't be railroaded into taking an interest in or develop much understanding of statistics, calculus and algebra either.

Unfortunately the geeks have to keep going with literature because it is deemed essential, despite a breathtaking lack of connection between English competence and later income, while the literati are allowed to duck out of maths and physics. English is retained as a compulsory subject because it has 'cultural benefits' but maths and physics are allowed to be dropped because they are considered non-essential.

As Gates says, money is a great way to keep score. In keeping with the Gates credo, simply splitting the self-made billionaires into those who chose subjects that were more numbers-based versus arts-based gives a staggering $118 billion to the numerate, $56 billion to the unclear and $14 billion to the arts-based. While there are statistical dangers in splitting such a small sample, this telling split indicates much better income results for those with a numerate bias as opposed to an arts bias. There may be an argument that literature has cultural value, but that is hard to measure.

There may be an argument that literature has cultural value, but that is hard to measure.

As interesting as this is, it is not the main proposition here. The main proposition is that there is some biological basis for different functional intelligences and that they are developed through interaction with a person's environment.

Second, there is the generally unexplored matter of people having a 'calling', or being attracted to one occupation or activity over all the rest and then excelling in it. This is more complicated to untangle because a calling will certainly be influenced by impacts in the environment. But there are two clear examples, in Icahn and Soros, of self-made billionaires whose innate intelligence or calling was stronger than the environmental pressures and these billionaires went against their early conditioning.

Icahn's degree was in philosophy but his mother passionately demanded he be a doctor. Icahn could handle medical theory well enough but fled the hospital ward when confronted by sick people. Obviously he wasn't a natural healer. A brief sojourn in the army introduced him to poker and he discovered his calling, so much so that he made sufficient money to provide an early stake. Poker led him to company trading, where he plays a kind of negotiation poker in his takeover games. He could only join that game if he reconciled the antagonism towards capitalists gained from his parents with making money, hence his need for punishing capitalists for his own gain.

Soros did not want to be a trader, he wanted to be a philosopher but discovered that he was not going to be a success in that occupation. Soros, however, had a natural talent for trading, so he traded despite his father insisting that he should not make money for money's sake. Soros could only reconcile this by using his innate intelligence, or calling, for trading to make a vast river of money and then giving it away.

In addition, most people have stories they can recall of the outsider made good, people who found their calling.

As a teenager, I worked in my father's small-town manufacturing and engineering works during vacations. He employed around fifty people. Most of the employees continued for all of their working lives in the occupations they started in, but two employees stand out in particular as not fitting this pattern.

One was a young man with a juvenile record and poor education. He had a prickly personality and was a loner. He was given a chance by my father and was employed as a storeman, soon to become a very good store manager. He could source any part, no matter how obscure. Out of hours he was always trading bits and pieces on his own behalf. He would buy an old car and fix it up, buy a piece of engineering equipment and find a profitable home for it, and so on. He was always trading, and aside from supporting a young family, always alone—an outsider in other words. After about five years he stopped working for my father, and continued trading on his own behalf, doing rather well in a shambling, opportunistic kind of way. He finally became quite a rich man, not that anyone would know by looking. He lived in a shanty adjoining what looked like a wrecker's yard but he had property and businesses all over town.

The second was a very good tradesman and a charming lad. He did his job exceptionally well but always bucked the administrative system. He too always had side deals going on. Fairly soon he left my father's works and began working for himself. His forte was starting new businesses just as that kind of business was beginning to get market acceptance. He built them up and sold them before the market topped or dropped, usually within five years of start-up. He had a garden-maintenance business, and he bought avocado and kiwi fruit orchards. He, like the first, had businesses and properties all over town but, being somewhat more socialised, had more of the trappings, such as a nice home and modest boat.

Both these men have become richer than my father. They weren't compulsive in the way the billionaires were. Neither of them ever had a stated goal to become rich, neither of them ever expressed jealousy or resentment towards my father and what he had when they worked for him. They just did what they did, traded and made money, while those around them stayed put, doing exactly what they did.

Lucas could easily have been exactly like these young men if he had stayed in his home town and not become obsessed with filmmaking.

My father, on the other hand, was a supremely competent engineer. He was a natural with steel and machinery but he was not a business natural. He did well enough, but never really flourished in business. In this book, he can be likened to an Allen. My father needed a trading partner like Gates to become really wealthy.

Most people would be able to point to people like this in their backgrounds. Teachers can often recall an unlikely student who made good. The dunce, the naughty student or the invisible truanting child, the student who out of school simply does what comes naturally, trades. Branson was like this; in fact, all the self-made billionaires were.

Some of the billionaires did it while in school and some were so good, like Buffett, that by the time they left they were earning more than their teachers. If Buffett hadn't much trading intelligence, given his numbers orientation he might have been an extremely good academic mathematician or been employed as an analyst in a stockbroking firm.

There are too many other environmental factors to form a clear picture of the genetic/environmental impact that operated on the others, but it is interesting to note that ten out of the seventeen billionaires have at least one biological parent who is a lawyer, stockbroker or business person, and the number increases if their grandparents are included.

Third, and this is strictly anecdotal, there is the experience of observing deals being negotiated and closed by natural traders. I have a moderate spread of intelligences, but unfortunately I am an unexceptional deal maker. It is not my calling. However, I have been fortunate to have participated in several deals as the person with technical abilities with a business partner who was an adept deal doer. Something happened during those negotiations but I'm not sure what it was. It was as if the negotiators were speaking a different language. It was exactly the same experience as watching any natural do what they do, be it a sportsperson, an engineer, an artist or an analyst. There is a kind of magic that goes beyond normal skill.

There is no doubt that there are multiple intelligences. And it is highly probable that intelligences exist that predispose people to pursue certain activities or perform certain functions associated with living. Trading is one such activity. In fact, there is no doubt that an innate trading ability exists in a large proportion of the self-made billionaires. All but Winfrey and Sperling exhibited strong trading abilities by their thirties. Some already showed it well before leaving school, others had it spring almost unexpectedly from nowhere.

Part V

LESSONS LEARNED

Chapter 26

Don't try this at home, folks

By now it should be clear that there is pain at the beginning of extreme wealth. It is absolutely certain that if offered the choice of a different start to life and the possibility of extreme wealth, every one of the self-made billionaires would have chosen a different childhood. None of the billionaires stated this, but what child would choose bullying and being ostracised over popularity and admiration?

Kids need love, not wealth

A baby needs love and certainty; the promise of wealth in the future is so far beyond its mental powers it is irrelevant. Acceptance and belonging to a peer group is much more important than future wealth to most children right up until leaving school—look at all the apparently senseless things that teenagers do just to belong. Remember all the stupid, dangerous and potentially self-destructive things you did as a teenager just to get that critical emotional sense of belonging you needed? If things had gone seriously wrong it could have had a negative effect on your future. Lucky you weren't caught!

Acceptance and belonging, rather than wealth, remains an enduring objective for much of the population right through their adult lives.

Money and happiness are uncomfortable bedfellows

There was certainly pain at the start of the billionaires' lives. There may be pain right through their whole adult life. There is no real way of telling this from the billionaires, as most put on a very good public face. But what are their emotional states behind the public face?

For well over fifty years, psychologists have been studying human happiness, and the result is very clear. Money does not bring happiness! But neither does it bring unhappiness. It merely brings money. Less than a certain amount may make a person miserable because they can't buy the essentials in life. More than a certain amount may also make a person miserable because of the demands to manage the money or demands from other people. The right amount is usually neutral.

But what people perceive as the right amount of money keeps growing, so more is required for people to feel the same. Studies of life satisfaction in the US over fifty years have shown that while the material wellbeing of US citizens has increased dramatically, their happiness has remained static. Being able to put a second, third or tenth car in the ever-growing garage doesn't actually make a person happier. Nor does air conditioning or a TV in every room, 500 pairs of shoes, twenty metres of clothes in a walk-in robe the size of the average house fifty years ago, a facial every second day, the latest mobile phone or a home entertainment system the size and quality of a major cinema. In fact, these things are more isolating than anything. Guards are needed to keep out the people who want to steal or just deface these people's property. To paraphrase comedian Billy Connelly, 'I have been poor and miserable and I have been rich and miserable. Rich is better'.

> Being able to put a second, third or tenth car in the ever-growing garage doesn't actually make a person happier.

To people with the hunger for money, making money provides a temporary relief to their hunger, so make money they will. No amount of money will be enough because money actually doesn't do anything but enable you to buy things and help define your status. Like heroin addicts, the volumes of money, possessions and status have to grow just to get the same fix.

Where increasing happiness with increasing wealth is most evident is usually in the lower income brackets. Small increases in income make big differences to the happiness of the poor. Once a person reaches the middle income brackets, the happiness to money curve flattens, and the more wealth increases the flatter the curve becomes, and according to some studies can even drop slightly. It is often the people with average family incomes that are the happiest. They usually have limited financial aspirations and the strongest family ties. Increasing wealth does not bring happiness.

Families and spouses are the real key to adult happiness

All the studies on happiness are clear on one fact. The key to happiness is a good family life followed by a good marriage — as if these two things aren't linked. Money comes a poor third to this, followed by housing, job, friendships, health and then leisure activities. Money tends to be associated with the latter sources of satisfaction but not much with the first two key factors.

People in any wealth bracket — from grinding poverty to extreme wealth — can have a happy family life and great spouses. It is probably less likely, but not impossible, at the grinding poverty end because of the harshness of day-to-day life. It is hard to be happy if your children are dying of malnutrition, disease or drug addictions.

As a group, the extremely wealthy are happier than the grindingly poor. Paradoxically they are less likely to be happier than people on average incomes because the characteristics needed to become extremely wealthy are also the ones that require family life to play second fiddle to money-making activities.

Ecclestone tries to spend half a day a week with his family. Lauren is reported to have an unhappy home life and few friends. Winfrey very publicly suffers. Buffett was a tourist in his home while his children were growing up. Geffen can't maintain a relationship and is constantly in therapy. Lucas lives without a partner as a luxury hermit on his ranch. Lowy is a loving autocrat. Sperling and Ellison can't sustain a marriage. Gates may have found true happiness now but was well out of contention until he married at thirty-eight; prior to that, he was reportedly unable to get a date despite his wealth. Ingvar Kamprad is a self-professed alcoholic given to publicly breaking down in tears.

Mortgaging kids' emotional present and future for the sake of their financial future

This book has shown that considerable pain is required in childhood to make colossal financial gains as adults. As adults, many of us make decisions to sacrifice our present for our futures — this is particularly so of those who choose to study. Many people do. They go back to school to study for that degree they had to have, or they work long hours at three jobs. But the quality of experience needed to become so extremely wealthy is completely different to that. It requires deep emotional trauma, such trauma that can only be gained in childhood. Such trauma that no-one would volunteer for it. As children, the billionaires wouldn't have volunteered for their own childhoods, even if the financial outcome was certain. And the financial outcome was always far from certain.

There is a rare class of parents who are excessively tough on their children for their 'own good'—to harden them up. Unfortunately, they are not rare enough. In the course of developing this book, I came across several people who were concerned that the book would provide a template for bad parenting—that it would encourage it. They were particularly concerned because their own parents had been deliberately neglectful or abusive in order to toughen them up. They carried deep emotional scars.

I was incredulous. As a parent, I know there are so many things that parents can get wrong without deliberately setting up harmful situations.

Of all the billionaires, Branson's mother abandoning her defenceless four year old to find his way home across country is the most pertinent example of making a child deliberately vulnerable to harden it for some future gain. There is no evidence that the parents of the other billionaires actually set out to provide 'beneficial' harm to their children in such a blatant way, but there are enough opportunities for things to go wrong in a growing child's life without deliberately setting out to do it.

There are a set of coded phrases that people use to justify beneficial harm to children. Two of these are 'You have to be cruel to be kind' and 'Spare the rod and spoil the child'. Undoubtedly the billionaires heard these and variations on these as they grew up, most particularly Winfrey, Lucas and Sperling.

A particularly pernicious one is 'If it was good enough for me, it is good enough for him'. Or variations on that theme. However, there is no guarantee that what parents perceive as having been beneficial to them will be good for the child. Actually, there is no guarantee that what a person perceives as being beneficial to themselves was actually beneficial at all. Most people can only guess at what was good or harmful in their lives.

Children are different from their parents. The times are different, the child has a different set of genes, has different mental and physical capabilities and has had different experiences. The child is a different person with different abilities and needs. If a child wouldn't naturally choose to do something then there may be something wrong with the experience it is being coerced into having.

A 'good' experience may actually harm them! For male children, harm can happen around sport where a particularly ambitious father wants his son to follow in his footsteps. Fathers forcing children into sport is not reported for the billionaires—it may or may not have happened. There are examples, however, of bullying parents trying to force their child into occupations they didn't want to be in. Lauren's mother tried to force him to be a rabbi and moved him from school to school to achieve it, and Icahn's mother tried to force him to be a doctor.

The ideal way to rear a child

Chapter 22 dealt with the ideal way to bring up a child. Simply put, a child requires—after food, water, shelter and temperature control—love and expressions of love through sound, sight and particularly touch. They also need predictability and a growing sense of being able to influence their environments, with a bit of uncertainty thrown in since life won't be predictable all the time.

An ideal upbringing is mostly loving, predictable and responsive, but sometimes not any of these things, whereas a 'perfect' upbringing has a sense of rigid order about it, which paradoxically isn't ideal.

The billionaires had far from ideal upbringings and suffered for it. They suffered as children and most likely still are, but at least now their suffering has been financially compensated.

Having given that health warning, I will now move on to the final chapter. Chapter 27 summarises why the billionaires became wealthy and what lessons ordinary mortals can take from their achievements.

Chapter 27

Hope for the future

In this book I have looked at seventeen self-made billionaires, and while there is no recipe or silver bullet it can be confidently stated from this research that for someone to become a self-made billionaire it is necessary to be a driven outsider with trading intelligence and direction. I am also confident that for every one of the self-made billionaires there must be tens of thousands of other outsiders who have trading intelligence and direction who *haven't* become billionaires, but many have become quite rich.

Outsiders have the edge

There are no statistics on this yet—this is a project I intend to undertake—but almost everyone I have spoken to about this project knows someone who has the trading outsider characteristics. It is a relatively common phenomenon. These people have made what appears to be an unreasonable amount of money out of unlikely projects or career transitions. I can name at least a dozen out of my own experiences, such as the electrician or the immigrant concrete worker who independently became one of the nation's greatest developers or the dyslexic brother of a poor academic who lives in a mansion.

But there is obviously more to becoming a self-made billionaire. The necessary conditions for making extreme wealth on one's own behalf appear to be for the person to be a driven trading outsider. The most wealthy self-made billionaires fit this model perfectly. They have difference, direction, drive and trading skills.

Moving down the list of billionaires, trading seems to decline somewhat while other talents are more prevalent. Lucas, Spielberg and Winfrey are all great talents in an industry that rewards talent extraordinarily well. Jobs is somewhat more of an inventor than a trader but has made much more money recently after taking a leaf out of Gates's book and has bought companies with a proven product rather than inventing his own. Sperling is a product champion and made money when he brought in a business manager.

The act of trading is easy. All it requires is for two people to transact in some way. But there is a popular misconception that any bright person can make money by trading. Not so. Many otherwise bright people trade very badly! Take a look at the stock market and you will see that this is so. Many very bright people get caught in the inevitable correction at the end of a long bull run and suffer large financial losses.

Returning to Gates and Allen, Gates would have done pretty much what he did without Allen — he would have found someone else to do the technical development work. Allen without Gates would probably be a senior manager in a computer company nearing retirement and certainly not the nineteenth richest man in the world with $18 billion. By any measure, Allen has done well by being in partnership with Gates and it is not a bad model for bright technical outsiders to follow.

At the time Microsoft started, there were hundreds if not thousands of people attached to the edge of the computer industry, all with exactly the same opportunity as Gates. Most of these people were technical people, more or less inventor types. They were fascinated with the processes, and if they thought about the market at all they expected the market to come to them because they had the best product. The market didn't. Gates recognised this and he cleaned them up! Even if Gates is years late into a market, as he was with the internet, he eventually wins.

Ellison had his first major win against a product-oriented company. They were slow to market and Oracle fast. They had the better product, Ellison had the better trading power. Ellison won.

Gates and Ellison are disliked in their own industries and Jobs is loved. All of them are tough, but more importantly the inventors are angry that trading beats technical superiority in the market. Gates and Ellison are traders, whereas Jobs appears to be one of them, an underdog inventor made good.

Trading almost always beats invention. Most inventors who make money are the ones that are good at both inventing and trading — Thomas Edison was such a man. The obvious solution for inventors is to find their own traders, as Sperling, Gates, Ellison and Jobs's partners did.

It is not just inventors who benefit from being associated with traders. Joni Mitchell and Don Henley, both 1970s pop music stars, observed that David Geffen was getting richer than they were. Ultimately Geffen was to become much, much richer than either of his famous talents. Joni Mitchell and Don Henley did very well from their time of fame. Both did better financially than if they hadn't been associated with Geffen, and if they aren't rich now it is because they didn't manage their wealth well. Geffen did and he always made money. When he didn't have famous talent to trade he traded property, movie studios, record companies and musical productions.

> Outsiders have an edge over the rest of the population because they are different.

Outsiders have an edge over the rest of the population because they are different. That coupled with direction and drive is a potent mix. If wealth is the required outcome, trading outsiders have an even bigger edge. If you are a trading outsider, then you are lucky. If you are an outsider who doesn't have good trading intelligence, then find a business partner who does.

Outsiders are everywhere

By my estimate it's possible that up to one-third of males and a slightly smaller proportion of females are outsiders to some extent. Yet there are relatively few self-made billionaires, so what of the rest?

Some extreme achievers in other fields have already been mentioned. These include Albert Einstein, Sigmund Freud, Sir Edmund Hillary, Amelia Earhart, Coco Chanel, Walt Disney, Jack Kerouac, Pablo Picasso, Andy Warhol, Winston Churchill, John F Kennedy, Elvis Presley and John Lennon. All of these are or were outsiders.

Stepping back from the rarefied company of the extreme achievers it is obvious that we really don't know what happens to the rest of the outsiders.

Drawing on personal experience, I have found outsiders everywhere, at the top and bottom of corporations or government and in all levels and occupations in between. Just like everyone else, they are in all walks of life — they run small businesses, are doctors, lawyers, artists, mechanics, managers, nurses, mothers and some are unemployed. They are strongly represented in the arts and media.

Since being a square peg in a round hole is not an easy path to success, outsiders seem to be over-represented among the highly unsuccessful. Too often they are misunderstood and shut out of opportunities because they won't be heard or their ideas seem too wacky.

Yet they also seem to be over-represented in the highly successful too. So being a square peg in a round hole may indeed have some benefits. Most blue-chip CEOs and board members I have met are outsiders to some degree, as are heads of government departments. These people have learnt to adapt to hierarchies and have made it. Many high-profile media personalities give the appearance of being outsiders — even some of the ones in sport.

It would appear that outsiders are everywhere!

Difficult beginnings can lead to extraordinary outcomes

The billionaires are both extraordinary and ordinary. Outside of their achievements they do very much the same things as anyone else and have similar requirements. Like everyone else, they can buy what they can afford but they can't buy everything, and the one thing they can't buy is happiness.

Childhood pain is at the centre of achieving extreme wealth. This fact has been hidden in plain sight because people don't think of the extremely wealthy as being more or less ordinary people with more or less ordinary beginnings. They think of them as exceptional people and so look at the exceptional things in their life. But exceptional things only occur to people after they become exceptional; anything before that is not exceptional so isn't noticed. It is only described, if at all, as a kind of background to their lives. But the billionaires' backgrounds do more than just set the scene, they are the key.

There are implications for parenthood and child rearing and there are some surprising implications for schooling. This group of individuals has achieved wealth on a heroic scale, yet not only are they not heroic now, but they were so far from being heroic at school that any suggestion of their future success would have been considered madness. They were the kids voted least likely to succeed. They were the little kids, the tall gangling kids, the ugly kids, the annoying kids, the invisible kids, the 'dumb' kids, the bright nerds, the strange kids from somewhere else. As a group they generally didn't play sport or have best friends, let alone date, and their academic achievement was irrelevant. They didn't make it into the yearbooks. They suffered through school.

For parents of difficult or learning-challenged children (mainly boys) or outsider children in general—success and/or popularity at school is not a precondition to achieving extreme wealth. Conversely, poor academic, social and sporting achievements may ultimately imbue people with attributes that lead them to unconventional success.

In addition, the attributes required to achieve massive wealth in a lifetime are so extreme that there is no point suffering from wealth envy. Take the pressure off a bit and enjoy yourself; there may be a halfway point that will provide you with everything you need.

There are no secret moves for becoming a self-made billionaire, no slavish formulae to follow; all of the billionaires made their money doing different things in different ways. Their achievements were dependent on being different from those around them. Having different personalities and dealing differently with the circumstances they found themselves in. Technology and media billionaires seem to get all the press but billionaires are being made in other industries at a far greater rate. We live in a time when change is accelerating at a rate never before seen and it won't slow down any time soon. The opportunities for finding new ways to make money are also accelerating—they can come from any place, any industry, any person and at any time.

Success in life is not just about wealth. Outsiders received a gift they had no wish to receive; being an outsider is a double-edged sword. Outsiders suffer socially, especially at school, but they often have qualities that are exceptional in all sorts of ways. There is evidence that many of the people who go on to achieve extraordinary success are, or were, also outsiders; for example, Winston Churchill, Albert Einstein and John Lennon to name three.

If the self-made billionaires hadn't made it so big in life they would have been the forgotten kids. They were the kid at the back of the class, or the kid sitting next to you. With a few differences they might even have been you. They weren't the kids others admired or envied.

All these billionaires were discriminated against for being different. They all suffered. Did this disable them? It did not! Did they sit around licking their wounds? They did not! Did they complain about injustice or seek revenge? If they did, the only revenge they sought was the best sort—extreme success!

There is a secret of extreme wealth. It is not a formula to be slavishly followed in any business book sense. The secret is deeply grounded in childhood! All these self-made billionaires were forced out of the mainstream when they were at school. They had to invent their own lives. Relatively unrestrained by the conservatism of group think promoted by schools and society in general, they all developed an unorthodox mix of skills, interests and personality traits that set them apart.

Starved of approval, they concentrated more on the few activities that gave them the approval they craved. This approval came from participating in unorthodox activities. So critical was this approval in their formative years that the activities became embedded in their personalities. Approval and unorthodox activities became inextricably linked in a self-reinforcing cycle. This cycle led them to develop their inner drive. Approval and differences powered them.

The billionaires developed the right tools to make their wealth during their school years. They didn't know they were the right tools and they didn't know where their difference, direction and drive would lead. They were lucky they weren't deflected into orthodox jobs because they couldn't flourish in someone else's hierarchy. They tempered their outsider's edge with fire and wielded it with spectacular results

The self-made billionaires remain as they have been all their lives—outsiders!

Bibliography

Baxter, J 1999, *George Lucas: a Biography*, HarperCollins, London.

Baxter, J 1996, *Steven Spielberg: the Unauthorised Biography*, HarperCollins, London.

Bower, T 2000, *Branson*, Fourth Estate, London.

Branson, R 2002, *Losing My Virginity*, Random House, Australia.

Bruck, C 1988, *The Predators' Ball: the Inside Story of Drexel Burnham and the Rise of the Junk Bond Raiders*, Penguin, Melbourne.

Cringely, RX 1993, *Accidental Empires*, Penguin Books, London.

Dearlove, D 2007, *Business the Richard Branson Way*, John Wiley & Sons, United Kingdom.

Forbes 'The World's Billionaires', <http://www.forbes.com/lists/>, accessed January 2007 to June 2007.

Gates, B 1995, *The Road Ahead*, Viking, United Kingdom.

Gross, M 2003, *Genuine Authentic: the Real Life of Ralph Lauren*, HarperCollins, New York.

Henry, A 2003, *The Power Brokers: the Battle for F1's Billions*, Motorbooks International, Minnesota.

Kador, J 2002, *Charles Schwab: How One Company Beat Wall Street and Reinvented the Brokerage Industry*, John Wiley & Sons, New Jersey.

Kamprad, I & Torekull, B 1998, *Leading by Design: the IKEA story*, HarperBusiness, New York.

Kaufman, MT 2002, *Soros*, Random House, New York.

Kilpatrick, A 2001, *Of Permanent Value: the Story of Warren Buffett*, McGraw-Hill, New York.

King, T 2000, *The Operator: David Geffen Builds, Buys and Sells the New Hollywood*, Broadway Books, New York.

Krohn, K 2000, *Oprah Winfrey*, Lerner Publications Company, Minneapolis.

Kurotani, K 2005, *George Soros: an Illustrated Biography of the World's Most Powerful Investor*, John Wiley & Sons, Singapore.

Lewis, E 2005, *Great IKEA! a Brand For All the People*, Cyan Books, London.

Lovell, T 2003, *Bernie's Game: Inside the Formula One World of Bernie Ecclestone*, Metro Books, London.

Lowe, J 1998, *Bill Gates Speaks: Insight From the World's Greatest Entrepreneur*, John Wiley & Sons, New York.

Lowenstein, R 1996, *Buffett: The Making of an American Capitalist*, Weidenfeld & Nicolson, London.

Manes, S & Andrews, P 1994, *Gates: How Microsoft's Mogul Reinvented an Industry and Made Himself the Richest Man in America*, Touchstone, New York.

Margo, J 2001, *Frank Lowy: Pushing the Limits*, HarperCollins, Sydney.

Moodie, A 1998, *Local Heroes: a Celebration of Success and Leadership in Australia*, Prentice Hall, Sydney.

Pollock, D 1999, *Skywalking: the Life and Films of George Lucas*, Da Capo Press, New York.

Singular, S 1997, *The Rise and Rise of David Geffen*, Birch Lane Press, New Jersey.

Slater, R 1996, *Soros: the Unauthorized Biography, the Life, Times and Trading Secrets of the World's Greatest Investor*, McGraw-Hill, New York.

Sperling, J 2000, *Rebel With a Cause*, John Wiley & Sons, New York.

Stevens, M 1993, *King Icahn: the Biography of a Renegade Capitalist*, Dutton, New York.

Stone, FM 2002, *The Oracle of Oracle*, Amacom (American Management Association), New York.

Symonds, M 2003, *Softwar: an Intimate Portrait of Larry Ellison and Oracle*, Simon & Schuster, New York.

Taylor, P 1999, *Steven Spielberg: the Man, His Movies, and Their Meaning*, Continuum, New York.

Trachtenberg, JA 1988, *Ralph Lauren: the Man Behind the Mystique*, Little, Brown & Co., Boston.

Wallace, J & Erickson, J 1993, *Hard Drive: Bill Gates and the Making of the Microsoft Empire*, HarperBusiness, New York.

Wilson, M 2002, *The Difference Between God and Larry Ellison*, HarperBusiness, New York.

Wilson, S 2001, *Steve Jobs: Wizard of Apple Computer*, Enslow Publishers Inc, New Jersey.

Wooten, SM 1999, *Oprah Winfrey: Talk Show Legend*, Enslow Publishers, New Jersey.

Young, JS & Simon, WL 2005, *iCon: Steve Jobs, the Greatest Second Act in the History of Business*, John Wiley & Sons, New Jersey.

Further reading

Allen, FL 1965, *The Great Pierpont Morgan*, Harper & Row, New York.

Anastasi, A 1976, *Psychological Testing*, MacMillan Publishing Co, New York.

Argyle, M 1985, *The Psychology of Interpersonal Behaviour*, Pelican Books, England.

Argyle, M 1987, *The Psychology of Happiness*, Methuen & Co, London.

Bibb, P 1997, *Ted Turner: it Ain't as Easy as it Looks*, Johnson Books, Colorado.

Blair, G 2000, *The Trumps: Three Generations That Built an Empire*, Touchstone, New York.

Breger, L 2000, *Freud: Darkness in the Midst of Vision*, John Wiley & Sons, New York.

Brian, D 1996, *Einstein: a Life*, John Wiley & Sons, New Jersey.

Brown, PH & Broeske, PH 1997, *Howard Hughes: the Untold Story*, Warner Books, Great Britain.

Brunskill, I 2005, *Great Lives: a Century in Obituaries*, Times Books, London.

Butcher, HJ 1968, *Human Intelligence: its Nature and Assessment*, Methuen, London.

Clayson, A 2003, *John Lennon*, Sanctuary, United Kingdom.

Davies, D 2004, *Child Development: a Practitioner's Guide*, 2nd edn, Guilford Press, New York.

Davis, R & Braun, E 1997, *The Gift of Dyslexia: Why Some of the Smartest People Can't Read ... and How They Can Learn*, Perigee, New York.

Dawkins, R 1989, *The Selfish Gene*, Oxford University Press, Oxford.

Gardner, H 1999, *Intelligence Reframed: Multiple Intelligences for the 21st Century*, Basic Books, New York.

Goldman, A 1982, *Elvis*, Penguin, England.

Goleman, D 1996, *Emotional Intelligence: Why it Can Matter More Than IQ*, Bloomsbury, Great Britain.

Gross, D 1996, *Forbes Greatest Business Stories of All Time: 20 Inspiring Tales of Entrepreneurs Who Changed the Way We Live and Do Business*, John Wiley & Sons, New Jersey.

Hillary, Sir E 1999, *View From the Summit*, Doubleday, New Zealand.

Johnson, P 1990, *Intellectuals*, Harper Perennial, New York.

Johnson, P 2006, *Creators*, HarperCollins, New York.

Kessler, R 1997, *The Sins of the Father: Joseph P Kennedy and the Dynasty He Founded*, Coronet Books, Great Britain.

Kline, P 1993, *Personality: the Psychometric View*, Routledge, London.

Lacey, R 1986, *Ford: the Men and the Machine*, William Heinemann, London.

Lovell, MS 1990, *The Sound of Wings: the Biography of Amelia Earhart*, Arrow Books, London.

Madsen, A 1991, *Chanel: a Woman of Her Own*, Henry Holt and Company, New York.

Marsh, L 2003, *The House of Klein: Fashion, Controversy, and a Business Obsession*, John Wiley & Sons, New Jersey.

Matthew, G & Deary, IJ 1999, *Personality Traits*, Cambridge University Press, Cambridge.

Mosley, L 1985, *The Real Walt Disney*, Grafton Books, London.

Myers, DG 1992, *The Pursuit of Happiness*, Avon Books, New York.

Pease, B & A 2000, *Why Men Don't Listen and Women Can't Read Maps*, Broadway Books, New York.

Pease, B & A 2004, *Why Men Don't Have a Clue and Women Always Need More Shoes*, Broadway Books, New York.

Plous, S 1993, *The Psychology of Judgement and Decision Making*, McGraw-Hill, New York.

Price, Glickstein, Horton, Bailey 1982, *Principles of Psychology*, Holt, Rinehart & Winston, New York.

Rich, L 2003, *The Accidental Zillionaire: Demystifying Paul Allen*, John Wiley & Sons, New Jersey.

Ridley, M 2004, *Nature Via Nurture: Genes, Experience and What Makes Us Human*, HarperPerennial, London.

Siegel, DJ 1999, *The Developing Mind: How Relationships and the Brain Interact to Shape Who We Are*, The Guilford Press, New York.

Shawcross, W 1993, *Murdoch*, Pan Books, London.

Storr, A 1988, *Churchill's Black Dog, Kafka's Mice & Other Phenomena of the Human Mind*, Grove Press, New York.

Walton, S & Huey, J 1993, *Sam Walton: Made in America*, Bantam Books, New York.

Wilson, C 1978, *The Outsider*, Picador, London.

Yates, FJ (Ed) 1994, *Risk-Taking Behavior*, John Wiley & Sons, Chichester.

Index

Printed and bound by CPI Group (UK) Ltd, Croydon, CR0 4YY

11/10/2023

08128986-0001